The Making of the Highlands

The Making of the Highlands

Michael Brander

Book Club Associates

London

For Evelyn

First published in 1980 by Guild Publishing
the Original Publications Department of
Book Club Associates

© Michael Brander 1980

Designed by Harold Bartram

Set in 11 on 13pt Monophoto Bembo
Printed and bound in Great Britain by
Morrison & Gibb Ltd., London and Edinburgh

Whilst every reasonable effort has been made to find
the copyright owners of the illustrations in this book
the publishers apologize to any that they have been
unable to trace and will insert an acknowledgment
in future editions upon notification of the fact

Frontispiece: The north shore of Loch Broom looking towards Ullapool
Endpapers: Herring gutters at Wick *c.* 1905

Contents

Preface

At first sight there might seem to be more than enough books already written on the Highlands. There are certainly plenty of local histories covering specific areas, as well as travel books and gazetteers. There are also numerous military and social histories dealing with various periods such as Montrose's brilliant campaign of 1645, Prince Charles Edward Stuart's role in the rebellion of 1745, and the notorious Clearances of the late eighteenth and early nineteenth centuries. There are economic histories dealing with aspects of Highland life such as whisky distilling, fishing, agriculture, and deer management. There are notable books on sport and natural history, on rock climbing and other outdoor activities in the Highlands. There are also general histories and geological surveys covering the whole of Scotland. Strangely enough, however, there are no general outlines of the development of the Highlands from their geological formation as the north-western tip of Europe to the present day covering the whole picture and putting it in perspective.

Inevitably a book of this nature is open to a charge of superficiality, since it is clearly impossible to deal in any depth with many of the subjects covered. On the other hand it is useful for the reader unacquainted with the Highlands to see them as a whole. Those aspects which appeal to the individual can then be followed up in greater detail by reference to the select bibliography which is included. It is to be hoped that even those readers who know the Highlands well will find something of interest to them in this overall picture.

Introduction

It is common practice when writing of the Highlands to include with them the Islands, as if the two were inseparable. The words roll easily off the tongue together and politicians from the days of the early James's in the fifteenth century have found it expedient to link the two together. It is true that for convenience of administration there are numerous bodies connected with both Highlands and Islands, but a glance at any relief map of Scotland must show at once that the Outer Isles, Orkney, and Shetland, at least, have little in common with the Highlands. For that matter their history and way of life, as well as their physical environment, are quite different.

In much the same way considerable areas of the east coast north of the Moray Firth, including the Black Isle, parts of Easter Ross and Sutherland, as well as almost all Caithness, are clearly Lowland rather than Highland. These are indeed generally included in the North-East Lowlands, a geographical description which also covers the low-lying parts of Aberdeenshire, Banffshire, and Morayshire. As with the Central Lowlands south of the Highland Boundary Fault, which runs from the Firth of Clyde to Stonehaven in the north-east, the different physical environment has had its effect on the inhabitants so that their history and way of life, their customs, and even language have differed radically from those of their Highland neighbours. In the North-East Lowlands the distinction may be to some extent blurred today, but physically and historically remains clearly defined.

Although this is a book specifically about the Highlands as such, occasional references must be made to other areas. Thus notice must be taken of parts of the North-East Lowlands and of some of the islands close to the mainland. There are also occasions when mention must be made of Highland forays into the Central Lowlands even to the Borders and beyond. All these, however, are only to set the central picture more firmly in perspective.

Chapter 1

The Coming of Civilisation

The isolation and remoteness, the remarkable scenic attractions and variety, the history and economic development of the Highlands in their unique physical environment all stem basically from their geological origins. Yet when discussing the geological formation of the Highlands there is a strong temptation to start 'Once upon a time . . .'. The facts are obscure because as yet the Highlands have not been fully and satisfactorily explored geologically. A great deal still remains pure conjecture and will have to remain pure conjecture since economically no other course is possible.

Originally the Highlands were formed by earthquakes and eruptions in such a way that with minor exceptions the general trend is for the mountains to lie in a north-north-east to south-south-west direction. The Highland Boundary Fault, along the line of the Ochils running from Helensburgh on the Firth of Clyde in the south-west to Stonehaven on the coast in the north-east, effectively dividing the Highlands from the Central Lowlands, is the obvious line beyond which the Highlands begin. This is, in effect, the frontier of the north-western tip of Europe.

Within the Highlands themselves one of the more obvious geological faults is to be seen clearly in Glen Mor, short for *Gleann mor na-h Albin*, or the Great Glen of Scotland, more often known simply as the Great Glen. It extends for 96 kilometres between Fort William on the shore of Loch Linnhe in the south and Inverness on the Moray Firth in the north and can also be traced along the straight coast of the Black Isle as far as Tarbat Ness. This Great Glen, or Great Fault, was probably the result of a wrench rather than a slip fault some 350 million years ago causing the northern mass to move some 144 kilometres south-west alongside the southern block. The movements of glaciers and erosion since then have resulted in a clear-cut break between the Grampians in the south-east and the North-West Highlands.

Another obvious geological feature is the Moine Thrust, which runs for some 192 kilometres north-north-east from the Sound of Sleat at the south corner of Skye to Whiten Head at the entrance to Loch Eriboll in northernmost Sutherland. In this case the older rocks were piled westwards

The Callernish stones on Lewis

over the more recent rocks and the result can be seen particularly clearly by the roadside near Inchnadamph in Sutherland at the end of Loch Assynt.

Less obvious is a fault which starts at the west end of Loch Tay and can be traced north-eastwards into Loch Garry and finally into the long straight valley of Glen Tilt in Blair Atholl. There are numerous other faults throughout the Highlands, some clear to the experienced eye and others hard to trace Not surprisingly these faults have on occasions shown signs of their volcanic origins. According to the *Gentleman's Magazine* of 1784:

On Sunday, September 12th, 1784, between the hours of eight and nine in the morning, the water at the east end of Loch Tay ebbed about three hundred feet, and left the channel, or bed of the loch, quite dry at that part where the water is usually three feet in depth and being gathered together in the form of a wave, rolled on about three hundred feet further to the westward until it met a similar wave rolling in a contrary direction; when these two clashed together they rose to a perpendicular height of four feet and upwards . . . Then this wave so formed took a lateral direction southward towards the shore, gaining upon the land four feet beyond the highwater mark of the loch . . . It continued to ebb and flow for about an hour and a half . . . It is to be observed that during this phenomenon there was absolute calm . . .

That notable eighteenth-century traveller and author Thomas Pennant recorded a similar event taking place on Loch Ness in 1755:

November 1st, 1755, at the same time as the earthquake at Lisbon, these waters were affected in a very extraordinary manner; they rose and flowed up the lake from East to West with vast impetuosity, and were carried above 200 yards up the river Oich, breaking on its banks in a wave near three feet; then continued ebbing and flowing for the space of an hour, but at eleven o'clock a wave greater than any of the rest came up the river, broke on the North side and overflowed the bank for the extent of 30 feet.

Over the past 200 years nothing as interesting as these phenomena has been observed in the Highlands. The strongest earth tremor ever recorded in Scotland was centred on Inverness in 1816, with an intensity of 8 on the Rossi-Forel scale. Although the shock was felt as far away as Glasgow and Edinburgh the total damage was negligible, consisting of a few chimney stacks loosened, some walls cracked, and numerous tiles and slates displaced. In 1839 there was a lesser tremor in the Comrie area of the Highland Boundary Fault which had similar effects to the earlier earthquake in Inverness, but which also produced some fissures in the ground some 200 metres long. Apart from this minimal damage these tremors had no other visible effect, beyond causing a good deal of alarm amongst those people living in the area.

Taking this into account it is understandably difficult for the layman assessing geological formations to grasp the amazing forces and time factors

The geology of the Highlands

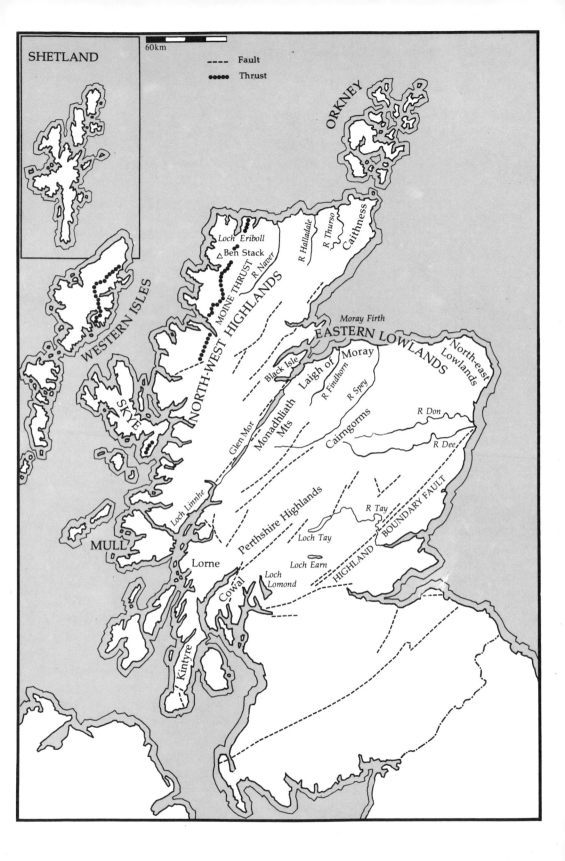

SHETLAND

60km

- - - - Fault
●●●●● Thrust

ORKNEY

Loch Eriboll
△ Ben Stack

WESTERN ISLES

MOINE THRUST

R Naver

NORTH-WEST HIGHLANDS

R Halladale

R Thurso

Caithness

Moray Firth

EASTERN LOWLANDS

North-east
Lowlands

Black Isle

Laigh of Moray

R Findhorn

R Spey

R Don

SKYE

Glen Mor

Monadhliath
Mts

Cairngorms

R Dee

Loch Linnhe

MULL

Perthshire Highlands

R Tay

Loch Tay

HIGHLAND BOUNDARY FAULT

Lorne

Loch Earn

Cowal

Loch
Lomond

Kintyre

involved. As examples, west of the Moine Thrust in Sutherland stands Suilven, an isolated mountain 732 metres high, known locally as the Sugar Loaf due to its strange shape, while further north stands Ben Stack, 721 metres high, each standing alone amid the greyish rocks and strange lunar landscape of this area. Each is formed of Torridonian Sandstone some 600 million years old yet resting on Lewisian Gneiss, amongst the oldest rocks in the world, dating from around 2,700 million years ago.

Standing amid this strange rocky landscape below Durness in Sutherland it is easier to understand how the Highlands took their shape, formed originally by earthquakes, eruptions, and basaltic lava some 40 million years ago, thereafter eroded, split, or smoothed by the four successive major Ice Ages. Erosion and weathering shaped the mountains, and the softer rocks gave way as the result of glacier action to form valleys. It was the straths and glens thus formed which were to provide fertile ground and shelter for man.

As the ice melted, changes in the sea level also resulted and as the vast weight of the ice was removed from it the land mass gradually rose, leaving in places round the coastline the appearance of raised beaches at 30-, 15-, and 7·5-metre levels. All three may be seen in well-developed form on the shores of the Moray Firth as well as round the west coast. They are of importance in often providing an area of fertile ground by the shore and also giving easy access to steep-sided sea lochs in the west coast.

The same processes which produced the Highland formations also produced the dramatic differences between west and east. It is due to them that the west coast is largely composed of sea lochs and a deeply indented rocky coastline with numerous islands, whereas the east coast has straight steep cliffs and sloping sand dunes rolling down to the sea. The west has ragged mountain peaks whereas the east has broader mountain plateaux. The west has a rainier, wetter climate, but the east is noticeably drier.

It is possible that between the later Ice Ages Paleolithic man penetrated as far as the Highlands and hunted prehistoric beasts such as the mammoth, or the great elk, but no trace of this has been uncovered. Certainly, as the last Ice Age receded and the climate altered sufficiently for it to survive, vegetation gradually spread north from Europe. Initially this consisted of mosses in the semi-arctic tundra, then dwarf birch and willow established themselves, to be followed, as the climate improved still further, by larger trees including such familiar specimens as alder, pine, oak, and elm. By somewhere around 7000 BC much of the Highlands was covered with forest, then a return of a wetter, wilder climate resulted in whole areas being blown down and covered with moss. By 5000 BC much of the Highlands was covered with peat bogs.

Inevitably, as the vegetation spread northwards it was followed by birds and animals, also by man himself. Wildfowl—swans, geese, ducks, waders, grouse, and ptarmigan—and birds of prey—eagles, hawks, kites, buzzards, and owls—all gradually established themselves. The smaller mammals, such as lemmings, voles, and mice were probably amongst the first to appear on land. They were followed by the elk, the reindeer and the red deer, the bear, the wild boar, the hare, the lynx, the wolf, the fox, the marten, the wildcat, and lesser predators.

The first Mesolithic men who penetrated the Highlands probably arrived from the south through Ireland. They were extremely primitive nomadic people, who remained close to the sea shore where they could obtain shellfish and a vegetable diet of berries, fruit, and fungi, eked out perhaps with the smaller mammals and occasional birds or larger prey eaten raw since they had not learned the use of fire. Traces of their presence have been found in Argyll in the form of shell middens, or heaps of shells thrown away after eating, and flint tools, knives, and arrowheads. One of the most important Mesolithic sites was found in caves near the sea at Oban, now long incorporated in the concrete of the main street. Such traces of their presence as have been found may be seen in the National Museum of Antiquities in Edinburgh, but little is really known about them.

Somewhere between 4000 and 3000 BC Neolithic man began rudimentary farming in Scotland and traces are to be found in Moray and Banffshire. Equipped with little more than stone axes they cleared areas of forest and planted grain, introducing wheat, barley, and rye into Scotland. It seems likely that they also introduced the small Neolithic cattle from the Continent, descended from domesticated aurochs, the *Bos Urus*. In addition they hunted the red deer, the reindeer, and the bear, possibly using some form of bolas as well as spears and arrows to kill their quarry. Accustomed to using fire, they also produced pottery, and, building small dug-out canoes, they caught fish in the river estuaries and the sea.

It would appear that Neolithic man indulged in a certain amount of trade with other parts of Europe, for apart from importing domesticated cattle from the Continent, which in itself argues the ability to build boats of some size and seaworthiness, he also obtained axe-heads from various centres, often quite far afield. There were certain areas regarded as particularly good for axe-head manufacture, due to the superior type of stone produced locally. For example, axe-heads from Great Langdale in Cumbria, from Penmaenmawr, Gwynned in Wales, and even ceremonial axe-heads from the Rhineland have been discovered in various parts of the Highlands. This would appear to indicate a considerable advance for no doubt with such trading ventures new ideas were also interchanged. Examples of axe-heads and similar artefacts of this period are to be seen in the National Museum of Antiquities in Edinburgh.

Some of the most outstanding Neolithic remains are to be found on Orkney. At Skara Brae a prehistoric village of ten stone-built houses was apparently overwhelmed by a sudden sandstorm some time around 1400 BC and was not discovered until it was exposed by another severe storm in 1850.

Camster Round Cairn, Caithness, one of the finest examples of chambered tombs still in
existence

There is also a remarkable series of chambered tombs to be seen on the island
of Rousay. Each tomb there is different, from the two-storied Taversoe
Tuick, to the multi-chambered Midhowe. Between Stromness and Kirkwall
is the chambered tomb of Maes Howe, regarded by many as the finest
example of its kind and probably the work of a single architect.

The most impressive remains left behind by Neolithic man in the
Highlands are in the form of chambered tombs. At Nether Largie in
Kilmartin, in mid-Argyll above the Crinan Canal; at Crarae on the west side
of Loch Fyne, some 14·5 kilometres south-west of Inveraray; at Clach na
Tiompan in Perthshire; and at Camster in Caithness there are well-preserved
examples of these chambered tombs to be seen. Perhaps the finest of these are
the two Grey Cairns of Camster, known as Camster Long and Camster
Round, which project like stone mounds from a bare, bleak moor in Caithness

about 9·5 kilometres north of Lybster. (Camster Round is pictured opposite.)

It has been calculated that tombs such as these at Camster must have taken some 7,000 man-hours to build, and huge stone blocks weighing several tons each were somehow hoisted into position by Neolithic man using no mechanical aids other than levers, wedges, and rollers. Bearing this in mind they are impressive erections, indicating that by 3000 BC the early inhabitants of the Highlands had attained considerable skills in working with stone. Since several groups must have worked together to build such tombs it is tempting to suggest that some form of clan system had already evolved.

Around 2500 BC the art of working copper was introduced to Britain and by about the year 2000 BC, by adding tin to form the alloy, work in bronze was being produced in Scotland. Bronze Age man in the Highlands left even more impressive remains behind him than his predecessors. The splendid pottery beakers produced in the early part of the period were a notable improvement on those of the preceding age. The art of the goldsmith also came to the fore at this period. Armlets, torques, and even decorated spearheads are amongst the golden ornaments which have been discovered.

During the Bronze Age the difficulty of producing an axe-head with a socket to fit the handle was finally mastered. Whether bronze shields manufactured at this time were used in warfare or solely for ornament is somewhat uncertain. It seems likely that leather shields were used in warfare,

Two Bronze Age pottery beakers to be seen in the National Museum of Antiquities of Scotland

the forerunners of the Highland targe, and the bronze shields were reserved for ceremonial use since they could not withstand blows as well as hardened leather. These and similar relics from this period may also be seen in the National Museum of Antiquities and elsewhere in museums throughout Scotland

With the Bronze Age came increasing trade and communication throughout Britain. Inevitably it also resulted in an increasingly complex social system. Skilled workers were required to smelt and cast metal. The less skilled looked after the beasts and tended the crops. The hunter warriors were the *élite* in each group and with the introduction of effective weapons and valuable ornaments the chieftains naturally found it necessary to fight to acquire control of larger groups, either for defence or attack. Those centres with easy access to copper and tin ore became rich and important at this period.

It is significant that in the Henges, or standing stone monuments, throughout Britain, from Stonehenge to the Stones of Stenness and the Ring of Brodgar in Orkney, the same measurement of 2·27 feet (0·692 metres)— known as the megalithic yard—is used, indicating that there was some overall control. At Kilmartin in central Argyll there are the most outstanding Bronze Age burial sites in Scotland where a linear cemetery extends for some 5 kilometres, starting from the Neolithic chambered tomb at Nether Largie. It should be appreciated that linear cemeteries are not common in Scotland, but are associated with the Bronze Age centres in Wessex. It is particularly noticeable that there are carvings of bronze axes on some of the tombs at Kilmartin which are only found elsewhere on the Stonehenge trilithons. There are a number of other resemblances to Stonehenge which indicate close links at this time between Argyll and Wessex.

As the Bronze Age gradually merged into the Iron Age around 1000 BC the pressures on the various groups in the Highlands began to intensify. With the arrival of the Celts in Britain around the seventh century BC the need for defence became paramount in places. The Celts were a warrior race, used to working in iron and skilled at making and using short iron swords, as well as at riding horses. As they settled in Scotland they shared their knowledge and customs with the inhabitants of the country. The Celticisation of Scotland took place gradually and imperceptibly.

During this period some notable brochs, or Iron Age forts, were built, purely for defence, in areas particularly subject to attack. A number of these are situated in Shetland, Orkney, and the inner isles, notably Skye, but there are two good examples in West Inverness-shire, Dun Telve and Dun Troddan, at Glenelg in splendid countryside some 13 kilometres from Kintail.

Opposite top: Loch Linnhe one of the many sea lochs in the Highlands

Opposite bottom: Brinn Trilleachan in the west of Scotland, a strath formed as a result of glacier action

Opposite top: Well-preserved examples of Pictish silver—a chain, brooch, plaque, and pin are illustrated

Opposite bottom: The Hunterston brooch *c.* AD 700. This together with the silver above can be seen in the National Museum of Antiquities

Above: Mousa broch, Shetland, resembling at first sight some form of primitive cooling tower

Even more impressive, perhaps, is Dun Dornadilla in Sutherland set beneath the towering presence of Ben Hope and commanding the vale of Strath More.

The basic method involved in building all brochs was much the same. In outward appearance circular and massive, they resemble at first sight some form of primitive cooling tower. The outer wall is generally some 3·5 metres thick surrounding an inner courtyard about 7·5 to 11 metres in diameter. The remains of those at Glenelg and in Strath More still stand about 9 metres high in places. With their own well, sleeping accommodation for the chieftain and his followers, and a stoutly barred entrance, they must have been completely impregnable unless taken by surprise. As a safe retreat against marauders they could hardly have been bettered, even likely to withstand disciplined invaders such as the Romans.

The Coming of the Romans

In the year AD 43 the Roman Emperor Claudius landed in Kent and within twenty-five years most of England was under Roman rule. Around AD 80 the Governor Agricola determined to bring Caledonia and the Caledonians under Roman rule as well. Fortunately the campaign was thoroughly, if somewhat flatteringly, documented by his son-in-law the historian Tacitus.

Initially Agricola advanced only as far as the Forth and Clyde valleys, where he established a chain of forts on the line of what was later to become the Antonine Wall. He then advanced systematically into Scotland. Marching beyond Perth his forces followed the line of the river Tay to Inchtuthil some 11 kilometres east-south-east of Dunkeld. Here he established his advanced headquarters in a 21-hectare camp capable of acting as a base or staging post for 5,000 men and strategically sited so as to be protected from the north by a bend in the river.

Although probing forces were sent out to the north-west establishing a camp as far north as Fortingal beyond Aberfeldy and above Loch Tay, it was soon obvious that he was unlikely to be able to advance in that direction. Turning instead north-east he advanced through Angus and the North-East Lowlands. In AD 84 he defeated a large force of Caledonians under their leader Calgacus at a place named as Mons Graupius by Tacitus, but never so far clearly identified, although placed by numerous self-styled experts variously between Forfar and Banff.

Despite the fact that this was not a total victory, Agricola was able to march on unopposed to Banff, through the territory of many of the tribes and take hostages from them. He also sent his fleet, which had accompanied his forces, round the north of Scotland, proving for the first time that it was an island. Owing to a mistake by his cartographers, which was perpetuated for centuries, the Scottish mainland was set at an angle to the rest of the country.

Before he could follow up his victory and consolidate his gains, Agricola was recalled to Rome. Due to trouble with the barbarians on the Danube some of his forces were also withdrawn. The remainder were compelled to make a strategic withdrawal in the face of renewed attacks by the Caledonians. Thus Scotland remained unconquered. Whether in fact Agricola would have been able to penetrate the Highlands and effect a lasting conquest is very much open to question. The terrain is such that it seems improbable. In any event the Caledonians continued to be a source of trouble to the Roman forces in the south with frequent raids over the border.

The Romans recorded the names of a number of different tribes in Scotland. In Caithness there were the *Cornovii*, or People of the Horn. In north-west Sutherland there were the *Cereni*, or Sheep People. In east

Prehistoric, Roman, and Dark Age sites

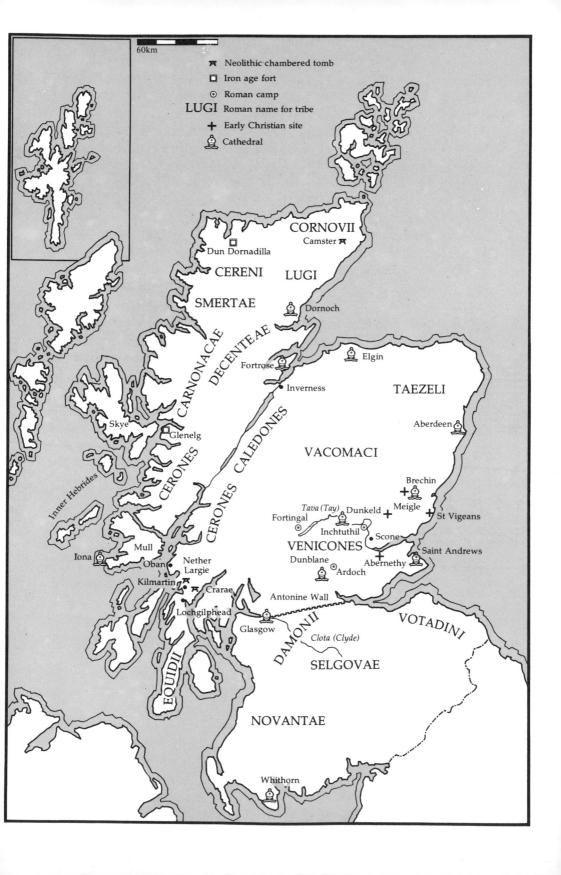

Sutherland were the *Lugi*, or Raven People, and in central Sutherland the *Smertae*, or Smeared People. In Wester Ross lived the *Carnonacae*, or People of the Rocky Hills, while in Easter Ross were the *Decenteae*, or Noble People. In the Great Glen lived the *Caledones* and in Ardnamurchan the *Cerones*, while the *Vacomaci* lived in the Cairngorms area and further south were the *Venicones*. In Aberdeenshire there were the *Taezeli* and in Kintyre the *Equidii*, or Horse People. South of the Forth and Clyde valleys were the *Damonii*, while south of them, below the Cheviots, were the *Selgovae*, or Hunting People. In the west were the *Novantae* and in the east the *Votadini*.

The defensive wall between the Solway and the Tyne known as Hadrian's Wall after the emperor who authorised its construction in AD 122 was never very effective in curbing the aggression of the northern tribes of Caledonia. Some two decades later, between AD 139 and 142, the Antonine Wall between the Forth and Clyde valleys was built by the governor of Britain, Lollius Urbicus. Some 59 kilometres long as opposed to the 117·6 kilometres of Hadrian's Wall, it should have been easier to defend, but it was abandoned after fifteen years. It was certainly occupied a second time for some five years around AD 158 and possibly yet again towards the end of the century, but the Roman forces on each occasion were forced to withdraw to Hadrian's Wall. During the third and fourth centuries there were innumerable revolts and uprisings accompanied by frontier battles on or around Hadrian's Wall. At last in AD 410 the Roman forces were finally withdrawn from Britain.

By this time the tribes, noted by the Romans earlier, had merged into larger groups. The Scots, a Celtic tribe from northern Ireland, had settled in Argyll with Dunadd as the capital of their Kingdom named Dalriada. They were constantly at odds with their neighbours in the west and north, the original Celtic inhabitants, the Picts. From the Clyde to the Solway was settled by Britons, also Celtic in origin, and subdivided into kingdoms based on the old tribal territories. From the Forth to the Tyne the Angles had steadily encroached and threatened the Britons on the west and the Picts in the north.

After something like 400 years of their rule it is not surprising that the Romans left behind them many customs and attitudes, some good and some bad, which were copied both by those tribes in the north which were friendly to them and by their enemies. The weapons they used and their methods of using them were to some extent adopted, particularly the Roman sword. The Roman methods of working metal were such an obvious improvement that they were accepted at once, but many everyday Roman objects had also become accepted by the tribes in the north. To a certain degree the Roman attitude of mind had also become accepted and the semi-Romanised tribes on the border attempted to hold the peace for some time even after the Romans had departed.

Amongst the remains left behind by the Romans and since uncovered, one of the strangest, perhaps, was at Inchtuthil, the frontier station on the Tay beyond Perth established by Agricola and subsequently abandoned and destroyed by the retreating Roman forces. In their haste to leave, the depleted Roman rearguard were unable to remove seven tons of iron nails, handmade and numbering over 750,000, ranging from 5 centimetres in size to 40 centimetres. To the Caledonians iron was regarded as a prize worth more than gold and the Romans knew the nails would instantly be turned into weapons in the primitive forges of the northern tribes. Determined to prevent them falling into enemy hands the Romans dug a pit 3·5 metres deep inside the shed in which the nails were stored. The nails were buried in the pit and covered with 2 metres of earth. The store was then demolished on top of the pit and burned to ensure no traces of the digging were found.

In the 1960s Professor I. A. Richmond, in the chair of Archaeology at Oxford, was making a routine dig at Inchtuthil when he uncovered the hoard. The top sheet of nails, when uncovered, proved to be rusted solid. Those underneath, however, proved to everyone's amazement to be in almost the identical condition they were when hidden some 1,900 years previously. Uncertain as to what to do with this enormous quantity of Roman metal, Professor Richmond finally sent it to the Iron and Steel Institute in London. After they had sorted and classified them, the Institute offered to sell sets of six nails of different sizes for £1·25, to raise funds for further excavation, expecting only something like a thousand applications. They were almost immediately swamped with over 10,000 applications, from far and wide, so that one aspect at least of the Roman occupation of Scotland may now be found in many parts of the world.

The most outstanding remains of the Roman occupation of Scotland are to be found on the edge of the Highland Boundary Fault at Ardoch in Perthshire. Here is one of the best-preserved fortified camps in Britain. It may be that its very position at the extreme northern boundary of the Roman Empire on the edge of the Highlands accounts for its fine state of preservation. Once it was abandoned and deserted there was little or nothing to encourage anyone to settle in that spot. The site is now adjacent to a comfortable hotel, but in the days of the Roman occupation it must have been bleak indeed for the southern troops shivering in the winter blizzards. No doubt a posting to Ardoch was regarded as a suitable punishment for those who had incurred imperial displeasure.

Of course, during their occupation of Britain the Romans were a stabilising influence, but Scotland as a whole and the Highlands in particular were beyond the scope of their direct influence. There was internecine warfare amongst the northern tribes, who together made up the so-called Picts. The Picts were in fact a diverse mixture, descended from the Neolithic aborigines and the Celtic invaders, speaking a Celtic dialect. Occasionally the various tribes would combine against the Romans, but more often than not they were at odds with each other.

The Roman camp at Ardoch, one of the best-preserved fortified camps in Britain

The Origins of the Scots

The Scots were originally the offshoot of a Gaelic-speaking tribe from northern Ireland, who established a foothold in Argyll. The name *Scotti* means bandits and the picture is one of the outlaws and pirates driven from their own home and forced to settle elsewhere. Some 150 Scotti under a leader named Fergus succeeded in establishing themselves in Argyll, where there were few inhabitants to withstand them. In AD 501 they carved out a small kingdom named Dalriada after their homeland in Ireland. Their base, for it hardly deserved the title of capital, was an isolated hilltop fort at Dunadd in the flat country north of the Crinan Canal and north-west of Lochgilphead.

Once established, in true Celtic style the Scots pressed home their advantage and waged continuous warfare against the Picts. In the year AD 559, however, they were decisively defeated by Brude Mac Maelchon, the paramount Pictish king, and it seemed as if it might not be long before they were driven back to Ireland. Having accepted a form of Christianity they were fortunate in receiving the support of St Columba at this critical time.

In AD 563 with the sacred number of twelve disciples accompanying him, Columba established a monastery on the island of Hi, also known as Ioua. This was subsequently misread as Iona, which has since become the generally accepted spelling. He approached Brude Mac Maelchon at his capital in Inverness, probably journeying by way of the Great Glen, and successfully took up both the cause of Christianity and that of the Scots with the king. The latter promised both to allow Columba to continue his missionary work and also to refrain from pressing home his attacks against the Scots.

In the Dark Ages which ensued there is little knowledge of what happened since virtually no records remain available. The only certainty is that by the eighth century the Scots, whether peacefully or by force, had extended their kingdom to beyond Oban in the north and possibly as far as Atholl in the east. At the same time there was a comparatively peaceful penetration by the Norse into the northern islands and mainland, also down the west coast. In the late eighth century, however, Viking raiders sacked Iona. In the early ninth century, they also decisively defeated the Picts with considerable slaughter. The weakened Pictish kingdom was then overcome and absorbed with little difficulty by Kenneth MacAlpin, King of the Scots, whose capital was by then at Dunstaffnage north-east of Oban. In AD 843 he was crowned King of Scotland at Scone near Perth, erstwhile capital of the southern Picts.

The Vikings meanwhile had established themselves in Orkney, Shetland, and the Hebrides, as well as in Caithness. They also continued to raid the mainland and even colonised a good deal of the west coast. The effective rule of the Scottish king at this period therefore extended little further than the Moray Firth in the north and the Firth of Forth in the south. To the west the mainland was occupied along the coast and the mountains prevented access except by sea.

As regards visible remains, the Picts left a wealth of metalwork in a variety of shapes and forms, from magnificent silver brooches to hanging bowls, sword pommels, and buckles. They also left numerous relief sculptures with mysterious symbols depicting wolves, boars, and deer, amongst other beasts. One suggestion has been that these symbols might have been clan badges, or possibly marks of ownership. They left few buildings and their habit was to occupy natural defences such as rocky outcrops which are now known as 'nuclear' forts. A good example is to be seen at Dundurn, 8 kilometres west of Comrie in Perthshire.

The Scots left little in the way of buildings beyond the remains at Dunadd. Near the top of the hill there is a boar carved in the rock close to the imprint of

a foot, where tradition holds that the kings of Scotland stood to be crowned. Close to these carvings in the rock is an indecipherable inscription, possibly Pictish in origin. Excavations on the site have produced clay moulds for casting bronze pins and brooches. Fragments of pottery show that they came in some instances from Europe, indicating a regular trade with the Continent.

The remains of early Christianity that are most impressive are the numerous sculptured stones. Perhaps the most outstanding collection of these is to be seen at Meigle in Perthshire. Another good collection is at St Vigeans in Angus. The early ecclesiastical buildings were of wood and have not left any traces. The oldest are a round tower close by the side of Brechin Cathedral in Angus and another tower at Abernethy in south-east Perthshire, standing beside the kirk above the Tay. The Vikings, against whom these were probably built as a defence, have ironically left few visible traces on the mainland. The remains of their settlements are almost entirely restricted to the northern isles.

Although the visible remains of early Christianity in the Highlands may not appear to amount to much, St Columba and his contemporary in the south, based on Glasgow, Kentigern, or St Mungo, and his followers successfully spread at least a form of Christianity throughout the Highlands. Primitive though it may have been and differing widely from the tenets of Rome, it skilfully blended the customs of the old pagan religions with those of Christianity. The early Celtic saints such as Maelrubbha, Cormac, Duthus, and Kessock founded shrines of importance across the Highlands from Applecross in the west as far as Tain in the east. Here the Culdee monks, spreading over from Ireland, established centres. Hence it was this form of primitive Christianity which dominated the Highlands for the next 500 years and which some maintained was to remain the underlying religion among the majority of Highlanders for more than a thousand years, even after the arrival of Presbyterianism.

A Pictish stone showing a figure on horseback possibly with a drinking horn, c. tenth century AD

Chapter 2

The Clans and the Years of Strife

In the year 1005 Malcolm II came to the throne of Alba as it was then known. His aim, like that of previous Scottish kings since MacAlpin, was to unify Scotland by defeating the Angles in the south-east and the Norse in the north and west. In 1018 at the battle of Carham on the banks of the Tweed, he defeated the Angles in such a decisive manner that they had no hope of recovery, thus bringing the Lothians as far as the Tweed under Scottish rule. He also regained the mainland and the Hebrides from the Norse. On the death of the King of the Britons, whose territory extended to Cumbria in the west, his grandson Duncan inherited the throne so that at this time Scotland very largely resembled its present-day boundaries from the Tweed to the Pentland Firth. For the first time it came to be known as Scotland, and inevitably the centre of power soon began to shift southwards from the Highlands, simply because of the easier access and communications.

In 1034 Malcolm's grandson Duncan I succeeded him, but in 1040 he was killed by Macbeth, who contrary to Shakespearian legend ruled well and wisely for seventeen years, extending Scotland's connections with England and the Continent, until defeated and killed by Duncan's son, Malcolm III, known as Malcolm Canmore, who had spent a year in exile at the court of the Saxon king Edward the Confessor where he had absorbed some southern influences. His reign lasted until 1093, but in 1068 he married a Saxon princess named Margaret as his second wife. Eldest sister of Edgar, child heir to the Saxon throne usurped by the Norman conqueror William I, she was a powerful personality who had been educated in Hungary and included a number of Hungarians in her following. She was responsible for introducing the Romanisation of the Church in Scotland, even if there may have been some lack of effective penetration in the Highlands.

Although her brother Edgar had been treated kindly by William I it was probably due to Margaret's influence that he fled to Malcolm Canmore for refuge. This resulted in Scotland becoming a haven for refugees and malcontents from England. Such names as Lindsay and Wallace came north

A romanticised view of the luxurious court of James I

with Margaret and Edgar and some of these at least, notably the Drummonds, later earls of Perth, originated in Hungary. Another notable name which emanated from Hungary was Alexander, ever since Scotticised as Sandy. It is significant that Malcolm Canmore had a Gaelic nickname, but his sons by Margaret who succeeded him had Saxon or non-Celtic names, Edgar, Alexander, and David. The process of Anglicisation of the south of Scotland had begun, although as yet the Highlands remained unaffected.

This process was enhanced when William the Conqueror, not belying his nickname, invaded Scotland in 1072, advancing in much the same manner as Agricola by land and sea simultaneously. Provoked by repeated invasions of Northumberland he was determined to make Malcolm Canmore swear fealty to him and claim the right of suzerainty that had existed under Saxon rule, which he considered now due to him. After defeating Malcolm's forces at Abernethy on the Tay he forced Malcolm to pay him homage. Here was the first round of the long-drawn-out conflict between England and Scotland which was due to last intermittently for nearly 600 years with the Lowlands and Borders providing the battlegrounds and the Highlands providing a reserve of fighting men when required.

This did not stop Malcolm Canmore invading Northumberland yet again in 1093 when he and his eldest son Edward were killed at Alnwick. Following his death Scotland had no less than four kings in the next four years. One result was that in 1098 the King of Norway, Magnus Barefoot, regained the Hebrides and by the treaty of Tarbert in the same year was granted all the islands round which he could sail. According to tradition he claimed Kintyre by sitting at the helm of a ship while it was dragged across the narrow neck of land between West and East Loch Tarbert.

After Magnus Barefoot's death in 1103, however, the Norse hold on the west coast gradually weakened and by mid-century they had been driven out of Argyll. Meanwhile the Norman influence in Scotland was strengthened. David I, who had spent his youth in England and was an admirer of Norman ways with an English wife, though unlike his predecessors not a vassal of the English king, brought with him numerous Norman advisers and supporters. High positions in both Church and State were granted to Normans who came north during this period. Such accepted Scottish names as Bruce, Chisholm, Cummings, Haig, Fraser, Sinclair, and Stewart owe their origins to Norman adventurers of this period who were granted estates in Scotland. Some notable Highland clans originate from this period.

It is somewhat ironic that it was thus under the leadership of a Wallace, probably of Hungarian origin, then of a de Brus, whose origins were Norman, that Scotland finally became united as one nation in opposition to an English king whose origins were also Norman. The immediate effect was to cause a division for the first time between Highlands and Lowlands, with the Gaelic-speaking Highlands becoming quite distinct from the more Anglicised

Lowlands where the speech was increasingly English. This was a distinction which was to grow more marked over the centuries as the more accessible Lowlands and Borders were ravaged by warfare and during the intervals of peace engaged in trade with the Continent, while the Highlands remained almost in a state of suspended animation, inaccessible and remote from the rest of Scotland in the south with whom increasingly they had less in common. The Gaelic speech of the Highlands was to become as much of a barrier to the English-speaking Lowlanders as the mountains themselves.

Another marked difference between Highlands and Lowlands developing at this period was that the Highlanders remained largely unaffected by the spread of feudalisation, which was a notable feature of the Lowlands. While the Lowlanders owned land in feu to their lord, or to the king, the Highlanders held their land as a clan, appointing their chieftains by popular vote—at least in theory. Certainly the earliest clan chieftains can be traced back to the twelfth century. Somerled, son of Gillebride, who drove the Norse out of Lochaber, Morvern, and the north of Argyll after the death of Magnus Barefoot, was the founder of the powerful clan Donald. The history of the MacDonalds dominates the early events in the Highlands. They became kings of the Isles and the Isle of Man, lords of the Isles, and the earls of Ross. At one period their power was almost equal to that of the Scottish king and they were involved in warfare against him. Eventually their power was broken and their territory dwindled to include Kintyre, the Isle of Islay, parts of Skye, and parts of the mainland, including Ardnamurchan and Glencoe. Somerled's son Dougall was the founder of the Clan MacDougall centred on Oban.

The clans tended to be founded in certain areas, grouped initially around a leader in that area. Thus Cormac, the Celtic bishop of Dunkeld, appointed by Alexander I, in 1107 had six sons to each of whom he granted church lands and it is claimed that each was the founder of a clan. Guaire was the progenitor of the Macquarries in Ulva, Fingon of the Mackinnons in Mull, Gilchrist of the MacMillans in Lochaber, Gille Adhamhan of the Lamonts in Cowall, Anrias of the Macgregors in Glenorchy, and Ferchar of the Mackenzies and the MacPhees in Applecross.

For various reasons, of course, a clan might move, or be forced to move from its original area. Shortage of good agricultural land, famine, or disease were all reasons for such movements. As branches, or septs, of the clan prospered elsewhere and the original line declined in power, so the clan might move its ground. They might also be driven out of their land by a more powerful neighbour. On occasions also the government might take a hand. Thus, Malcolm IV, who succeeded to the throne of Scotland at the age of twelve in 1153, was responsible in 1160 for moving the Mackays, the old royal house of Moray, after dissension in that area, *en masse* to Ross-shire, whence they were given lands in the north-west of Sutherland by the bishop of Caithness and duly prospered exceedingly.

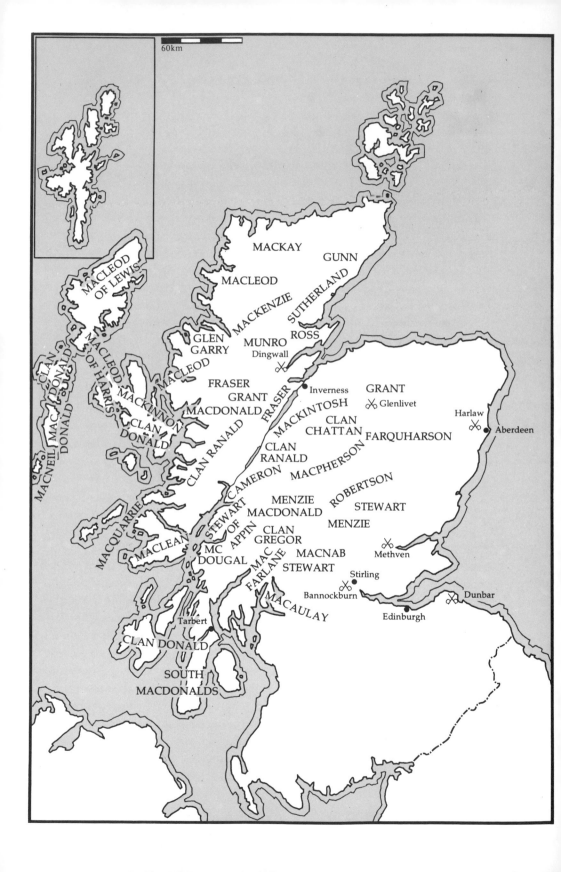

60km

MACLEOD
OF LEWIS

MACKAY

GUNN

MACLEOD

MACKENZIE

SUTHERLAND

CLAN MAC DONALD
MACDONALD
MACLEOD OF HARRIS
MACKINNON

GLEN
GARRY

MUNRO
ROSS

Dingwall

MACLEOD

CLAN
DONALD

FRASER
GRANT
MACDONALD

FRASER

Inverness

GRANT

Glenlivet

MACNEIL

MACKINTOSH

CLAN
CHATTAN

Harlaw

Aberdeen

CLAN RANALD

MACPHERSON

FARQUHARSON

CLAN
RANALD

MACQUARRIE

CAMERON

ROBERTSON

STEWART

MENZIE
MACDONALD

MENZIE

STEWART
OF
APPIN

CLAN
GREGOR

Methven

MACLEAN

MC
DOUGAL

MAC
FARLANE

MACNAB

STEWART

Stirling

Tarbert

MACAULAY

Bannockburn

Dunbar

Edinburgh

CLAN DONALD

SOUTH
MACDONALDS

When surnames came to be introduced, the form Mac, or 'son of,' was added to the original name. Thus the son of Donald became MacDonald. This was in effect a variant of the Irish habit of adding Ua, or O' to the surname. The same meaning was intended, thus the son of Hagan became O'Hagan. It was not until the twelfth century that names began to become important in the Highlands as the clans were formed and in general the tendency was for those without a name to take that of their clan chief or of their most powerful neighbour to ensure his protection.

There were, naturally enough, numerous clans which originated from the descendants of the Dalriadic Scots. The MacAlpins were, of course, Celtic in origin with their clan seat originally at Dunstaffnage and later east of Loch Awe. The Macaulays, to the south-east of Loch Lomond, were a branch, or sept, of this clan. Prominent also were the Campbells, whose land stretched from the sea at Benderloch as far inland as Loch Tay. The Macgregors of Glenorchy claimed descent from Grogar, son of King Alpin, and another clan of Celtic origin was the Macarthurs from Argyll, while in the twelfth century Fergus, Prince of Galloway, founded the clan Fergusson of Atholl and Balquhidder.

The clan Chattan was an ancient and loose federation originally composed of some seventeen clans which claimed Pictish origins. The main constituent members were the clans Davidson, south of Inverness; Farquharson by Braemar; Macbean near Inverness; Macgillivray alongside the Davidsons; Mackintosh to the east of them; and the Macphersons to their south along the river Spey. The clan Cameron in Lochaber was originally reputed to have belonged to the clan Chattan, but to have broken away. For centuries the Mackintoshes and Macphersons disputed as to who should produce the head of the clan Chattan and eventually it was decided in favour of the Mackintoshes. The name dates from the eleventh century and is derived from the title of the chief, Gilliechattan Mor, or the Great Servant of St Catan, that is the bailie of Kilchattan Abbey in Bute.

The clan Ross is thought to have been Celtic in origin, descended from the earls of Ross who held sway around the Dornoch Firth in the clan area, although alleged by some to be of Norse descent. The Macleods, established on the mainland below the Kyle of Lochalsh, were definitely Norse in origin, being descended from Magnus. the last King of the Isle of Man. There were other clan origins, naturally enough, such as that of the Leslies, who can trace their descent back to Bartolf of Hungary, who came over with Margaret.

Families of Norman origin such as the Chisholms, who finally settled in Strath Glass, the Cummings, above Loch Ericht, the Frasers, encircling the north of Loch Ness, the Gordons, surrounding Huntly and the Stewarts

The development of the clans and battles of the Middle Ages and the sixteenth century

spreading below Perth were examples of southerners granted, or acquiring through marriage or by other means, estates in the north round which eventually a clan was formed. In such cases it might be said that not only did they cease to practise their feudal system of government, but that gradually they became more Highland than Highlanders themselves. Whether by marriage or by grant each of these originally Norman families founded clans which by the late thirteenth or fourteenth century were recognisable and powerful political forces.

The clan was a patriarchal form of society and had its own laws regarding succession and land-holding, which had evolved over the centuries. The leader was followed as chieftain of the clan and as a representative of their common ancestors, not as under the feudal system because they were the tenants of the landowner and bound to him. There was generally a blood tie, as well as a common living area, or habitat, so that there was mutual respect rather than subservience between the chief and his followers.

The habit of fosterage, common to both Celts and Norse, helped to perpetuate this clan feeling. By this a child of the chief, or lesser personages, might be sent to a family to keep until he or she had reached the age of puberty, to be brought up by the foster parents as their own. In return the child was expected to maintain his or her foster parents in their old age and naturally to look after his foster brothers and sisters. It was a system which was maintained until the late eighteenth century in many parts of the Highlands. Living under such a system the clan chieftains had to prove themselves worthy of their place and never lost touch with their clan.

By mid thirteenth to mid fourteenth centuries the clans had mostly evolved in their modern form. The Highlands were populated by groups of semi-tribal inhabitants in each glen and strath. The larger the clan, in general, the greater the number of dependents, branches, or septs, which were formed and allied to it. Frequently quarrelling, but equally often uniting with each other in battle against a common foe, they shared a language and customs which steadily divorced them from their southern neighbours. Although generally accepting a common king the Gaels did not feel bound to him by the same feudal ties as the Lowlanders. This is the explanation for the fact that the Highlanders could be found fighting on each side at almost every major battle in Scotland from Bannockburn to Culloden.

During the long reign of Alexander III from 1249–86 the Highland clan system was able to take shape during a lengthy period of comparative peace. In 1263 King Hakon of Norway attempted to assert his overlordship of the Western Isles by sailing round the north of Scotland with a fleet of 160 ships and some 20,000 men. He anchored by Largs in the Firth of Clyde off Arran

John Balliol, Bruce's rival for the Scottish throne, portrayed with his wife

Johñe Baliell 1292

when an unfavourable gale blew up and the Scots army awaiting them on the shore were able to defeat them with ease. From the Norwegian viewpoint it was an unmitigated disaster and King Hakon himself died in Orkney on his way home. By the ensuing Treaty of Perth in 1266 the Western Isles and the Isle of Man, together known as the Sudreys, were ceded to Scotland, while Orkney and Shetland, known as the Nordreys, remained under the rule of the Norwegians.

An Alliance with France

With Alexander III's death in 1286 his three-year-old granddaughter, Margaret, daughter of King Eric of Norway, and known as the Maid of Norway, became his heir. Guardians were appointed to govern Scotland during her minority and when Edward I proposed that she be married to his son this was strongly approved. Unfortunately she died at the age of seven and the Guardians then were unable to make a choice between the thirteen claimants to the Scottish throne and appealed to Edward I to act as a mediator. Edward chose Balliol on condition that he swore fealty to him, but when Edward declared war with France in 1294 Balliol, urged by his advisers, chose to make the historic treaty of alliance with France in 1295 which was to affect Anglo-Scottish relations for the next 400 years.

In 1296 Edward I led an English army into Scotland and after defeating the Scots resoundingly at the battle of Dunbar led Balliol captive with him back to England. All the major castles throughout Scotland were garrisoned with English troops, and the Stone of Destiny, on which every Scottish king had been crowned at Scone since MacAlpin, was taken back in triumph to Westminster. Edward returned to England convinced, with good reason, that he had finally conquered Scotland.

In fact resistance was still very much alive, particularly in the Highlands, which had barely been affected by these events. It seems likely also that even in the matter of the Stone of Destiny Edward was misled. Tradition had it that this was the stone on which Jacob laid his head when he dreamed of the angels and it was reputedly brought back from Bethel in the Holy Land to Ireland and thence to Scotland. The probability is that it was meteoric fragment of hard rock and tradition has it that it was carved. The Stone of Destiny in Westminster is of plain soft sandstone such as may be obtained around Scone and the probability is that the original was replaced with a local substitute which Edward unwittingly took back to England.

William Wallace led a spirited revolt against the English occupying forces

David II after his defeat at Neville's Cross (1346) with Edward III

The Great Seal of Robert the Bruce

in 1297. Successful in the first stages of the Wars of Independence, he continued to wage guerrilla warfare until his betrayal and execution in 1305. His defiance, however, encouraged Robert Bruce to follow suit and in 1306 he was crowned King of Scotland at Scone.

After the defeat of his army at Methven near Perth in the same year as his coronation Bruce was forced to fly for his life. He was pursued relentlessly by MacDougall of Lorn, who was related to the Red Comyn whom Bruce had killed at Dumfries, so that there was a blood feud between them. The MacDougall clan pressed Bruce hard, but he received refuge and aid from Angus, King of the Isles, at Dunaverty Castle in the south of Kintyre, who provided him with a ship in which he escaped to Ireland and shelter.

The following year, 1307, Bruce returned to defeat the English forces at Loudon Hill. Edward I, returning to Scotland yet again to fulfil his nickname of 'the Hammer of the Scots', died at Burgh Sands as he prepared to cross the Solway Firth. In 1308 Bruce revenged himself on the MacDougalls when he defeated them in a battle in the Pass of Brander between Loch Etive and Loch Awe. The MacDougall lands were then given to Ian Campbell, one of his strongest supporters, and this saw the start of the Campbell rise to power in Argyll during the ensuing centuries. With the knack of backing the winning side the Campbells became one of the most powerful clans in the Highlands.

For the next six years Robert the Bruce was able to range the country more or less at will, systematically recapturing all the castles which had been occupied by the English. Finally only Stirling Castle remained holding out against him, upthrust like a mailed fist from the plain on its granite base guarding the gateway to the Highlands. Sir Philip Moubray, the English commander, besieged by Edward Bruce, Robert Bruce's brother, agreed to surrender the fortress if he was not relieved by 24 June 1314.

By 10 June the English army had assembled to march on Stirling to the relief of the garrison. There were between 2,000 and 3,000 armoured knights and around 17,000 foot soldiers against which Bruce had only some 5,000 foot soldiers and 500 light horse. There were, however, twenty-one clans who followed Bruce into battle. In alphabetical order they consisted of the Camerons, Campbells, Drummonds, Frasers, Grants, Macdonalds, Macfarlanes, MacGregors, Mackays, Mackenzies, Mackintoshes, Macleans, Macphersons, Morrisons, Munros, Robertsons, Rosses, Sinclairs, Stewarts, Sutherlands, and those under the Earl of Randolph of Moray. Aiding the English were the Cummings, the MacDougalls, and the MacNabs.

Although heavily outnumbered Bruce was able to choose a strong strategic position in front of Stirling above the Bannock burn, a narrow but deep tidal tributary of the Forth. The English army was very slow-moving and it was not until 23 June that they approached Bruce's position. It took them most of the night to cross the Bannock burn by improvised bridges and by morning their morale was low. It was then that a Scottish knight, Sir Alexander Seton, slipped away from their forces and approached Bruce with the epic words: 'Now's the time and now's the hour.'

The Scots attacked while the English were still on a narrow front, unable to use their full strength. The Scottish forces were deployed in four divisions, or batals, with about 1,000 pikemen in each. These pikemen fought in schiltrons, or companies of 500, and presented an almost impenetrable hedge of steel against which armoured knights were of no avail. Forced gradually back against the Bannock burn, the English finally lost heart when Edward's banner was seen leaving the field. Then, scenting victory, the Scots camp followers streamed down the hill behind Bruce's army and, thinking they were fresh troops, the English army broke and fled. The victory was overwhelming and only Edward with a small escort succeeded in escaping by boat from Dunbar.

Following the battle of Bannockburn Bruce ensured that those clan chiefs who had fought against him forfeited their lands. He was more concerned, however, with unifying Scotland as one nation than with disciplining the Highlands although latterly he made moves to curb the power of the Highlanders in the west, particularly attempting to gain more control over Kintyre by rebuilding the castle at Tarbert. Unfortunately Scotland was frequently fated to have a minor succeeding to the throne at critical periods in her history and on Bruce's death in 1329 he was succeeded by his five-year-old son David II.

Edward III was not slow to take advantage of this and actively supported Edward Balliol, son of John Balliol, as claimant to the Scots throne. In 1332 with a largely English army Balliol invaded Scotland, defeating the Scots forces under Donald, Earl of Mar, at Dupplin Moor near Perth and was crowned at Scone. Two years later in 1334 Balliol acknowledged Edward's

Opposite: A delightfully primitive evocation of the battle of Bannnockburn (1314) from Fordun's Scotichronicon

Below: The memorial to Robert the Bruce on the site of the battle of Bannockburn, erected in 1964

overlordship and ceded the Lowlands, from East Lothian to Dumfries, to England, which resulted in a hundred years of warfare before they were regained. Only the outbreak of the Hundred Years War with France in 1338 relieved the pressure on Scotland at least temporarily. Throughout this century, the Highlands provided the reserve of fighting men essential to Scotland's survival, even if in the period following Bruce's death the Highland chieftains were largely a law unto themselves.

In 1346 David II, aged twenty-two, invaded England, but, though not lacking in personal courage, he had none of his father's abilities as a general. He was defeated at Neville's Cross and taken prisoner, only finally being released on payment of a vast ransom in 1356 after Edward himself had invaded Scotland in a vain effort to impose his rule. On David II's death in 1371 he was succeeded by his nephew Robert II, the first of the Stuarts. In 1390 he was succeeded by his middle-aged son Robert III, who died in 1396, not long after his son James, destined to become James I, had been captured by the English at sea. His captivity lasted eighteen years until 1424, during which time his uncle the Duke of Albany was virtually ruler.

During this period of uncertainty and turmoil, the Highlands mirrored the chaos prevalent in Scotland. An example of the general lawlessness prevalent in the Highlands towards the end of the fourteenth century was the behaviour of Robert III's younger brother Alexander, Earl of Buchan, whose nickname was 'the Wolf of Badenoch'. Although appointed Justiciary of the Northern Lowlands he led the Highlanders in raiding the area.

He was eventually deprived of the Justiciary, but in 1390 he sacked Elgin Cathedral. At the same time one of his bastards, named Duncan, led a force of Highlanders into Angus and killed the sheriff of the county along with other notables. Duncan's brother, Alexander, another of the Wolf's bastards, married the widowed Countess of Mar by force and thus duly acquired the title of Earl of Mar.

Armed with bows and well-barbed arrows, with broadswords and leather targes, or shields, the Highlanders were lightly equipped and could move fast and far. They usually fought only as long as was required to load themselves with enough booty to take home. They had brought the art of acquiring booty in battle to a high degree, usually vanishing from the scene when the fighting became too severe and the prospects of loot were poor.

This was by no means always the case, however, especially when a blood feud was involved. In 1396 there was an epic meeting involving thirty champions a side from, it is thought, clan Chattan and clan Cameron on the North Inch, a meadow on the banks of the Tay at Perth. A large crowd of spectators, including Robert III and many of his court, attended the combat. The representatives of each clan fought fiercely to the death and when all had been wounded or killed the sole surviving Cameron only escaped with his life by diving into the Tay and swimming to safety. Whether the King acquiesced

A medieval illustration of Robert II (1371–90)

in the combat as one way of disposing of the best warriors of the rival factions and hence one way of curbing their power is open to question. There were certainly few enough curbs on the Highland clans and their conflicts during this period.

In 1411, during Albany's regency, Donald MacDonald, Lord of the Isles, assembled a huge force of Highlanders, including the clan Chattan, the Camerons of Lochaber, the Macleans of Mull and of Skye, and many of the Macdonalds, estimated at well over 10,000 strong. Ostensibly this was to ensure that his claim to the earldom of Ross was confirmed, but he was clearly using it as an excuse to extend his power, and in the absence of his kinsman James I it is possible that he even had aspirations to the throne. At Dingwall his forces encountered the Mackays and the Rosses from Sutherland led by Angus Mackay and defeated them. He then sacked Inverness and marched on into Aberdeenshire.

At Harlaw, 22·5 kilometres north-west of Aberdeen, they were met by Alexander, the Wolf of Badenoch's bastard son, now Earl of Mar, together with the Provost and burgesses of Aberdeen and a small force of knights and Lowland gentlemen. After a long and bloody day's struggle the Highland forces melted away in the night leaving the field to the Lowlanders. Aberdeen was saved and the affair went down in ballad and folklore as 'Red Harlaw' for it was said the ditches ran red with blood. Although sometimes referred to as the last encounter between Saxon Lowlander and Highland Gael there were, of course, Gaels on both sides and this continued to be the case until the final battle at Culloden.

Donald of the Isles died in 1420 to be succeeded by his son Alexander. With the accession of James I in 1424 there came a new determination to assert the rule of law both in the wild Borderland and in the Highlands. Aged nearly thirty when he at last gained his throne, James I was determined to prove that the king's rule was paramount. In 1427 he held a Parliament in Inverness and summoned the Highland chieftains to attend. As soon as they appeared he had them imprisoned and some of the less important hanged as an example. Alexander was treated as an honoured guest and released in 1429, when he promptly showed his gratitude and his real feelings by burning Inverness. Thereupon James led an army against him and soundly defeated him in Lochaber, imprisoning him again, this time at Tantallon on the East Lothian coast at the opposite end of the realm to his homeland. Finally he was confirmed as Earl of Ross and freed once more, after which he remained quiescent until his death in 1449.

Although a certain degree of control had been imposed on the Highlanders by these measures, raids on the rich Lowland farmlands bordering the Highlands, resulting in the loss of cattle and sheep, remained periodic occurrences and a good deal of internecine warfare continued. The clan Chattan and clan Cameron, to take only one example, were frequently at odds with each other although there were also periods of uneasy alliance against others, followed, as likely as not, by acts of treachery and violence. The general spirit of the times throughout Scotland, not only in the Highlands, was brutal, treacherous, merciless, and savage.

James I's assassination in 1437, butchered unarmed in front of his Queen and her ladies-in-waiting, was in keeping with the age and he was succeeded by his son James II, aged six. By the time that he had come of age and begun to establish control over his kingdom relations with England had deteriorated. The 'auld enemy' once again claimed sovereignty over Scotland. It was necessary once more to renew the 'auld alliance' with France and in 1460 during the ensuing border warfare James, aged only thirty, was unexpectedly killed by the explosion of a cannon—ironically one from his own side. His son, James III, who succeeded him, was aged nine.

The Queen Mother and Bishop Kennedy of St Andrews acted as guardians,

A nineteenth-century painting of James I's assassination

or regents, for the young king, but in 1461, seizing his opportunity as he thought, Edward IV of England negotiated with John, successor to Alexander as Lord of the Isles and Earl of Ross, to attack from the north, while the attainted Earl of Douglas backed by English forces attacked from the south. The attempt failed when Douglas was defeated in 1463 by a force led by Bishop Kennedy. A truce with England was then concluded in 1464, but the part played by the Lord of the Isles was not forgotten. Tried for treason by his peers—Argyll, Atholl, Huntly, and Crawford—in 1476 he forfeited his earldom of Ross and his lands in Inverness, Knapdale, Kintyre, and Nairn. He was allowed to retain his lordship of the Isles, although his son Angus and grandson Donald Dubh remained intractable and rebellious until the death of the latter in Ireland. The lordship of the Isles was finally forfeited and annexed to the Crown in 1493.

In 1464, while the Highlands still remained without any firm rule of law, there was a typical incident between the Keiths and the Gunns, who had long been feuding with each other. Deciding to settle the dispute with a match between twelve horse from each side they agreed to meet in a remote part of Caithness. The Keiths arrived with two men mounted on each horse and in the fight which followed only five sons of the Gunn chieftain survived. The three least wounded followed the victorious Keiths and while they were relaxing at a banquet with their neighbours the Sutherlands, the Gunns killed the Keith chieftain and several others with well-aimed arrows before beating a retreat. Naturally such actions merely intensified their blood feud.

One of the difficulties facing any historian regarding such clan battles is that there were never any independent or unbiased eyewitnesses present to record details. They all passed into clan history, or legend, through the medium of the clan bards, who were perfectly capable of distorting the facts and even turning defeat into victory to suit their own ends. Thus hardly any two versions of the same event are likely to agree. All one can be sure of was that there was generally a great deal of violence, bloodshed, and treachery.

In 1469, when James III was eighteen, he married Margaret, daughter of the King of Norway, as a result of which the Orkneys and Shetland Isles came under Scottish rule once again. Unfortunately James showed none of the character of his father and grandfather and during his reign the rule of law in the Highlands and in the Borders deteriorated yet further. His reign was bedevilled by internecine quarrels as various noble houses contended with each other for power.

A manuscript illustration of James III and his queen, Margaret, daughter of the King of Norway

In 1488 James III's eldest son was proclaimed James IV by a group of nobles consisting of the Humes and Hepburns in the south and the earls of Angus and Argyll in the north. The earls of Huntly, Crawford, Errol, and Buchan in the north with their respective clans remained loyal and the two sides clashed at Sauchieburn near Bannockburn. James III, galloping from the battlefield, was thrown from his horse. While lying semi-conscious, he was quietly knifed by an unknown assassin, probably in the service of Lord Gray, one of his oldest enemies. Yet again the clans were to be found fighting on both sides and yet again the Campbells had shown their predilection for choosing to ally themselves with the winning faction.

For the next twenty-five years there was a welcome period of law and order with a corresponding increase in trade and prosperity and a fresh outlook in the world of arts and scholarship. James began to pacify the Highlands effectively. He spoke Gaelic, the last Scots king to do so, and in the Highlands he wore the Highland garb. During his reign he accomplished considerable changes, establishing Edinburgh as the capital of the realm where the Parliament was based, rather than moving from place to place. In 1502 he agreed to a treaty of 'perpetual peace' with England prior to marrying Henry VII's eldest daughter, Margaret Tudor. Despite considerable provocation from Henry VIII after his accession in 1509, peace with England was maintained until 1513.

In 1512 Henry VIII joined in a Holy Alliance with Spain and Venice on the side of Pope Julius II against France. The Pope, who was more concerned with uniting Italy under his own temporal rule than with religion, had intrigued to get the French into Italy to crush the power of the Venetians. At this stage he was attempting to drive the French out of Italy and had formed the so-called Holy Alliance for this purpose. Eager for military honour and glory, Henry needed little persuasion to join the coalition against France.

When England invaded France in 1513, James IV, also eager for military honour and glory, renewed the 'auld alliance'. Against the advice of his counsellors he decided to invade England. Unfortunately although personally highly courageous, James was no sort of a general. Hot-headed and impetuous, he had no grasp of strategy or tactics. Although he had an army of 30,000 men, including Highland clansmen under Argyll and Lennox, they were poorly trained and indifferently armed with pikes and short swords and heavy but inefficient artillery. The English were commanded by the Earl of Surrey and his son Lord Thomas Howard. They had only 21,000 men but they were well armed with 2·5-metre-long axes with curved heads known as bills. The result was disastrous for the Scots and for Scotland. Not only was James himself killed, but 6–10,000 Scottish fighting men also died on the battlefield, including twelve earls, fourteen lords, one archbishop, three bishops, and sixty-eight knights and gentlemen.

Once again Scotland was left with a minor on the throne, for James V was

A contemporary illustration of the battle of Flodden (1513) where James IV died

only eighteen months old at the time of his father's death. The result on this occasion was even worse than on most previous such occasions since the bulk of the nobility were also dead. There was no restraining influence on the Highlanders and the rule of law soon began to deteriorate sadly in the Highlands.

In 1516 there was a dispute between John and Donald Mackay, the bastard sons of Roy Mackay, and his brother Neil for the possession of the Mackay lands in Strathnaver in Sutherland. With the help of the Earl of Caithness, Neil gained control of the Mackay lands, but his forces were ambushed by Donald, who killed both his sons and many of his men. John obtained help from the clan Chattan and together the brothers had Neil beheaded by his foster-brother. In 1517, growing even bolder, the brothers invaded Sutherland, but were defeated by the earl and 250 of their men were killed as well as some forty of the Sutherland supporters.

There were further minor battles between John Mackay and the Murrays in the 1520s, although nothing involving as much loss of life. The Gunns, however, not having forgotten or forgiven the treachery of the Keiths over fifty years earlier, took advantage of the prevailing climate of violence to further their blood feud. In an act of revenge the grandson of the chieftain killed Keith of Akregill along with his son and twelve of his clansmen.

In 1526 the chief of the clan Chattan, Lauchlan Mackintosh of Dunnachtan, was murdered by a kinsman James Malcolmson who with his followers was duly chased and killed by the outraged Mackintosh clansmen. Lauchlan Mackintosh's son being a minor, the clan elected Hector Mackintosh, Lauchlan's bastard brother, as captain of the clan until the boy came of age. The Earl of Moray took over the young Mackintosh's care and education. His uncle Hector, however, wished to have him in his power and committed several violent outrages to this end, in particular killing twenty-four Ogilvies. The Earl of Moray obtained power from the king's council to put a stop to this flagrant lawlessness. He then attacked and defeated Hector Mackintosh and his men, hanging his brother William and a considerable number of his followers at Forres. Hector managed to escape, but was subsequently killed by an assassin in St Andrews.

Another example of the general lawlessness of the Highlands during this period was the case of Ian Moydertach, the Captain of the Clanranald. In 1531 and 1534 he was granted Crown charters recognising him as chief of the clan. These charters were intended to impress on the chiefs that they held their position and land as the king's vassals and were contemptuously termed 'sheepskin grants' by the older chiefs. In Moydertach's case Dugal, chief of the Clanranald, had been summarily executed by his clansmen due to his oppressive rule, and his uncle, Alastair, set in his place. Moydertach was Alastair's bastard son and accepted by the clan on his father's death.

Ranald, Dugal's son, had been brought up by Lord Lovat, chief of the clan Fraser. On his coming of age Lovat attempted to instal him as chieftain, restoring him to his father's place, but the clansmen did not like him, nicknaming him Ranald Gallda, or 'Stranger'. In 1544 Moydertach, with the support of Macdonald of Keppoch and Cameron of Lochiel, drove him out and laid waste Lovat's land, capturing Urquhart Castle on Loch Ness. With the aid of the Earl of Huntly, Lovat drove his opponents back and replaced Ranald as chief.

Near Loch Lochy Moydertach ambushed the Frasers, killing nearly 300 of them, including Lord Lovat and his heir, the Master of Lovat, as well as Ranald Gallda. The Earl of Huntly promptly invaded the Clanranald land and killed many of the leading clansmen. Mackintosh, acting on his behalf, captured Macdonald of Keppoch and Cameron of Lochiel, with each of whom he had a feud, and they were both executed in 1546. Three years later in 1549 Mackintosh was accused of plotting to kill Huntly and was also executed. Moydertach, although outlawed, was eventually pardoned and regained his place as chief of the clan. There was indeed little justice in the Highlands at this period.

This was, of course, a period of general turmoil in Scotland. In 1523, when the offer of his daughter Mary in marriage to the young James V had been rejected, Henry VIII sent an army over the border, burning Jedburgh and Kelso. In 1542 he sent another army into Scotland with the same result. When

Opposite: Urquhart Castle on its promontory above Loch Ness

Above: The front and back of a gold and enamelled pendant with the arms of Mary Queen of Scots in crystal *c.* sixteenth century

James V then tried to retaliate his army was defeated at Solway Moss and he returned to Edinburgh to die just seven days after his French queen, Mary of Guise, had given birth to a daughter, Mary. Thus yet again a minor inherited the Scottish throne.

Henry VIII promptly pressed for the marriage of the infant Mary to his son Edward, destined to become Edward VI. This was agreed by a treaty of 1543, which the Scots then annulled. Determined on a policy of 'rough wooing', Henry then sent invading armies over the border in 1544 and 1545, burning Edinburgh, Holyrood, Leith, Dryburgh, Melrose, and Kelso. Even after Henry's death in 1547 the Protector, Somerset, sent yet another army of 12,000 men over the border. At Musselburgh they met a Scots army under the earls of Angus, Arran, and Huntly, each with 10,000 men. Overconfident and suffering from divided command the Scots were soundly defeated, losing 10,000 men.

A rare contemporary print of Darnley and Mary, engraved by R. Elstracke

A Catholic Queen

Once again the Scots turned to the 'auld alliance' to give support and it was agreed that in return for military assistance Mary should be brought up in France and marry the Dauphin. By this time, however, there was a strong body of national feeling in favour of the English and the Protestant faith, rather than France and the old religion. When Mary returned to Edinburgh as Queen of Scotland on the death of the Dauphin in 1561 she was a Roman Catholic in a largely Protestant country, at least in so far as the Lowlands were concerned. The Reformation had barely touched the Highlands since the barriers of language and the trackless mountains were sufficient to deter even the most ardent proselytiser.

It was nevertheless a leading Roman Catholic, Gordon, Earl of Huntly, who first turned against Mary. Angered by the favour she was showing to her Protestant half-brother, Lord James Stuart, and suspecting that she had secretly granted him the title of Earl of Moray despite the fact that he, himself, had enjoyed the honours and income of the title since 1548, Huntly determined to take action. In 1562 when the Queen and James Stuart were making a royal progress in the North-East Lowlands Huntly prepared an ambush for the royal party at a place known as Corichie or the Hill of Fare about 29 kilometres west of Aberdeen. Obtaining warning Stuart summoned help and the royal escort proved sufficient to withstand the assault. Huntly was killed in the attack and his eldest son was hanged in Aberdeen. Lord James Stuart was then duly made Earl of Moray.

Mary's son, destined to become James VI and I, was born in 1566, and later that year she made a journey from Jedburgh to Hermitage Castle to visit the sickbed of the Earl of Bothwell, who had been wounded in an affray with a border reiver, 'Little Jock' Elliot. From then onwards the tragedy of her reign developed remorselessly. The next two years saw her husband Darnley's murder, her abduction and marriage to Bothwell, her capture at Carberry Hill near Musselburgh by a junta of nobles, her enforced abdication and incarceration in Lochleven Castle, her escape, and the defeat of her supporters at the battle of Langside in 1568 followed by her flight over the border for refuge to Elizabeth, Queen of England. Eighteen years of imprisonment followed and finally the executioner's axe.

In 1567 James VI and I was crowned King after Mary's enforced abdication. A period of civil war followed, which extended to the Highlands and resulted in further lawlessness amongst the clans. Regent followed regent and at times near anarchy prevailed. It was not until 1587, when Mary had finally been executed, that James, aged twenty-one, could be said to be the ruler of the realm in name and deed. Even then he proved weak and ineffectual, especially when faced with the misdeeds of the Earl of Huntly for whom he had what was politely termed a 'tendresse'.

In 1589 the Catholic earls of the north, Huntly, Errol, and Angus plotted

THE ROIAIL PROGENEI OF OUR MOST SACRED KING IAMES BY THE grace of God King of E.S.F & I. &c. Decended from ye victorius King Hy 7 & Elizabeth his wife wherin ye 2 deuided families ware vnited together

HONI SOIT QVI MAL Y PENSE

Iames King of England Scotland France and Ireland

Anna Daughter to Frderik 2 King of Denmark

Francis the second King of France

Mary Queene of Scotland maried furst

Secondly Henry Lo: Darley D. of Albany K. of Scotland

Iames the fift King of Scotland

Mary sister to ye D. of Guis & Duches of Longevill

Margret mar. Mathew Steward Earl of Lennox

Mathew Steward Earl of Lenox

furst Iames the fourth King of Scotland

Margret eldest daughter to K. Henry ye 7 maried

Secondly to Archabold Don gall Earle of Agwish

The familie of Lancaster.

The familie of Yorke.

Henry the 7 are of the family of Lancaster

Elizabeth eldest daughter to K. E. ye 4 are of york

Beniamen Wright fecit

Comp: Holland excu Lon 1619

with Philip II of Spain to land troops in Scotland with a view to invading England. Elizabeth demanded their punishment on learning of this correspondence, but James treated them with considerable leniency. They then rose against him, but faced with James's army at the Brig o' Dee surrendered. Again, however, they were very leniently punished with merely a few months 'in ward' in Edinburgh Castle. In 1593, after yet further plots by Huntly and Errol were revealed, they were told they must renounce Roman Catholicism or forfeit their estates. Ignoring either alternative they remained in the north. In 1594 they enforced the release of a Papal agent in Aberdeen and finally, incensed beyond measure, James began to raise an army to march against them.

Before the King could take action the Earl of Argyll advanced to attack Huntly and Errol with Maclean and his men from the Western Isles as well as a strong force of Campbells, making altogether some 7,000 men. In his own stronghold Huntly was quickly able to raise 1,000 Gordons and some 300 horsemen under the Earl of Errol. At the ensuing battle of Glenlivet in 1594, with the decisive aid of a battery of six cannons, Huntly resoundingly defeated the attackers. Argyll was forced to leave several hundred dead on the field, but when faced by an army led by James shortly afterwards the earls abjectly surrendered. Even then they were merely banished for a couple of years before returning to favour once more. Throughout the Highlands the catalogue of treachery, murder, and rapine continued, but finally in 1603 with the death of Queen Elizabeth, James VI of Scotland became also James I of England. A new chapter was about to begin.

An illustrated royal family tree, dated 1619, showing the Tudor connection

Chapter 3

The Road to Union

James VI of Scotland and I of England had barely received the news from the south of Elizabeth's death, and of his impending accession to the throne of England in her place, when he received unwelcome news from the north. This was a report of a serious affray between the Macgregors, who were renowned for their lawlessness, and the Colquhouns of Luss. It was alleged that during this pitched battle between the two clans at Glenfruin over 200 Colquhouns and sundry burgesses of Dumbarton, who had been innocent spectators, had been killed by the Macgregors for the loss of only two of their number.

The King was in no mood to trifle over such matters. The Macgregors' reputation was a bad one and he had little hesitation in passing an act through the Scots Privy Council outlawing the entire clan. The very name Macgregor was banned by law and any Macgregor persisting in using the name might be killed with the full backing of the law. Whether the Macgregors were peaceable or bloodthirsty made no difference. Such a savage sentence, branding the innocent and the guilty alike, had never before been imposed. Unfortunately for the Macgregors they had more enemies than friends and no one stood up in their favour.

The Macgregors, claiming descent from Grogar, third son of King Alpin, had for their motto 'Royal is my name'. Initially they had possessed wide lands stretching from Glenorchy through Argyll to Perthshire and encompassing Glenstrae, Glenlyon, and Glengyle. They were thus perfectly placed for swift raids on the rich lands around Stirling and the Clyde valley followed by equally swift retreat into the rocky fastnesses above Loch Katrine or the vast expanse of the moor of Rannoch.

Unfortunately for the Macgregors their lands in Glenorchy particularly were bounded by those of the increasingly powerful clan Campbell. During the fifteenth century the Campbells employed every tactic of the law they could find, including the newly introduced land charters. Gradually the Macgregors' lands were eroded, according to the strict letter of the law, even if far from fair dealing was involved. The Macgregors constituted a threat to

Glencoe, site of the infamous massacre in 1692

the rich and powerful landowners round Stirling and Perth and as such they were attacked by every means available. Any outrage by outlaws, or mixed clansmen, was at once attributed to them. Their reputation for lawlessness was in itself held against them by their enemies.

In 1519 the Campbells had successfully insinuated their own nominee, Ian Macgregor of Glenstrae, as seventh chief in succession to the rightful sixth chief. With insufficient land to support his clan he was in an unenviable position. Within two generations his grandson, the tenth chief, Gregor Macgregor of Glenstrae, was merely a tenant of Campbell of Glenorchy with whom he was frequently at odds, to the extent of armed battles. In 1570 when captured by Glenorchy he was duly beheaded in the presence of Murray of Atholl and others as a salutory lesson to the clan Macgregor.

Thus using the law and the statutes to suit themselves the Campbells successfully evicted the Macgregors from Glenorchy and Glenstrae, but the clan Macgregor did not take this lightly. Amongst their reprisals for the death of their chief was the killing of thirteen Campbells. They unfortunately went on to compound this lawless behaviour by killing John Drummond, one of the King's foresters. Although denounced for this the Macgregors were granted a pardon within two years.

The quarrel with the Colquhouns of Luss which finally ended in their being declared outlaws arose from a raid in 1602 which was led by Duncan, Macgregor of Glenstrae's brother, on the Luss lands. Amongst the items stolen, apart from household goods, were 300 cows, 100 horses, 400 sheep, and 400 goats. In the process two Colquhouns were killed. It is only fair to assume that the figures mentioned were grossly inflated for it was also alleged that the Colquhouns, to gain the King's support, displayed a number of shirts said to belong to Colquhouns slain by the Macgregors, which were in fact merely dyed with sheep's blood. The effect was that James VI gave Colquhoun of Luss a commission to take action against the Macgregors without requiring him to refer to the Earl of Argyll.

There are various versions of the events which led up to the battle of Glenfruin, which took place the following year in 1603, just prior to James VI and I's departure to England. The most probable is that a conference was held at which, predictably, no agreement was reached and the Macgregors started homewards followed by Colquhoun of Luss and his men. The numbers on either side are open to question as in so many such clan affairs. The result was a particularly bloody mêlée at the end of which the Macgregors had two dead and the Colquhouns lost over 200. This apparently was accomplished by the Macgregors splitting their force in two and, when the Colquhouns were fully engaged with their main force, the other party of Macgregors led by John Macgregor, brother of the chief, worked round to the rear of the Luss forces unobserved and attacked them from behind. Amongst the Macgregor casualties was John Macgregor himself, killed by an arrow. However their victory was achieved, the end result was that James passed his savage act of reprisal against the Macgregors.

Although the punishment decreed was indeed savage, it is, of course, questionable to what degree it was implemented. Macgregor of Glenstrae, the clan chieftain, was hanged along with anything from ten to thirty of his clansmen who were hostages. The women were reputedly branded and transported and the children sent as cattle herds to northern Ireland, which was then being colonised, on pain of death if they returned to Scotland. It seemed impossible for the clan to survive in the circumstances, but survive it did, even though the members were widely separated and often travelling or living under assumed names.

It must be admitted that some of the clan were accustomed to living in such remote parts of the Highlands that they were known as 'The Children of the Mist', but at the same time it is clear that if the edicts against them had been fully observed the clan could not have survived. The only possible conclusion is that once the principals had been hanged as an example the other punishments were not fully or rigorously enforced. With the considerable degree of intermarriage between the clans and having regard to the Highland respect for blood relationships, however remote, this is not surprising. As in so many of the clan decrees this was probably more honoured in the breach than in the observance.

By the turn of the sixteenth century the clans were more or less settled into their modern form, even if still by no means settled in peaceful terms. The practice of levying 'Black Meal' or a payment in meal, or in money, from Lowlanders bordering their part of the Highlands, was fairly widespread amongst the clans. By this means the Lowlanders paid for the protection of the clan neighbouring their land and, should any other clan attempt a raid, they could call on them for armed assistance. This primitive but effective form of the modern protection racket is possibly the origin of the word blackmail.

One venture which had been promoted in 1598 with James VI and I's approval ended in 1605 in complete failure. The Crown had granted powers to a number of Fife merchants and others terming themselves the Adventurers of Fife, to take over the Isle of Lewis from the clan Macleod. As if settling a colony in the new world, a party of artisans and soldiers sailed to Lewis and built a small township. Their arrival united the Macleods who had been quarrelling amongst themselves over the succession to the chieftainship for the previous fifty years or more. In 1605 they drove the settlers out forcibly and ended this experiment which had been seen as a possible method of pacifying the Highlands.

The earliest attempt at industrialisation in the Highlands followed soon afterwards when in 1607 a considerable ironworks was built at Letterewe alongside Loch Maree in Wester Ross. A colony of Englishmen was established there in order to make iron and cast cannon. Haematite ore was apparently imported from Cumberland and landed at Poolewe, being transported thence to the furnace. The earliest ironwork furnace in Scotland, built of brick and Torridonian sandstone, still stands, although extremely vitrified, on the side of the Furnace burn flowing into Loch Maree. A grant of the woods at Letterewe for the purposes of fuel was made in 1610 to Sir George Hay of Kinfauns in Fife who had been one of the moving figures behind the Lewis fiasco. Throughout the sixteenth and seventeenth centuries increasingly vast amounts of timber must have been destroyed in the Highlands for use as fuel or building domestically, to prevent robbers or wolves finding shelter, or for such occasional industrial purposes.

In 1609 the Statutes of Icolmkill were promulgated, nine in number and aimed specifically at the Islanders, but viewed as measures which could be successfully extended to the Highlands. On the face of it they were apparently concerned merely with improving the lot of the Highlanders and Islanders. In fact they had the more direct intention of changing the Highland way of life and forcing the Highlanders to accept the Lowland life-style. The first was obedience to the reformed kirk and it was in fact through the urgings of the kirk that the statutes were passed.

Under these statutes the importation of *aqua vitae* was prohibited, for it was claimed that 'one of the special causes of the great poverty of the Isles, and of the great cruelty and inhuman barbarity, which has been practised by sundry of the inhabitants upon their natural friends and neighbours, has been their extraordinary drinking of strong wines and aqua vitae brought in among them, partly by merchants of the mainland and partly by traffickers among themselves'. Despite this ban on importing *aqua vitae* the Islanders were permitted to distil it themselves or brew ale.

The sixth statute dealt with the question of education and the 'continuance of barbarity, impiety and incivility' in the Isles and the Highlands was attributed to lack of understanding of English; thus it was decreed that every gentleman must send his eldest son, or daughter, if he had no son, to the Lowlands to learn 'to speik, reid and write Englische'. The long-term intention, however, was revealed as being that the 'Irishe language which is one of the chief and principall causis of the continewance of barbaritie and incivilitie amongis the inhabitants of the Isles and Heylandis may be abolisheit and removeit'.

As early as 1609 James VI and I, already King of England for six years, was acting in conjunction with his Lowland advisers to effect what was nothing more or less than a long-term plan to extinguish the Gaelic language in the Highlands. For the next 200 years or more this was still the intention behind numerous actions taken by the Lowland government. At this time it was clearly aimed at breaking up the clan system and the Highland way of life. To be fair it must have seemed at this time a reasonable and logical way to prevent the warring clans from continuing to commit murder and mayhem. The

Statutes of Icolmkill were, however, in effect pointless, since they were generally unenforceable, but they were the first of their kind and the thin end of the wedge.

The Introduction of Whisky

As will be gathered from the statutes quoted above there had been one introduction to the Highlands during the sixteenth century which had been steadily increasing in popularity as being ideally suited to the climate and the countryside. This was initially known as *aqua vitae*, the water of life, translated in the Gaelic as *usquebaugh*. *Aqua vitae*, or brandy, distilled from wine, was known in the fifteenth century, but the first mention of it as definitely being made from malt, like the modern whisky, was in an entry in the Exchequer Rolls for 1494 noting: 'Eight bolls of malt to Friar John Cor, wherewith to make aqua vitae.' Since this was half a tonne of malt, which would have produced some 318 litres of whisky, it is clear that already by this early date distilling of whisky had reached considerable proportions.

Throughout the sixteenth century there is no doubt that the popularity of the new drink increased in the Highlands. In 1555 there was an act specifically forbidding the export of 'aqua vitie' amongst other goods. In 1579 during a year of disastrous harvests it became necessary to prohibit the making of 'aquavitae'. It was not, however, until early in the seventeenth century that the first reference was made in 1618 to the drinking of 'Uisge beatha', or the water of life, at a Highland chieftain's funeral. The shortening of the Gaelic 'Uisge' to whisky was a mere matter of time. Having regard to their climate and conditions of life the eagerness with which the Highlanders took to the drink is very understandable.

By this time the Highlanders had reached the stage where they were accustomed to using firearms as well as bows and arrows, although the latter were still their mainstay. While bears were long since extinct there were still wolves as well as foxes, martens, polecats, and wildcats to be found in the Highlands. The red deer, roe deer, hares, red grouse, blackgame, and ptarmigan were the mainstays of their diet when hunting and salmon and trout were readily available in the rivers and lochs. Geese in the winter in the straths and glens and capercailzie in the ancient forests were also a part of the Highlanders' diet.

There is some argument as to how the Highlanders dressed at this period. Their basic garment appears to have been the *leine croich*, or a long kilted shirt of saffron-coloured cloth with long sleeves. Over this was worn the *feileadh*, or woollen plaid. This could be from 5 to 5·5 metres of double-width cloth, which was worn folded in pleats and buckled round the waist with a belt, while the remainder was carried over the left shoulder, fastened with a

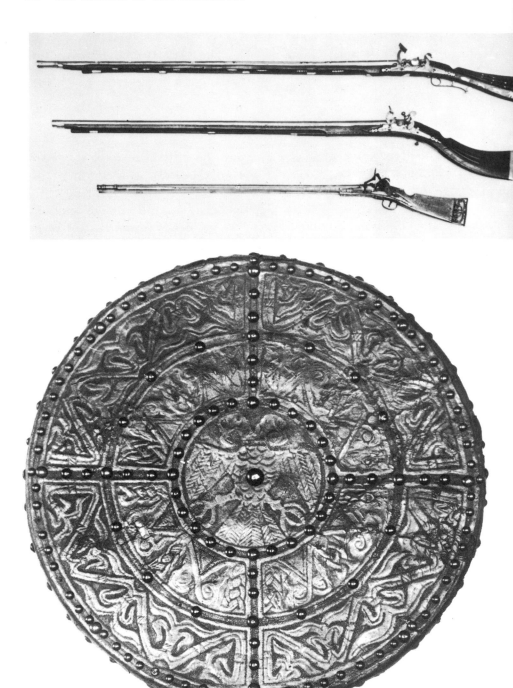

Top: Examples of seventeenth-century Scottish gun-making

Above: A fine embossed leather targe with the double-headed eagle of the Macdonalds *c.* seventeenth century

brooch, and used as a cloak when required in the Highland winters.

This useful garment could also double as a sleeping bag, or blanket, at night and it was the Highlanders' custom when benighted in the open in freezing conditions to dip it in a convenient burn, or pool of water, then wring it out and wrap the damp garment round them. Cocooned thus in a film of ice they were effectively protected against the elements. The full-length *feileadh* was, however, generally discarded by the Highlanders whenever they were about to go into battle, as being something of a hindrance in close-quarters combat. The *feileadh beg,* or short kilt, also variously written as *philibeg,* or *filibeg,* was worn much as the present-day kilt, leaving both hands free for use; but when it was evolved is a matter of contention.

The trews, a garment like close-fitting trousers with the foot attached, more akin to tights, were worn by the chieftains and gentry when riding. In addition a jacket might be worn, either with the trews or with the *feileadh.* Hose, or stockings, were worn on the legs and the feet were shod, if at all, with deerskin shoes cut round the foot and worn with the hair outside and tied round the ankle with a leather thong.

One of the best early descriptions both of the Highlanders' garb and of their methods of hunting was provided by that early English traveller in the Highlands, John Taylor. This eccentric Elizabethan Thames waterman and inn-keeper, prolific rhymer and pamphleteer, made a *Pennyless Pilgrimage* to Scotland in 1618. In Stirling he made friends with the Earl of Mar and followed him by way of St Johnston or Perth, then via Bréchin and Glenesk to join him at the Braes of Mar where he attended a *Tainchel,* or Highland deer hunt. His account of this and of his journey, written in his usual exuberant style, is of considerable interest. He recorded:

I did go through a countrey, Glaneske . . . where the way was rocky and not above a yard broad in some places, so fearful and horrid it was to looke down into the bottome, for if either horse or man had slipt, he had fallen (without recovery) a good mile dowenright . . . and withall, a most familiar mist embraced me round, that I could not see thrice my length any way. Thus, with extreme travell, ascending and descending, mounting and alighting, I came at night to . . . the Brea of Mar, which is a large country all composed of . . . mountains . . .

Once in the yeere, which is the whole moneth of August, and sometimes part of September, many of the nobility and gentry of the kingdome (for their pleasure) doe come into these high-land countries to hunt, where they doe conforme themselves to the habits of the Highlanders, who for the most part speake nothing but Irish . . . Their habit is shoos with but one sole apiece; stockings (which they call short hose) made of a warm stuffe of divers colours, which they call Tartane; as for breeches, many of them, nor their forefathers, never wore any, but a jerkin of the same stuff that their hose is of, their garters being bands or wreaths of hay or straw, with a plead about their

Overleaf: Red deer in the snow near Blair Atholl, Perthshire

shoulders, which is a mantle of divers colours, much finer and lighter stuff than their hose, with blue flat caps on their head, a handkerchiefe knit with two knots about their necke; and thus they are attyred . . .

Their weapons are long bowes and forked arrowes, swords and targets [i.e. targes], harquebusses, muskets, dirks, and Loquhabor-axes . . . As for their attire, any man of what degree soever that comes amongst them, must not disdaine to wear it; for if they doe, then they will disdaine to hunt, or willingly to bring in their dogges; but if men be kind unto them, and be in their habit, then are they conquered with kindnesse and the sport will be plentiful . . .

Describing the ancient Highland method of hunting, which was the age-old method, probably dating back to pre-history and the Neolithic hunters, he. went on:

Five or sixe hundred men doe rise early in the morning, and they doe dispose themselves divers ways, and seven, eight or tenne miles compasse. They doe bring or chase the deere in many herds (two, three or four hundred in a herd) to such a place as the noblemen shall appoint them; then when day is come, the Lords and gentlemen of their companies doe ride or goe to the said places, sometimes wading up to the middles through bournes and rivers, and . . . doe lie downe on the ground till those foresaid scouts, who are called the Tinchell doe bring down the deere . . . After we had stayed there three houres or thereabout, we might perceive the deere appeare on the hills round about us (their heads made a show like a wood) which, being followed close by the Tinchell, are chased down into the valley on each side being way-laid with a hundred couple of strong Irish greyhounds, they are let loose as occasion serves upon the heard of deere . . . With dogges, gunnes, arrowes, dirkes and daggers, in the space of two hours fourscore fat deere were slaine, which after are disposed of some one way, and some another, twenty and thirty miles, and more than enough left for us to make merry withall at our rendezvous.

Despite Taylor's rather charming picture of a peaceful Highland hunting expedition and despite the fact that James VI and I had considerable forces available to control the Highlands, there were still occasional feuds and inter-clan conflicts. It is noticeable that these were often inspired by the very clan chieftains supposedly in a position of authority. For instance in 1615 the Earl of Caithness was responsible for persuading members of the clan Gunn to burn the cornfields of a certain William Innes, who had aroused his displeasure. The Gunn chieftains felt this was rather beneath them, but one of them offered instead to kill Innes. The corn finally being fired, the Earl then blamed the Mackays, but although the truth eventually came out no action was taken.

In 1624 the Mackintoshes of the clan Chattan quarrelled violently with the Earl of Moray. As their chieftain was only a minor the Mackintoshes took advantage of this fact to lay waste the Moray lands, although without much loss of life. More bloody was a feud between the Grants of Ballindalloch and those of another branch of the clan in 1628 when numerous Grants on both sides were killed. This was the consummation of a clan feud which had been simmering for over eighty years since John Grant of Ballindalloch had been murdered by a bastard son of John Grant of Glenmoriston.

It should not be imagined from such incidents that the Highlands, in some parts at least, had not attained a considerable degree of civilisation by this time. Sir Duncan Campbell, Laird of Glenorchy for forty-eight years prior to his death in 1631, for instance, was a very advanced landlord and estate improver. He bred excellent horses; established fallow deer and a rabbit warren on the Isle of Innischonan on Loch Awe; planted numerous trees, including oak, fir, and birch; and maintained a small flock of sheep. His household books show that the family enjoyed food such as chickens, brawn, venison, mutton, smoked ham, wildfowl, rabbits, salmon, herring, and butter, with spices such as saffron, mace, ginger, sugar, and pepper. They drank claret, white wine, ale, and *aqua vitae*. They slept on feather beds, with bolsters, blankets, linen, and bed hangings. All of this was luxurious living by the standards of the day.

Among the regulations laid down in the Court Book of Glenorchy at this time were some points of good estate management. These included:

1   Moors only to be burnt in March.
2   No man to shoot at roe deer, or blackgame, etc., or to kill salmon kelts without permission.
3   All head and fold dykes to be repaired each year with turf and stones.
5   Peats to be cut with proper peat spades.
6   All dwellings to be in as good repair when tenants and cottars leave as when they took possession.
7   All tenants to plant six young trees yearly in their kail yard for each merkland held and every cottar three trees to be oak, ash or plane.
10 60 loads of earth to be applied yearly to each merkland as manure.
11 No swine to be kept.
15 Every tenant must make yearly four iron traps for killing wolves.
16 No tenant to allow rooks, hooded crows, or magpies to nest on their holding.
17 No quarrelling.
27 No young trees to be destroyed.
35 Fine for cutting wood without licence.
36 No one to drink at a brewhouse unless they have travelled eight miles thereto.
39 Tenants obliged to cut and lead fern and thatch for the laird's houses.

Although their aims were decidedly enlightened there is a feudal note about these regulations which was alien to the old Highland way of life, fore-shadowing the changes in the relationship between chieftain and clansmen which were to take place in the eighteenth century. The court cases at Glenorchy recorded about the same time included murder, cattle and sheep stealing, shooting at deer and grouse, selling ale to drunkards, and cutting trees. A pointer to the still unsettled nature of the countryside was the number of weapons listed in the household books. Even so it must be accepted that

Overleaf: The genealogical tree of the Campbells of Glenorchy

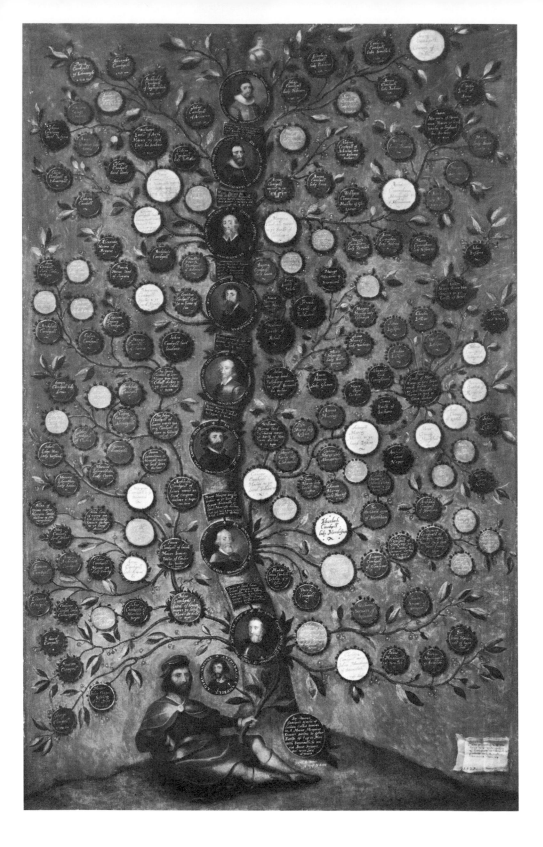

during James VI and I's reign the Scottish Borders were finally tamed and there was at least a fair semblance of order in the Highlands.

The National Covenant

With the accession of Charles I in 1625, however, the familiar Stuart lack of judgement became apparent. He attempted to impose uniformity of religion in England and Scotland, thus effecting unity amongst Presbyterians of all classes and prompting a riot in St Giles Cathedral in 1637. In a spontaneous upsurge of emotion the National Covenant of 1638 was signed by thousands of Scots. While professing loyalty to the Crown the Covenant rejected these innovations in Church affairs. Those who signed the Covenant at this stage were those who, like the majority of Lowland Scots, had accepted Presbyterianism at the Reformation as an austere religion suited to their life-style and rejected Episcopacy as too close to Roman Catholicism. In the trackless Highlands, for the most part, Roman Catholicism still held sway.

In 1638 the General Assembly continued to sit, despite being prorogued by the King's Commissioner, and deposed the bishops and abolished Episcopacy. The so-called Bishops' Wars of 1639 and 1640–1 ensued in the course of which the Covenanters drew up lists of those termed 'enemies of religion'. The Committee of Estates commissioned the Earl of Argyll to pursue the people listed with 'fire and sword' until 'brought to their duty, or rooted out and utterly subdued'. The fact that the unpopular clan Campbell led by the Earl of Argyll was on the side of the Covenant was enough to cause most of the other Highland clans to oppose it, quite apart from the fact that the Reformation had barely touched many parts of the Highlands and to a great extent they remained Roman Catholic.

Amongst those named by the Covenanters as 'enemies of religion' was the Roman Catholic Earl of Airlie. Leaving Airlie Castle in the charge of his eldest son, Lord Ogilvie, he discreetly left for England. The Earl of Montrose, whose duty it was to invest Airlie Castle for the Covenanters, was content to enforce its surrender. The Earl of Argyll, however, insisted on it being pillaged and destroyed. He further saw to it that the other Ogilvie castle at Forthar was also looted and destroyed. It was typical of Argyll's dealings that in a letter dated July 1640, to one Dugald Campbell giving instructions for this act, he wrote: 'You need not let them know you have directions from me to fire it.'

Such double dealing was anathema to a man of honour like Montrose, inspired leader and poet, capable of acting as he wrote on the lines:

He either fears his fate too much,
    Or his deserts are small,
That dares not put it to the touch,
    To win or lose it all.

By 1641 it was clear to Montrose that Argyll was aiming at obtaining supreme power in Scotland. In attempting to expose him, being no match for Argyll as an intriguer, he was himself made the subject of an investigation by the Committee of Estates. While Argyll was made a marquis by Charles I, Montrose was imprisoned and unable even to gain an interview with the king. In 1642, however, he was freed and his case closed since Argyll clearly thought he had nothing further to fear from him; but by this time Montrose was thoroughly opposed to Argyll and the Covenanters' cause.

In 1643 the General Assembly agreed to send an army south to assist the Parliamentary forces against the king. The General Assembly and the Estates also signed the Solemn League and Covenant which supposedly superseded the National Covenant, but included the significant difference that those who failed to sign were liable to forfeit their estates and suffer imprisonment. Already the Covenanters' cause had been skilfully manipulated by Argyll with a political bias apparent and in the same year Montrose offered his services to Charles and urged him to allow him to raise a rebellion in the Highlands.

Throughout 1643 Charles prevaricated, but finally in February 1644 he appointed Montrose his Lieutenant-General in Scotland. After capturing Dumfries without support he then went to take Morpeth in May with the aid of six cannon from the Duke of Newcastle's army. In the same month he was made a marquis, but he was no nearer breaking through to the Highlands.

Taking the bold course, as ever, Montrose, whose features were well known, slipped through the Covenanters' forces in disguise and after four days' journey reached Perth with two companions. There he heard that Alasdair Macdonald had come over from Ireland with 1,600 followers and after attacking the Campbell lands in Ardnamurchan had marched into Lochaber. Macdonald then appealed to the King's Lieutenant for assistance and Montrose sent orders to meet him at Blair. He arrived at Blair just in time to prevent a confrontation between Macdonald's men and those of Atholl. Both sides on seeing him joined in acclaiming him enthusiastically.

Their combined forces only amounted to 2,200 men. Alasdair Macdonald's force, by this time reduced to 1,100 men, was armed with pikes, clubs, claymores, bows and arrows, and matchlocks. Seasoned fighting men, they were divided into three regiments. Although poorly armed the Highlanders were lightly equipped and amazingly fast movers across country. In August, while marching south, Montrose encountered his brother-in-law, David Drummond, Master of Madderty, with a force of 500 bowmen, who also joined him. Thus equipped he met the Covenanters' force under Lord Elcho at Tippermuir west of Perth. Elcho's army consisted of some 7,000 men with 700 cavalry and nine cannon.

Montrose, a brilliant natural strategist, using the latest tactics developed by Gustavus Adolphus of having three lines, one kneeling, one stooping, and one

i 6   a Solemn   4 3
LEAGVE AND COVENANT,
for Reformation, and defence of
Religion, the Honour and happinesse
of the king, and the Peace and safety, of the
three kingdoms of
ENGLAND, SCOTLAND, and IRELAND.

We Noblemen, Barons, Knights, Gentlemen, Citizens, Burgesses, Ministers of the Gospel, and Commons of all sorts in the Kingdoms of England, Scotland, and Ireland, by the Providence of God, living under one king, and being of one reformed Religion, having before our eyes the Glory of God, and the advancement of the kingdome of our Lord and Saviour Iesus Christ, the Honour and happinesse of the kings Maiesty and his posterity, and the true publique Liberty, Safety, and Peace of the Kingdoms, wherein every ones private Condition is included, and calling to minde the treacherous and bloody Plots, Conspiracies, Attempts, and Practices of the Enemies of God against the true Religion, and professors thereof in all places, especially in these three kingdoms ever since the Reformation of Religion, and how much their rage, power and presumption, are of late, and at this time increased and exercised; whereof the deplorable state of the Church and kingdom of Ireland, the distressed estate of the Church and kingdom of England, and the dangerous estate of the Church and kingdom of Scotland, are present and publique Testimonies; We have now at last (after other means of Supplication, Remonstrance, Protestations, and Sufferings) for the preservation of our selves and our Religion, from utter Ruine and Destruction; according to the commendable practice of those kingdoms in former times, and the Example of Gods people in other Nations; After mature deliberation, resolved and determined to enter into a mutuall and solemn League and Covenant; Wherein we all subscribe, and each one of us for himself, with our hands lifted up to the most high God, do sweare;

The Solemn League and Covenant which superseded the National Covenant

standing, all discharging a volley as one, was to win the day even against the Covenanters' vastly superior force. Within a short time the Fife levies, ill-trained and ill-prepared, were on the run. The Covenanters' casualties were variously estimated as being from several hundred to as many as 2,000. Soon afterwards Montrose entered Perth, which at once surrendered, but the Highlanders had obtained so much booty that they promptly withdrew to take it home and Montrose was left with little more than his original Irish regiments.

By September he was outside Aberdeen with some 1,500 men and 75 horse opposed by 2,500 Covenanters under Lord Burleigh, which included 500 horse. After a battle of some hours Montrose ordered his men to charge and as the Covenanters were routed Aberdeen was taken. Contrary to his custom Montrose then allowed his men to pillage the city in revenge for the death of a drummer boy who had been killed when sent forward with an envoy.

Montrose soon received further reinforcements including 500 Macdonalds from Clanranald, Glengarry, Keppoch, and the Isles, also Macleans from Morvern and Mull, Farquharsons from Braemar, and Stewarts of Appin, all of whom hated the Campbells. With the aid of these fresh forces Montrose decided to attack the Campbells at Inveraray. By way of Loch Tay, past

Crianlarich, through Glenorchy and on past Loch Awe, raiding and burning Campbell lands and dwellings as he went, taking the cattle with him, he made remarkable speed. Indeed he moved so fast that Argyll barely had time to board a boat and take flight down Loch Fyne before Inveraray itself was being looted.

Montrose then led his men on to Kilcumin, the site of Fort Augustus at the southern end of Loch Ness. Once again the majority of his force had departed with their loot and he was again reduced to some 1,500 men. Nevertheless he intended to attack Seaforth and his rabble of some 5,000 levies in Inverness, confident that he could beat them. Then he learned that Argyll with 3,000 men, including Lowland levies, was a mere 48 kilometres behind him at Inverlochy.

Montrose promptly made a cross-country detour by way of Culachy and Glen Roy, past the famous Parallel Roads, the notable Ice Age formation there. Skirting the lower edges of Ben Nevis in the snowy winter of 31 January 1645 he came out above the Campbell forces on 1 February. Charging downhill his forces overthrew the Lowlanders, who had been thoroughly unnerved by the sight of the Highlanders charging down at full speed. Although the Campbells fought hard they could not have been inspired by the sight of their chief sailing for safety down Loch Eil. Their casualties were said to be around 1,500 and those of Montrose's men in single figures.

Campbell power never fully recovered from this devastating set-back and Montrose then marched on past Inverness to Elgin where he was joined by 300 Grants and 200 Gordon horse led by Lord Gordon. His forces by this time amounted to 2,000 men and 200 horse. He then moved on to Aberdeen once more and burned Brechin. He went on to capture Dundee, but while his men were pillaging the city he learned of the imminent approach of Generals Hurry and Baillie with an army of 3,000 men and 800 horse. Sending the bulk of his hastily gathered men on ahead, Montrose then withdrew slowly leading Baillie and his men in the direction of Brechin. Taking advantage of the moonlight he then slipped away into the hills. He thus extricated his forces in a masterly fashion leaving the attacking force pursuing him in the wrong direction.

His next successful battle was at Auldearn about 3 kilometres east of Nairn. By this time his force consisted of 2,000 men and 250 cavalry. General Hurry who was pursuing him had something like 4,000 men and 400 cavalry. Unfortunately for Hurry, Montrose's scouts heard Hurry's men discharging their muskets to clear them of wet powder the night before their attack on Auldearn. Thus Montrose knew what to expect and had time to prepare a trap to draw Hurry's force into the unsuitable boggy ground in front of Auldearn where they would have little ground for manoeuvre.

Battles and road building in the seventeenth, eighteenth, and early nineteenth centuries

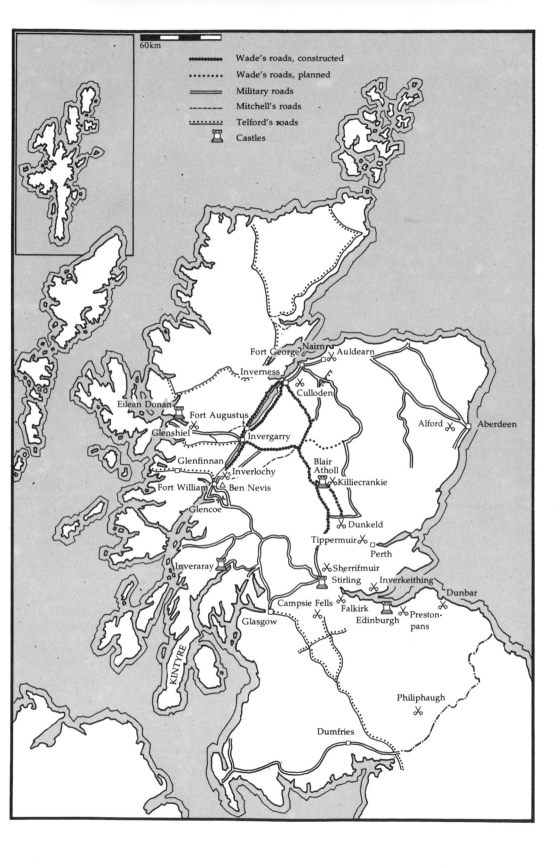

60km

Wade's roads, constructed
Wade's roads, planned
Military roads
Mitchell's roads
Telford's roads
Castles

Fort George
Nairn
Auldearn
Inverness
Culloden
Eilean Donan
Fort Augustus
Alford
Aberdeen
Glenshiel
Invergarry
Glenfinnan
Blair
Atholl
Inverlochy
Killiecrankie
Fort William
Ben Nevis
Glencoe
Dunkeld
Tippermuir
Perth
Inveraray
Sherrifmuir
Stirling
Inverkeithing
Dunbar
Campsie Fells
Falkirk
Preston-
pans
Glasgow
Edinburgh
KINTYRE
Philiphaugh
Dumfries

Montrose—a masterly leader

Montrose posted 300 Irish under Macdonald in the castle with his standard and kept the bulk of his force concealed in cover on the left. The Irish were attacked by four regiments, but due to the boggy ground three had to remain in reserve. Although driven back by weight of numbers, when Montrose charged with his cavalry and then his entire force on the unprotected flank of Hurry's army, Macdonald managed to summon enough reserves to charge as well. This sent the Campbells, who were attacking him, reeling backwards. The effect was catastrophic for Hurry. His four regiments were slaughtered and his reserves fled. He himself escaped with about 100 horse, but he lost some 2,000 men.

In June of 1645 Montrose defeated General Baillie in a battle at Alford, when their forces were about equal with some 2,000 on each side, although the Covenanters had 500 cavalry to Montrose's 250. Nevertheless Baillie and Argyll only escaped by a hairsbreadth, although much to Montrose's distress Lord Gordon was killed. With this battle Montrose's success in the Highlands was complete for he had defeated both Hurry and Baillie, the two Covenanter generals, within a couple of months.

After waiting some time at Dunkeld amassing fresh reinforcements, Montrose finally took the field again with 4,500 men and 500 cavalry. In August he advanced towards the Campsie Fells above Kilsyth where he finally clashed with Baillie leading an army of 6,000 men and 800 cavalry. The rival armies met at the head of the glen and the battle went in Montrose's favour from the start when the Covenanter army was virtually cut in half during their advance. After a stubborn resistance the charge of Montrose's cavalry proved decisive. The Covenanters' army was broken and few of the 6,000 survived. This was Montrose's final victory and the most decisive of the campaign. The whole of Scotland was now defenceless before him.

Typically, as soon as Montrose advanced south, although Edinburgh submitted, his Highlanders vanished back to their straths and glens. It was fatal, as he now found, to rely on them in the Lowlands. Once again his forces were diminished and he was left with only 1,200 foot and 1,000 cavalry. Of the foot some 500 were the remains of his original Irish forces.

In September his forces were encamped at Philiphaugh, near Selkirk. Here they were surprised by Leslie with 2,000 foot and 4,000 cavalry. Caught unawares by these greatly superior forces his men were utterly overwhelmed. Although Montrose rallied about 150 horse and twice charged the enemy to no avail he was at last persuaded to withdraw and save himself.

His brilliant year of success was finally over, but what a wonderful year of victories it had been. Had the Gaels supported him in success as they had in adversity he would have carried all before him, but this was the clearest example of the difference between Highlander and Lowlander. Unfortunately, despite his success, Montrose had caused a greater division between Highlander and Lowlander than had been known before and the Lowlanders were determined that never again would they be put in fear of another Highland onslaught.

For the rest of 1645 and the first half of 1646 Montrose did his best to raise another army in the Highlands with little success. In May of 1646 Charles I placed himself in the hands of the Scots as a last resort against Cromwell and commanded Montrose to cease fighting the Covenanters. Montrose was forced to go into exile on the Continent.

At the instigation of Argyll Charles was then surrendered to Cromwell by the Scots. With his execution in 1649 there was a strong revulsion of feeling in Scotland and Charles II was proclaimed king on condition that he signed the two Covenants. In 1650 Montrose was summoned from the Continent and embarked on an ill-fated expedition in the north.

Landing in Caithness from Orkney, in an area he barely knew, with ill-prepared forces awaiting him, the result was a foregone conclusion. Surprised by a superior body of horse at Carbisdale in Ross and Cromarty he was forced to take to the hills. Betrayed by Neil Macleod of Assynt, whose name became a byword for treachery, he was taken to Edinburgh and executed, but such was his dignity and presence that even in his march to the scaffold he triumphed over those who had come to jeer. Although not himself a Highlander he certainly deserved his place amongst the finest Highland leaders of any age.

The clans continued to fight against Cromwell's forces along with the Covenanters. At the battle of Dunbar in 1650 Cromwell soundly defeated the Covenanting forces under Leslie who opposed him. With these were a force of cavalry under Campbell of Lawers who had been amongst those defeated by Montrose at Auldearn. After Dunbar several clansmen rallied to fight with the Scots forces at Inverkeithing against General Lambert and Cromwell's Ironsides. Hector Maclean of Duart was killed on the battlefield and one after another his foster brothers were killed in the forefront of the struggle crying as each fell in turn 'Another for Hector'. The Frasers and Macleods were among the clansmen who followed Charles II to defeat at Worcester in 1651.

General Monk then waged a short, sharp, and decisive campaign to subdue the clans in the Highlands. It was not long before most of the chieftains submitted. The notable exception was Cameron of Lochiel, who stood out for some time against the garrison stationed at Inverlochy near Fort William. On several occasions he succeeded in ambushing and killing a matter of a hundred Cromwellian soldiers at a time. Once when grappling with a much larger Cromwellian soldier Lochiel bit his throat out and killed him. It is claimed that he regarded this as 'the sweetest bite he had ever taken'. Finally, however, even the bloodthirsty Lochiel was persuaded to accept terms and Argyll stood surety for him. Although the Highlanders were allowed to carry arms under the Commonwealth, while the Lowlanders were not, during the years 1653 to 1660 when Monk was in charge of the Highlands there was an assured peace for almost the first time in memory.

On Charles II's Restoration in 1660, Montrose's head and limbs were gathered together, nine years after his execution, and given a state funeral. By a quirk of irony Argyll, who had been condemned for treachery due to his dealings with General Monk, was executed at the same time and his head replaced that of Montrose on the spike above the Edinburgh Tolbooth. There was a certain poetic justice in this, which must have pleased many in the Highlands.

Cameron of Lochiel marched with Monk to London at the Restoration and was received with acclaim at court. When Charles II asked him for his sword to award him a knighthood, he found to his utter chagrin that it had rusted in its scabbard during the journey south and, unable to draw it, he burst into tears. Seeing his distress, Charles tactfully assured him that he was certain it would have been drawn in his defence if required as it had been in the past and presented him with another.

The story goes that Lochiel was also nearly the victim of poetic justice. One day he visited a barber and as the razor removed the lather from his chin the man enquired:

'You are from Scotland, sir?'

'Yes,' replied Lochiel. 'Have you ever been there?'

'No, and I have no wish to do so,' was the startling reply. 'They are all savages. Do you know, sir, one of them actually tore out my father's throat with his teeth. I only wish I had him where I have you now.'

Thereafter Lochiel vowed never to enter a barber's shop again.

In 1663 the Duke of Lauderdale was responsible for the restoration of Argyll's eldest son to his father's estates as the Earl of Argyll, but not as Marquis. Although the new earl tried to regain certain debts which were due to his father from the Macleans and resorted to armed force for the purpose, he was not successful. The Macleans, aided by the Lamonts and Macdougalls, proved too strong for him. Very few of the clans who had been loyal to the Stuarts had any love for the Campbells.

For the rest of the seventeenth century the dislike, lack of understanding, and distrust which existed between Highlander and Lowlander was steadily accentuated. The fear which the Lowlanders had felt since Montrose's successful campaign of 1645 led them to take every opportunity to curb the Highlanders' freedom. Few Lowlanders ever penetrated into the Highlands themselves and it was the language barrier as much as the fact that there were no roads which made interchange of ideas almost impossible. The Highlanders for their part regarded the Lowlanders with contempt and distrust, tinged in some cases with a little fear of governmental interference in their way of life.

With the growth of religious fanaticism and bitterness in the south, especially in Ayrshire and Galloway, the name Covenanter took on a subtly different connotation, implying extremist rather than merely someone who supported the Covenants. Since the Highlands were largely unaffected, the government in Edinburgh tried an unusual remedy. They gathered together 6,000 Highland clansmen led by Atholl and Perth. In 1678 this 'Highland Host' marched south and occupied Clydesdale, Renfrewshire, Kyle, and Carrick, being allowed freedom to pillage and being billeted on suspected Covenanting families. Despite their freedom and the loud complaints of the Covenanting Lowlanders there were no records of any loss of life. However, the distrust and dislike of the Lowlanders for the Highlanders was accentuated.

In 1681 a Test Act was introduced, which excluded the Royal family, but amongst the more prominent personages caught by this piece of legislation was the Earl of Argyll. He was tried and sentenced to death, but while imprisoned in Edinburgh Castle was allowed, with official connivance, to escape to the Continent. When James VII and II succeeded to the throne on his brother's death in 1685, he was initially opposed by Monmouth in the south and Argyll in Scotland. Royal forces defeated Monmouth and he was executed after the battle of Sedgemoor in the south. Meanwhile Argyll had landed in Kintyre with 300 men in May 1685. Gathering around him 2,500 Campbells and supporters he invaded the Lowlands. Inevitably the bulk of his following evaporated and he was soon captured and executed on the grounds that he had already been found guilty of treason.

The year 1688 saw one of the last clan conflicts in the Highlands when MacDonell of Keppoch quarrelled with Mackintosh of Mackintosh. Mackintosh had obtained a sheepskin charter to the lands of Glenroy. MacDonell of Keppoch met Mackintosh and his men in pitched battle in Lochaber and defeated them, taking Mackintosh prisoner. He was then compelled to renounce his claim to the land. It was typical of the changed times that MacDonell of Keppoch's lands were then subsequently laid waste by a force of troops sent for the purpose.

In 1688 William of Orange was brought over to England where James's attempts to restore Roman Catholicism as the national religion had led to widespread dislike and distrust. With typical Stuart vacillation he failed to take action when it was still possible, even though urged to do so. The clans and indeed much of Scotland were behind him, but with his disappearance to the Continent and the coronation of William and Mary the clans were left leaderless. Finally Viscount Dundee of Claverhouse, a kinsman of Montrose, raised his banner in the Highlands. At the battle of Killiecrankie Claverhouse defeated a force under General Mackay, but was mortally wounded.

On Claverhouse's death command was taken over by Colonel Alexander Cannon of Galloway, who had been sent over by James with a force of Irish troops. The Highlanders wished to have the Earl of Dunfermline as their leader but on referring the matter to James with unerring lack of judgement he nominated Cannon for the command. It says much for the loyalty of the Highlanders to the Stuarts that they accepted this decision. Cannon proved a disastrous leader and was finally defeated in 1690 at the Haughs of Cromdale when his forces were surprised and he himself captured by an unexpected dawn attack. Thus ended all resistance in the Highlands to William and Mary.

The Massacre at Glencoe

To enhance the yoke of government in the Highlands it was decreed that free pardons would be granted to all those chiefs who took an oath of submission to the Crown before 1 January 1692. MacIan, the chieftain of the Macdonalds of Glencoe, was six days overdue owing to heavy snowfalls and a misunderstanding about where the oath was to be taken. The Lord Advocate in Edinburgh, the Master of Stair, who loathed all Highlanders, and the Earl of Breadalbane, who neighboured Macdonald and had frequently suffered his depredations, particularly during the Montrose campaign, persuaded William III to sign an order to extirpate the clan. In a letter, Stair wrote plainly enough:

Glencoe hath not taken the oath at which I rejoice . . . it will be a proper vindication of the public justice to extirpate that sept of thieves . . . It were a great advantage to the nation that thieving tribes were rooted out and cut off. It must be quietly done, otherwise they will make shift for both men and their cattle . . . Let it be secret and sudden.

In the end it was an extraordinarily muddled and botched affair, a piece of amazingly cold-blooded bureaucratic inefficiency. On 3 February 1692, 120 soldiers, mostly Campbells, led by Campbell of Glenlyon who was related by marriage to MacIan, were billeted on the Macdonalds. It was planned that on 13 February at a specific hour at night further forces would arrive from Ballachulish and Breadalbane to block both ends of the Pass. They were then to kill every man, woman, and child in the glen. It all seems somewhat involved preparation for killing some fifty fighting men and a total population of around 150.

In the event it all went wrong. The soldiers might have been deliberately chosen as Campbells and hereditary enemies of the Macdonalds, but after ten days as guests of the clan they could hardly be expected to look forward to their grisly task with any pleasure. Several took care to give their hosts indirect warnings of what was in store for them and others ensured that they made plenty of noise approaching the houses on the fateful night to give the occupants due warning and a chance to escape. Apart from that blizzards prevented the troops arriving to block the pass as planned. In the event only thirty-eight men, women, and children including MacIan were assassinated by government order, although probably as many again perished in the snow, and enough escaped to spread the infamous story through the land.

The cold-blooded planning of the massacre and the breach of trust involved aroused a thrill of horror throughout the country, but particularly in the Highlands. Here in particular it greatly added to the fear and distrust the Highlanders felt for the authorities in Edinburgh and London and contributed in part to the rebellions of 1715 and 1745. William III, who had signed the order for the action taken, became the most hated man in the Highlands and the Campbell name, not altogether deservedly, became a byword for treachery. Yet despite widespread condemnation of the affair the authorities were somewhat naturally reluctant to probe too deeply into the matter. After a belated and rather perfunctory enquiry in 1695 the Master of Stair was removed as Lord Advocate, but soon afterwards became the Earl of Stair. The

Establishment looked after its own, but the Massacre of Glencoe passed into Highland legend as an unforgiven and unforgotten wrong. Six years of poor harvests and famine followed, which were always remembered in the Highlands as 'King William's lean years'.

About 1695 Martin Martin, born on Skye, wrote a book entitled *A Description of the Western Isles of Scotland*, which taken in conjunction with Taylor's description gives a reasonably clear idea of the development of the Highland dress and the tartans worn at the turn of the seventeenth century. He wrote:

The Plad worn only by the Men, is made of fine Wool, the Thred as fine as can be made of that kind; it consists of divers Colours . . . Every Isle differs from each other . . . thro the main Land of the Highlands, in-so-far that they who have seen these Places, are able at the first view of a man's Plad, to guess the place of his Residence . . .

This is the first mention of the difference in *setts,* or patterns, of tartans as varying in different localities. It seems likely that each glen would have its favourite vegetable dyes, which predominated locally, and these would be most commonly used in that area, thus anyone who knew the Highlands well would know roughly to which locality a man belonged. As for the kilt it is plain that by this time there were many ways of wearing it and it seems to have been common for a different tartan to be worn with the jacket or waistcoat. The belted plaid still seems to have been in widespread use, rather than the short kilt, or *philibeg,* although there must have been many variations according to the few illustrations in the seventeenth century.

An interesting report of an observation made by Lord Cromarty about this time was recorded in 1699, indicating the surprising speed with which peat bogs could apparently develop in some places:

In the year 1651, his lordship being then 19 years of age, he saw a plain in the parish of Lochbroom, covered over with a firm standing wood, which was so old, that not only had the trees no green leaves, but the bark was totally thrown off, which he was there informed by the old people, was the universal manner in which fir woods terminated; and that in 20 or 30 years the trees would cast themselves up by the roots. About 15 years afterwards he had occasion to travel that way and observed that there was not a tree, nor the appearance of a root of any of them; but that, in their place, the whole plain where the wood stood, was covered with a flat green moss, or morass; and on asking the country people what was become of the wood, he was answered that no one had been at the trouble of carrying it away, but that it had been overturned by the wind; that the trees lay thick over one another; and that the moss, or bog had overgrown the whole timber, which they added was occasioned by the moisture, which came down from the high hills and stagnated upon the plain; and that nobody could yet pass over it, which however his Lordship was so incautious as to attempt and

Captain Robert Campbell of Glenlyon, commander of the government troops at the Massacre of Glencoe

In Testimony Whereof the Commissioners for the respective
Kingdoms Impowred as aforesaid have sett their hands and Seals
to these Articles contain'd in this and the Twenty five foregoing
pages At Westminster the day and year first abovewriten

Seafield Chancellor   Tho: Cantuar:

Queensberry. C.P.S.   Wm Cowper C:S.

Mar ~ S.   Godolphin

Loudoun S.   Pembroke. P.

Sutherland   Newcastle C.P.S.

Morton   Devonshire

Wemyss   Somerset

Leven   Bolton

Stair   Kingston

Rosebery   Sunderland

Glasgow   Orford

Arch Campbell   Townshend

slipt up to the arm-pit. Before the year 1699 that whole piece of ground was become a solid mass, where the peasant dug turf or peat, which however was not yet of the best sort.

If by the turn of the seventeenth century the Highland distrust of the Lowlanders was considerable, the Scottish dislike for the English had reached its peak. The Scottish attempt to found a colony on the Isthmus of Panama, or Darien as it was then known, between 1698 and 1700 failed largely owing to the determined hostility of the English commercial interests opposed to it. Although originally intended as a joint venture, the English withdrew their support and refused to participate, so that it ended as a uniquely Scottish enterprise. Even in Darien it should be noted, however, that there were clashes and misunderstandings between Gaelic-speaking Highlanders and Lowlanders unable to understand them. The attempt ended with much loss of life due to disease and attacks by Spanish troops and the shareholders throughout Scotland lost large sums of money.

Following the failure of this venture there was violently bitter anti-English feeling all over Scotland at what was regarded as a deliberate betrayal and for some time the union of the Crowns seemed in jeopardy. After Anne's accession in 1702 the moves towards complete union were at last successful with the aid of considerable political chicanery behind the scenes. Many of the Scots nobility had considerable English interests and were to some extent dependent on English ministers' good offices for advancement. Argyll, the High Commissioner in 1705, and the Duke of Queensberry, along with Seafield, Tullibardine, and Tarbat were in favour of the union. The opposition was divided and weakened by political manoeuvring although the popular weight of opinion was on their side.

In 1707, despite the considerable opposition throughout Scotland, union of the Parliaments was in the end achieved. Under the title of Great Britain the two countries were finally united. In the apparent security and isolation of the Highlands the news might have seemed of little importance, but it meant that control had moved from Edinburgh to Westminster and Whitehall and ultimately to the heavy-handed rule of the House of Hanover.

The Act of Union, 1707. The Scots' signatures are on the left, the English on the right

Chapter 4

The Last Rebellions

By 1707, compared with previous centuries, the Highlands had become a reasonably settled, if still completely isolated, part of Scotland. Yet although comparatively peaceful the Highlanders, no less than the Lowlanders, disliked the Act of Union, if for no other reason than the fact that it had the backing of Argyll and the hated Campbells. Indeed throughout the entire country the Act of Union was almost uniformly opposed. One of the numerous spies sent to Scotland by Harley, Queen Anne's principal commissioner for negotiating the Union and later Earl of Oxford, sent a report to him in London stating:

In Edinburgh and to northwards especially, they cry so bitterly against the Union, cursing those great men of theirs that gave consent to it, that one may see fifty men before one that is for the Union, in South or North.

The principal organiser of the spy network set up by Harley was, of course, none other than Daniel Defoe, who, on the whole, thoroughly disliked the Scots, referring to them as 'a hardened refractory people'. His particular detestation was reserved for the Highlanders in Edinburgh. Although he was later to write a tour of Scotland claiming to encompass the Highlands, the probability is that he never actually penetrated beyond the Highland Line. Of the Highlanders in Edinburgh he wrote with a degree of venom which indicates that he had probably come off worst in some personal encounter:

They are all gentlemen and insolent to a degree. But certainly the absurdity is ridiculous to see a man in his mountain habit, armed with a broadsword, target, pistol or perhaps two, at his girdle a dagger, and a staff, walking down the street as upright and haughty as if he were a lord . . . and withal driving a cow.

Considering the immense popular feeling against the Act of Union it is not surprising that the French seized their opportunity in 1708 to distract the attention of the English from the War of the Spanish Succession, which was

A simple romantic conception of the battle of Culloden, with kilted rebels opposed to red-coated soldiers

being waged during most of Queen Anne's reign, by sending a fleet with 6,000 troops to the Firth of Forth under the leadership of James VIII and III, the Old Pretender. They were intercepted by the English navy and lost a warship and some transports before returning ignominiously to France. In the opinion of many observers at the time, if James had landed successfully, even without the support of troops, he would have been hailed with popular acclaim, despite the kirk's distrust of his religion, so great was the general Scottish discontent with the Union.

With the end of the war in Europe, following the Treaty of Utrecht in 1713, there was an attempt by Parliament to introduce a tax on malt, which was taxed in England but not in Scotland and had been specifically exempted by the Act of Union, with a qualifying clause stating 'during the present war'. The pressure from the English farmers was such that the clause was put before Parliament and approved, although vetoed by the House of Lords. Nevertheless the attempt raised an outcry in Scotland and was rightly viewed as a pointer to the future.

On Queen Anne's unexpected death in 1714 George I of Hanover was proclaimed King without opposition. The Jacobites were taken completely by surprise and unready to take action. Belatedly as usual, James VIII and III was only finally proclaimed King in September 1715. It was only then that the Earl of Mar, vainglorious, ambitious, and wavering, having stood by the Union, but discontented not to find himself recognised by George I, raised the Jacobite standard on the Braes of Mar, after sounding out the Highland chieftains at his annual hunting party in August. Unfortunately for James, Louis XIV, who might have provided him with military support, had died shortly before the news of this event and Louis XV's advisers were not inclined to assist him. Even so it is a measure of the loyalty he commanded in the Highlands and of the general discontent with the Union that 6,000 Highlanders flocked to join Mar.

Since there was only Argyll with 2,500 men opposing him in Stirling Castle, Mar could easily have bypassed him, leaving him powerless; but vacillating as ever, he waited two months in Perth, admittedly doubling his forces to 12,000. Finally, in November, after some hesitant moves, Mar's force encountered Argyll's at Sheriffmuir near Stirling. Argyll's right wing defeated Mar's left wing and Mar's right wing as decisively routed Argyll's left wing, so that neither side could claim a decisive victory, but Argyll remained based in Stirling blocking the route to the Lowlands. On the same day as this another smaller Jacobite force, which had bypassed Stirling and joined up with a small group of Lowland Jacobites, was decisively defeated at Preston in Lancashire.

George Keith, Earl Marischal of Scotland, in his *Memoirs* gave an account of the aftermath of Sheriffmuir and Mar's reasons for retreating after the battle as follows:

Next morning the Duke of Marr, finding most of our left had run away and was not returned, retired towards Perth, as the enemy had already done towards Stirling; he resolved there to reassemble those who had run away, and although a considerable number of them were there before us, yet they were of no use having lost their cloaths in the action. To explain this, one must know the habit of the Highlander and their manner of fighting. Their cloaths are composed of two short vests, the one above reaching only to their waste, the other about six inches longer, short stockings which reaches not quite to their knee snd no breetches; but above all they have another piece of the same stuff, of about six yards long which they tie about them in such a manner that it covers their thighs and all their body when they please, but commonly it's fixed on their left shoulder, and leaves their right arm free. This kind of mantell they throw away when they are ready to engage, to be lighter and less encumber'd, and if they are beat it remains on the field, as happened to our left wing, who having lost that part of their cloaths which protects them most from the cold and which likewise serves them for bed cloaths, could not resist the violent cold of the season, and were therefore sent

A Dutch contemporary print of the Old Pretender landing at Peterhead, 1716

with their officers home, not only to be new cloathed but also to bring back those who had fled straight from the battle to the mountains.

It is clear from this that already the winter had set in and despite the fact that James himself at last arrived at Peterhead in late December, his forces were clearly dispirited and on the retreat. In January Argyll received reinforcements and advanced on Perth. The Jacobites withdrew to Dundee. From thence they retreated yet again to Montrose and in February, after little more than a month in Scotland, James VIII and III sailed once more for France. The Old Pretender had failed yet again and the Rising of 1715 had come to an inglorious end.

Yet, uninspiring leader that he may have been, it is indicative of the general unrest in the Highlands that this was not the last attempt to raise rebellion on James's behalf. After intriguing in both Sweden and Spain the Jacobites received aid from the Spanish as an act of revenge for the defeat of their fleet at Cape Passaro. In 1719 two fleets sailed from Spain, one of 3,000 men led by the Duke of Ormonde and one of 300 led by George Keith, the Earl Marischal of Scotland. Encountering adverse storms the Duke of Ormonde and his fleet returned to Spain, while the Earl Marischal's fleet, consisting of only two frigates, reached the western isles. There Keith learned that, tactless as ever, James had appointed Lord Tullibardine as the commander of the Jacobite forces, a post which he had confidently assumed would be his. Relationships between the two quickly reached the stage where they were hardly on speaking terms.

On 25 April the small force landed on the shores of Loch Alsh, taking Eilean Donan Castle as their base on the mainland. The two commanders by this time were quarrelling so violently that they camped 5 kilometres apart. Although an incorrect rumour that Ormonde was coming with his reinforcements after all brought some 1,000 Highlanders to their support they still had little cohesion or discipline. On the approach of General Wightman with a force of 1,100 Government troops up Glenshiel they took up strong positions on each side of the river Shiel, but when the two forces met on 10 June they were subjected to long-range attack by four small mortars. During the evening darkness the Highlanders fled to their homes. In the morning the Spanish troops surrendered and the battle of Glenshiel was at an end. Once again the Jacobite hopes had been shattered.

It would be wrong to imagine, simply because of these uprisings, that all the Highlanders were in favour of restoring King James and concerned only with fighting the Hanoverians. This was in fact far from the case. Nor were all the Highlanders interested only in bearing arms and cattle-stealing. There were examples, other than Campbell of Glenorchy, of chieftains interested in improving farming practices, in planting timber, or rearing cattle, horses, and other stock.

One of the difficulties facing the Highlanders was the complicated social hierarchy which had developed over the centuries, for the clans were in effect still organised on a basically tribal basis. Wealth was largely measured still by the number of cattle which were possessed and by the number of men who could be raised to arms at any time to defend the cattle in the event of a raid, or when necessary to embark on a raid. There was thus a considerable pressure of population on the land available and in years of bad harvest the effects of famine must have been catastrophic.

The social divisions beneath the chief consisted firstly of the principal tenants, or tacksmen, who were his lieutenants in time of war and the entrepreneurs, or capitalists of the clan in time of peace. The tacksmen sublet the land they rented to sub-tenants on the feudal basis, which was not abolished until 1747, that they were to provide service when required for a certain number of days each year to the tacksmen or chieftain, as well as for a rent generally paid in kind, by oatmeal, peat, eggs, or the like. Even lower in the social scale were the cottars, who received land in return for services. On this land they might grow grain, or graze a cow or other stock. Although craftsmen such as weavers, leatherworkers, or millers, might also be employed, the average Highlander was remarkably self-sufficient and was generally able to work in metal and turn his hand to most crafts, as many observers noted.

In general the Highland farming methods were remarkably primitive at this time, as indeed they were throughout most of Scotland. The land in permanent use for agriculture consisted of the infield, nearest the farmstead, and the outfield, separated from the moorland by a head-dyke of stones or turf and itself usually divided into two portions. These consisted of the folds, generally the smaller area, in which the cattle were folded in the year before cropping to provide manure. They were then cropped until they yielded little return, when they were allowed to lie fallow for five or six years. There were also the faughs, generally the larger area, which never received any manure but were cropped in the same way.

The infield was kept in permanent tillage, divided into three equal parts with a crop rotation of bere, a type of barley; oats; and then bere again, with manure applied only prior to planting the bere. Furthermore each field was divided into seven or eight ridges 6 to 12 metres wide and the ridges belonging to each tenant were not necessarily adjacent, changing hands often enough to discourage attempts at improvement. Not surprisingly the crops were extremely poor, even in a good year.

The system of cattle-rearing was peculiar to the Highlands and similar to

Overleaf: Eilean Donan castle where the Spanish force landed in 1719 under George Keith the Earl Marischal

that still employed in Scandinavia, Switzerland, and Austria. In the spring the bulk of the beasts were sent in the charge of cottars and their families to the upper slopes of the mountains, where temporary shielings, or shelters, were built while they fattened on the new grass. During the winter they were expected to survive on the rough grazing on the moorland beyond the outfield, or else on the lower pastures, or haughs, in the strath bottoms, or on hay if any had been made successfully. During the winter months the beasts must often have suffered from short rations, and the Highland habit of bleeding them and mixing their blood with oatmeal to provide food for themselves frequently left them so weak they could hardly stand in the spring.

Once fattened, at any time from June to September, the surplus cattle not required for breeding were either killed and salted for the winter, or driven in herds by various well-known drove roads down to the collecting centres at Crieff and later Falkirk, where they were sold. The routes taken depended on several factors. In a particularly wet year it was necessary to avoid fords which might be swollen with rain. In a particularly dry year it was desirable to be sure there would be enough pasture by the wayside. At any time the drovers were armed and tried to avoid routes which would take them through areas where known cattle thieves were likely to be present. It is scarcely surprising considering the unsettled state of the Highlands that this trade only began to develop in the latter half of the seventeenth century because of the hazards involved previously, especially in such lawless areas as Lochaber and Badenoch. With the Act of Union this was a trade which soon developed on a large scale. According to John Macky in his book, *A Journey Through Scotland*, published in 1723: 'The Highland Fair at Criff happening when I was in Stirling, I had the curiosity to go to see it. There were at least thirty thousand Cattle sold there, most of them to English Drovers . . .'

During the early eighteenth century there were also several attempts at industrial ventures in the Highlands. An ironworks was started at Bonawe at the foot of Loch Etive as early as 1711, initially attempting to use peat as a fuel, but forced finally to use charcoal. At much the same time lead mining was started at Strontian by Sir Alexander Murray, a Lowlander from Stanhope in Peeblesshire, who bought the Ardnamurchan peninsula. He built a township called New York, populated mainly by Englishmen working in the mines. Predictably the local inhabitants decided he was an English spy and raided his livestock and burned his buildings.

Of considerable importance in the development of the Highland economy were the effects of the Act of Annexation after the rebellion of 1715, which resulted in the sale of the forfeited estates of the Earl of Mar, Macdonald of Sleat, Mackenzie of Applecross, and the Earl Marischal. Few Scots and no Highlanders would buy estates forfeited by ancient families and they were mostly sold to the York Buildings Company, a speculative London investment company prepared in their innocence to tackle the problem of

Eighteenth-century lead workers from a painting by David Allan. They are shown weighing lead bars

introducing industry into the Highlands. Not altogether surprisingly they eventually went into liquidation.

In 1728 they took a lease of the Abernethy pine forest from Sir James Grant of Grant, purchasing 60,000 trees as masts for the navy. When these proved too small they were used instead for charcoal and an ironworks was built on the spot. Haematite was obtained from Tomintoul, being carried the 30 or so kilometres by pack horse. A sawmills was also built at Abernethy and logs were floated down the Spey very successfully for many years, proving to be one of their few economic ventures. When Sir Alexander Murray gave up his lead mining at Strontian in despair he successfully leased the mines to the York Buildings Company, who sank a number of shafts and also built hearths to smelt the ore. In addition they constructed roads and numerous outbuildings, including peat barns, stables, and a brewhouse.

About 1727 some Cumberland ironmasters also decided to start an ironworks at Invergarry, initially using a deposit of local haematite. Later they were faced with the enormous expense of importing haematite from Cumberland via Corpach on Loch Linnhe and then transporting it overland and by boat to Invergarry before the days of the Caledonian Canal. As a result the furnace closed down after only six and a half years. Even so, taking into account the fact that a furnace consumed around 168 tonnes of wood a week, or over 48 hectares of mature timber a year, it can be appreciated that these furnaces accounted for a great deal of deforestation in the Highlands and it is scarcely surprising that after a few years they proved uneconomic.

There are good grounds for the belief, which is hotly contested in some quarters, that the ironmaster of the Glengarry works, Thomas Rawlinson, who had adopted Highland dress with enthusiasm, was in part the originator of the modern short kilt, or *philibeg*. Being conveniently placed between Fort Augustus and Fort William he was frequently visited by officers and men from the garrisons. Amongst his visitors, so the story goes, was a regimental tailor named Parkinson, who on seeing a Highlander indoors in a wet belted-plaid and being new to the district, enquired why he did not remove his 'cloak'. On it being explained to him that it was all one piece of cloth and was re-pleated each day he promptly suggested cutting it in half and sewing in the pleats in the bottom half. Rawlinson was impressed with the idea and, it is said, promptly arranged for the tailor to stay and make him a 'little kilt' in which he appeared two days later. John MacDonell, the chieftain of Glengarry, on seeing the design promptly had one made for himself and from this the idea soon spread around the Highlands.

Whether this version of the introduction of the little kilt is true or not is of little importance. It was certainly in common use in the first half of the eighteenth century in the Highlands. Its convenience compared with the *feileadh mòr,* or belted-plaid, in leaving the wearer free to use both hands is immediately apparent. It has certainly been worn for over 250 years and it was merely an adaptation of an older style of dress so that its origins do not really matter. If it is based on fact then Rawlinson's innovation undoubtedly had much greater impact on the Highlands than the early attempts at introducing industry of which he was a part.

To Tame the Highlands

There is little question that the man who had the most far-reaching effect on the Highlands in the first thirty years of the eighteenth century was the Irish General George Wade, who was appointed commander-in-chief of the Highlands in 1724. Until his appointment the problem of the perennial unrest in the Highlands had left the authorities at a loss. On taking up his command his first action was to order a thorough survey of the Highlands.

He then produced a report proposing the building of Fort Augustus at the foot of Loch Ness and Fort George beyond Inverness, in addition to Fort William which was already built. By this means he had a line of forts cutting off the west from the east. He also proposed building 400 kilometres of roads, which involved constructing forty bridges. His plan was put into action in 1725 in conjunction with a Disarming Act forbidding the Highlanders to carry arms and ordering them to hand in those they possessed. This Disarming Act was not very effective, but the military roads provided access to the Highlands for the first time. It was the first step towards taming the Highlanders and introducing them to contemporary civilised life. Governor Caulfield of Fort George produced a much-quoted, but extraordinarily poor couplet, which ran:

'Had you seen these roads before they were made,
You'd lift up your hands and bless General Wade.'

The Irish general, George Wade, commander-in-chief of the Highlands in 1724

Wade also revived the idea of arming loyal groups of Highlanders and forming them into Independent Companies. Initially, in 1725, six companies of some 500 men were formed from the clans Campbell, Grant, Fraser, and Munro, known to be loyal to the Government. These were known as the Black Watch, because of their dark tartan and the fact that their task was to keep a watch on the Highlands. They were posted throughout the Highlands with the exception of Caithness, Argyll, and the Islands, the two former being regarded as peaceful and the latter as no danger to the mainland.

According to Wade's report in 1724 the Macgregors on the borders of Argyll, the Campbells of Breadalbane, the MacDonalds of Keppoch, the Camerons in Inverness-shire, and the Mackenzies in Ross were the most

Opposite: Wade's bridge over the River Tay at Aberfeldy in Perthshire as it can be seen to-day

Below: A colourful figure in his day, Rob Roy remained a favourite subject for painters and illustrators up to the end of the nineteenth century

unruly and the worst thieves in the Highlands. The Macgregors, it may be noted, had been rewarded for their loyalty to the Stuarts at the Restoration by the repeal of the enactment of James I proscribing the use of their name. As they remained loyal to James II the law was re-enacted against them in 1695 by William III, yet it seems they continued to ignore it and were recognised by their own name even by the authorities. Like the Disarming Act of 1715 and so many other laws in the Highlands it simply does not seem to have been applied with any real intention of enforcement

Rob Roy Macgregor, of course, was the prime example of the law being flouted with apparent impunity. Around 1710 he was a respected cattle dealer and farmer. A deal involving the Duke of Montrose as a third party gave the latter the opportunity to foreclose in payment of a debt he claimed was due. Outlawed and outraged, Rob Roy went on to support the 1715 rebellion; thereafter he was determined to exact his revenge and with a following of some twenty men he plagued the Duke of Montrose whenever possible. Based on the Braes of Balquidder he was actively aided by Argyll, no friend to Montrose.

A typical exploit was when he heard that Montrose's factor had a rent collection in progress at a certain house. Setting off with only one follower he reached the house as it was growing dark. The factor, with a bag full of money collected, had just announced that he would cheerfully give it all to have Rob Roy in front of him. The latter promptly gave orders in a loud voice to imaginary men posting two at each corner, two at each window and four at each door. He then marched in boldly with his companion, each armed with a pistol in their left hand and a sword in their right. Taking the bag from the trembling factor he saw that some of the tenants had not received receipts. He at once insisted on the factor making them out and handing them over: 'To show his Grace that it is from him I take the money, and not from these honest men who have paid him.'

On another occasion two of his men had been captured and were being marched by a file of red-coated soldiers to Perth gaol to be tried and almost certainly hanged. Rob Roy and his men discreetly followed the prisoners and escort as they marched down the side of Loch Tay. It is easy to imagine them racing through the heather above, unseen and unsuspected, but unable to think of any way of releasing their friends.

As the soldiers prepared to cross the river Tay an ambush was prepared. A herd of goats was hastily slaughtered and Rob Roy and his followers draped the bloody carcases over their shoulders with the heads and legs dangling loose. At an agreed signal they rose from the roadside in the half light of the gloaming and bounded forward on the terrified escort with wild yells. Their companions were released without a shot fired and the demoralised soldiers were sent on their way unharmed after having been relieved of their weapons. Thus yet another story was added to the legend. One biographer wrote:

Rob Roy's grave in the Balquhidder churchyard

In this manner did this extraordinary man live, in open violation of the laws and died peaceably in his bed when nearly eighty years of age. His funeral was attended by all the country round, high and low, the Duke of Montrose and his immediate friends only excepted . . . He never hurt or meddled with the property of a poor man and . . . was always careful that his great enemy should be the principal, if not the only sufferer.

It is only necessary to replace the Duke of Montrose with the Sheriff of Nottingham to have an almost exact parallel with another folk hero, but the Scottish version lived as late as the eighteenth century and died in bed at a ripe old age. The story goes that on his death-bed he heard of the approach of an old enemy and insisted on being dressed and helped into his armchair where he greeted the man with his sword at his side and his pistol in his belt. As soon as the man had gone he announced that he was now prepared to die in peace.

In many ways Rob Roy was the epitome of the Highlander, embodying all his virtues and failings. Immensely proud of his lineage and ancestry, he was also hospitable and generous to a degree, fiercely loyal to those who stood by him, were dependent on him, or were related to him—no matter how distantly—and as fiercely determined to revenge himself on those he considered had wronged him, or his family. A good swordsman, active and brave, capable of feats of remarkable endurance, he was also capable of procrastination and idleness unless suitably spurred in an emergency, when his native cunning often came to his assistance.

With an intrinsic appreciation of music and poetry, like so many Highlanders, he was a good piper and extempore Gaelic rhymer. Possessing a fine sense of humour, except in so far as his own person, or family pride, was concerned, he would be happy to pass an evening amongst friends round the whisky barrel indulging in singing, mirthful story-telling, reciting, or dancing to the sound of pipes or fiddle. Yet he would still be prepared at a moment's notice to rise and rob the Duke of Montrose of his cattle or sheep, purely to gratify his sense of revenge.

In practice Rob Roy Macgregor lived during the last period in the Highlands when such behaviour could have been tolerated, or would have been possible. By 1736 Wade had completed his task and the Highlands at last had a system of roads. Edward Burt, his chief surveyor, described them thus:

One of them begins from Crieff, which is about fourteen miles from Stirling. Here the Romans left off their works, of which some parts are visible to this day; particularly the camp at Ardoch, where the vestiges of the fortifications are on a moor, so barren that its whole form has been safe from culture, or other alteration besides weather and time.

The other road enters the hills at Dunkeld, in Athol, which is about ten miles from Perth.

The first of them according to my account, though the last in execution, proceeds through Glenalmond . . . and thence goes to Aberfeldy. There it crosses the river Tay by a bridge of free-stone, consisting of five spacious arches (by the way, this military bridge is the only passage over that wild and dangerous river), and from thence the road goes on to Dalnacardoch.

The other road from Dunkeld proceeds by the Blair of Athol to the said Dalnacardoch.

Here the two roads join in one, and as a single road it leads on to Dalwhinny, where it branches out again into two; of which one proceeds towards the north-west, through Garva Moor, and over the Coriarach Mountain to Fort-Augustus, at Killichumen, and the other branch goes due north to the barrack of Ruthven in Badenoch, and thence by Delmagaray to Inverness. From thence it proceeds something to the southward of the west across the island to the aforesaid Fort-Augustus, and so on to Fort-William in Lochaber.

The length of all these roads is about 250 miles.

Burt was the author of a book published under the title of *Letters from a Gentleman in the North of Scotland*, written between 1725–6, but only published in 1754. He was a keen observer, if strongly biased against the Highlanders and the Scots as a whole, but his reasons for writing the letters and publishing them were probably as genuine as his observations. He noted:

The Highlands are but little known, even to the inhabitants of the low country of Scotland . . . to the people of England . . . the Highlands are hardly known at all; for there has been less that I know of written upon the subject than of either of the Indies...

There can be little doubt that some Highland chieftains were inclined to use their considerable powers in a manner which hardly accorded with justice. He wrote:

The heritable power of *pit* and *gallows,* as they call it, which is still exercised by some within their proper district, is, I think, too much for any particular subject to be entrusted with.

He noted one chieftain's abuse of power thus:

I have heard say of him, by a very credible person, that a Highlander of a neighbouring clan, with whom he had long been at variance, being brought before him, he declared upon the accusation, before he had seen the party accused, *that his very name should hang him.*

Although many of the chiefs acted in a just and paternal way towards their clansmen the subsequent actions of many of them during the latter part of the century more than justified his summing up:

. . . in general it seems quite contrary to reason, justice, and nature, that any one person, from the mere accident of his birth should have the prerogative to oppress a whole community for the gratification of his own selfish views and inclinations.

In Inverness he noted two churches 'one for the English and one for the Irish tongue, both out of repair'. He found the cant and hypocrisy of the ministers nauseating, for already the narrow-minded Calvinism of the early Presbyterian religion was spreading to the Highlands. The Society for the Propagation of Christian Knowledge, taking the same view as James I and successive governments, was determined to 'root out the Erse language' as being a barrier to the spread of religion. They continued to send selected ministers from the south to parishes in the Highlands. Naturally these 'Whig' ministers, as they were termed, were disliked by the Highlanders and, paradoxically, in order to make themselves understood their first task was to learn Gaelic themselves. Many proved utter failures, for it was only men of character and muscle who could succeed and very often these tended to become more Highland than the Highlanders.

A good example was Aeneas Sage, who accepted the ministry of Lochcarron in 1726. A man of immense stature and strength, his parishioners at first regarded him as a southern interloper and were not prepared to listen to him. As his grandson wrote subsequently:

To show their dislike, the people assembled every Lord's day, on a plot of ground about twenty yards from the church door for the practice of athletic games . . .

Sage was not the sort of man to be easily disheartened. He persuaded one of his reluctant parishioners to attend church each Sunday and listen to him preach in return for a pound of snuff. Each week for nearly a year this ritual took place and after Sage had preached to his lone audience he duly handed over the bribe. Finally, after a particularly powerful sermon on the text of 'What shall profit a man . . .' the Highlander broke down and refused to take the snuff 'for listening to the Lord's word'. Thereafter he became one of Sage's leading parishioners.

When it came to blows, as it occasionally did, Sage was more than capable of holding his own. Nor was he alone in such methods. A neighbouring minister, also of considerable personal strength, used to carry a cudgel, which he nicknamed 'the bailie' (i.e. magistrate). Sage remained minister of Lochcarron until his death in 1774 and it is apparent that the Highland atmosphere had its effect on him to the extent that he was rebuked by the General Assembly in 1759 for his 'heresy hunting disposition' after a quarrel with a neighbouring minister had been brought to their attention. Yet despite such heroic figures there were certain areas where Roman Catholicism persisted notwithstanding the efforts of the Kirk.

Another feature of Highland life which aroused Burt's ire was the Highlanders' pride in their family ancestry. He wrote:

This kind of vanity . . . in people of no fortune, makes them ridiculous . . . Thus you see a gentleman may be a mercenary piper, or keep a little ale-house where he brews his drink in a kettle; but to be of any working trade would be a disgrace to him, his present relations and all his ancestry . . .

He was also scathing about whet he termed the 'gentlemen soldiers' of the Independent Companies:

I cannot forbear to tell you . . . that many of these private gentlemen soldiers have gillys, or servants, to attend them in quarters, or on a march, to carry their provisions, baggage and firelocks . . .

It is clear that Burt simply did not understand the Highland mentality. The Disarming Act introduced after the 1715 Rebellion was galling to the spirited Highlanders and many men of good family and education joined the ranks of the Independent Companies simply for the opportunity of bearing arms and possibly seeing some action. This was not something that a southerner could readily understand.

Nor could Burt forbear passing on a joke which was clearly going the rounds at that time:

The Captain of one of the Highland Corps entertained me some time ago at Stirling with an account of a Dispute that happened in one of his Corps about Precedency. The Officer among the rest had received Orders to add a Drum to His Bagpipe as a more military instrument for the Pipe had to be returned because the Highlanders could hardly be brought to march without it. Now, the Contest between the Drummer and the Piper arose about the Post of Honour and at length the Contention grew exceedingly hot, which the Captain having Notice of, he called them both before him, and, in the End decided the matter in favour of the Drum; whereupon the Piper remonstrated very warmly:

'Ods wuds, sir,' says he, 'and shall a little Rascal that beats upon a Sheepskin tak' the right hand of me that am a Musician?'

Here again Burt had missed the point and an important one that the Whitehall mind also took a long time to grasp, namely that the Highlanders had to have their bagpipes rather than the drum favoured by the English regiments. By this time the bagpipes had long ousted the ancient clarsach, or harp, as the instrument of the Highlander. Although the violin, or fiddle, was to become extremely popular in the late eighteenth century, the Highlanders' blood thrilled to the sound of the bagpipes in war in a way which to the southern mind was past understanding.

Major General David Stewart of Garth in his epic two-volume work entitled *Sketches of the Character, Manners and Present State of the Highlanders of Scotland with details of the Military Service of the Highland Regiments,* which was published in 1822, wrote of the bagpipes as follows:

Playing the bagpipes within doors is a Lowland or English custom. In the Highlands, the piper is always in the open air; and when people wish to dance to his music, it is on the green, if the weather permits; nothing but necessity make them attempt a pipe dance in the house. The bagpipe was a field instrument intended to call the clans to arms and animate them in battle, and was no more intended for the house than a round of six-pounders. A broad-side, from a first-rate or a round from a battery, has a sublime and impressive effect, at a proper distance. In the same manner, the sound of the bagpipe, softened by distance, had an indescribable effect on the minds and actions of the Highlanders. But as few would choose to be under the muzzles of the guns of a ship of the line, or of a battery, when in full play, so I have seldom seen a Highlander whose ears were not grated when close to pipes, however much his breast might be warmed, and his feelings roused, by the sounds to which he had been accustomed in his youth, when proceeding from the proper distance.

In 1739, George II authorised the Independent Companies to be formed into a Regiment of Foot. The first parade was held in a field between Taybridge and Aberfeldy and Major General David Stewart of Garth recorded:

The type of dress worn by gentlemen in the Highlands in the early eighteenth century. A point of interest is that he is wearing a tartan jacket and trews together with the *feileadh mór* or belted plaid. (Here not pleated at the waist.)

The day before the regiment was embodied at Tayhbridge, five of the soldiers dined and slept in my grandfather's house at Garth. The following morning they rode off in their usual dress, a tartan jacket and truis, ornamented with gold lace embroidery, or twisted gold cords, as was the fashion at that time, while their servants carried their military clothing and arms.

General Stewart's own great uncle, Mr Stewart of Bohallie was one of these gentlemen soldiers:

This gentleman, a man of family and education, was five feet eleven inches in height, remarkable for his personal strength and activity, and one of the best swordsmen of his time . . . and yet with all these qualifications, he was only centre man of the centre rank of his company.

The 43rd, later to become the 42nd, Highland Regiment, or Black Watch, was thus formed from a hand-picked body of men, fully trained in the use of arms before they were ever recruited. They were certainly fully enough armed. In addition to the Government issue of musket, bayonet, broadsword, cartouche box, and belts, they carried a *tuagh,* or Lochaber axe, a dirk, a pair of 'dags' or steel pistols, and in some cases a *targaid* or shield. These, together with the original small leather sporran, were provided by the men themselves. Their proficiency in handling this formidable personal armoury was soon proven in action.

In 1743 the regiment was ordered south, with the intention of sending them over to Flanders to take part in the War of the Austrian Succession in which Britain had become involved. The reason they were given was that they were to be inspected by George II. Many of them, however, felt indignant on the grounds tht they had not volunteered to serve outside the Highlands. On their arrival in London matters were not improved when it was learned that George II had gone abroad. They were inspected by General Wade on 14 May, the King's birthday, but the rumour had been spread, possibly by Jacobite agents, that the intention was to send them to the West Indies, famed as the fever-ridden graveyard of white soldiers. The Highlanders felt that 'after being used as rods to scourge their own countrymen they were being thrown into the fire'.

There followed the famous mutiny, when 200 of the Highlanders slipped away by night, heading for Scotland. Keeping to the country between the two main roads north, marching by night and lying low by day, they reached Oundle, almost 160 kilometres from London, before they were discovered and surrounded by dragoons. After some negotiation they agreed to surrender and marched to the Tower to be imprisoned. So perfect had their discipline been throughout that there was a public revulsion of feeling in their favour, but military justice was not prepared to be lenient.

Although the majority could not understand English and relied on interpreters at their trial 107 men were tried by court martial and condemned to be shot. Finally three were chosen as ringleaders and shot in the presence of the others, behaving with exemplary calm. They were probably more fortunate than the remainder who were posted to the fever-ridden outposts they had hoped to avoid. Inevitably all those who were punished were regarded by their fellows as victims of perfidious double-dealing by the Government, but the remainder of the regiment embarked for Flanders and acquitted themselves with distinction, winning the regiment's first battle honours at the battle of Fontenoy in 1745, when even the French were loud in their praise. Ironically, the commander of the British forces was the Duke of Cumberland who was later to earn the nickname of 'Butcher' Cumberland for his dealings with their fellow countrymen after Culloden one year later.

In 1744 the French had planned an attack through the Highlands with 3,000 troops, who were to be supported by an uprising of the clans. At the same time another force of 12,000 was to be put ashore near London under the leadership of Prince Charles Edward Stuart, the Young Pretender, son of James VIII and III, by this time a well-built young man aching to recover what he regarded as his father's throne. A combination of a violent storm which wrecked many of their transports and a British fleet off-shore put an end to the French plans.

Bonnie Prince Charlie and the '45

Despite this fiasco the determined young Prince announced his intention of landing in Scotland in the summer of 1745. His supporters in Scotland were appalled at the idea and sent word for him to abandon the plan, but with typical Jacobite inefficiency the message never reached him. In July he set off in a privateer escorted by a French warship of 60 guns. The warship was involved in a naval action with an English ship, but the privateer continued alone and on 23 July, against all odds, Prince Charles Edward Stuart landed at Eriskay in the Outer Hebrides. He had nine companions, of whom only three were Scots. It was an unlikely beginning for such an ambitious attempt.

Despite initial rebuffs his charm and confidence must have been considerable for within three weeks he had won over Cameron of Lochiel, chief of the influential clan Cameron, and felt confident enough to announce his intentions publicly. On 19 August the Jacobite standard was raised at Glenfinnan at the head of Loch Shiel and James VIII and III for the second time was formally proclaimed King. At this stage his total following probably amounted to only some 1,300 men, but this was reported to the authorities in the south as being fully double this number. Already some small parties of prisoners had been taken by clansmen on their way to Glenfinnan and the confusion in the south was considerable as to the Prince's whereabouts and the numbers of his forces.

Ironically the military roads planned for use by Government forces were now used almost entirely by the Jacobites. Sir John Cope, the Government forces' commander, was not even sure of the Prince's arrival in the Highlands until 8 August. Ordered to march north to nip the rising in the bud, he was only able to raise around 1,400 raw troops, but on 20 August he duly marched northwards from Stirling. By the 25th he had reached Dalnacardoch and received first-hand, but inflated, reports of the strength of the Jacobite forces. His alternatives were to march on to Inverness in the hope of raising further forces, or to turn back for Stirling, in which case he might well have been overtaken or bypassed by the Jacobites. Making the right choice he pressed on to Inverness and it was no fault of his that he could find no volunteers there. On 4 September, while he was urgently demanding shipping from Edinburgh, Prince Charles entered Perth triumphantly.

In Perth Charles was joined by James Drummond, third Duke of Perth and

The landing of Charles Edward Stuart on the Scottish mainland in 1745

Lord George Murray, brother of the Whig Duke of Atholl. These two were promptly appointed the Lieutenant-Generals of the Jacobite army, in addition to John William O'Sullivan, who had been appointed adjutant and Quartermaster-General. One of the nine companions who had accompanied Charles from France, O'Sullivan was a captain in the French army and was accordingly supposed to have some knowledge of staff work. On these slender grounds he had been appointed to this important post when it was found that none of the clan chieftains, except for Keppoch, who had served in the French army, had any military experience.

O'Sullivan was the Prince's evil genius. The Duke of Perth, modest, kind-hearted, and brave, but with little military experience, tended to hold the balance between O'Sullivan and Lord George. The latter had fought in the Fifteen and at Glenshiel, with his elder brother, Tullibardine. After being pardoned he had settled down to a peaceful country life on his brother's estates at Athol. It was only a sense of duty which had impelled him to join the Prince's forces and he was at odds not only with O'Sullivan but also Murray of

Broughton, the Prince's secretary who openly cast aspersions on his loyalty. Despite the fact that the Prince never entirely trusted him Lord George was undoubtedly the principal strategist on the Jacobite side.

From their arrival in Perth onwards, Cope was always a little too late in his efforts to check the Prince and his forces. On the 11th Cope and his men embarked for Edinburgh from Aberdeen. On the 17th they arrived in the Forth in time to learn that Edinburgh except for the castle had fallen to the Prince with little or no bloodshed the night previously, when Lochiel at the head of a small force of Highlanders slipped in through the Netherbow Gate as it was opened to allow a coach to pass through. The guard had promptly fled with practically no resistance. In the morning the story goes that an Edinburgh citizen seeing a Highlander lounging on the ramparts enquired where the guard was, to be told: 'She is relieved.'

Cope was thus forced to disembark at Dunbar on the 17th and take the road for Haddington, preparatory to attacking Edinburgh. On the 20th they met the advance guard of the Jacobite forces just beyond Tranent. Cope rightly chos the open ground just outside Preston and beneath Tranent to fight, for the flat ground there provided him with ground to manoeuvre his dragoons, although the latter were in no real state to fight, for their commander, Colonel Gardiner, was an extremely sick man and the horses were in poor condition while the men themselves were all but out of control.

The two armies were of much the same size, about 2,300 men apiece. The Jacobites occupied the high ground around Tranent and Cope's army was drawn up below them on the plain. Initially Cope had expected the Jacobites to attack from the west and was drawn up facing that direction. When he saw them in Tranent at 2 pm he merely wheeled his men round to face them and thus the two armies remained until nightfall for between them there was an almost impassable morass and the Prince's advisers saw that despite the fact that they had the high ground they were unable to use it to advantage.

In the evening fortune favoured the Prince. A local man named Anderson agreed to guide part of his force along a route which though narrow in places would take it within 1,000 metres of Cope's east flank. During the early morning the Highlanders cautiously made their approach. Although Cope had fires burning throughout the night and patrols out, the Highlanders managed to make their approach unseen. When a patrol of dragoons finally challenged the advancing Highlanders at about 6.30 in the morning, Cope just had time to order his forces to wheel into position to prepare for the surprise attack.

It is probable that the Highlanders were able to advance very close under cover of the morning mist which frequently clings a few feet from the ground

Opposite: A youthful Bonnie Prince Charlie

Overleaf: The battle of Culloden, 1746

in the east coast areas. Then the speed of their attack must undoubtedly have confused raw troops unused to their methods of warfare. It was the Highland habit to charge at full speed and fire their muskets at close range, throwing them aside and then firing their dags, or heavy-butted pistols, which they immediately hurled at the enemy, following up instantly with their sword in the right hand, targe on their left arm, and dirk in their left hand. Dropping on one knee to take the bayonet thrust of the enemy on their targe they would then raise their arm and with it their enemy's point and rushing in on the defenceless man despatch him with a blow, following this by thrusting right and left with sword and dagger, frequently killing two men at once.

To raw troops it must have been totally demoralising and it was literally all over within five minutes. The panic-stricken Government infantry broke at the first charge and started running in all directions, despite the efforts of Cope and his officers to rally them. The dragoons were no better, being seized with the general panic. The discomfited officers, after attempting to rally a squadron of dragoons at pistol point, were forced to retreat at a trot up Birsley Brae to Tranent on a track still known as 'Johnnie Cope's Road'. The wretched Cope, by no means the poltroon he has been made out to be, was faced with the humiliation of reporting the defeat of his army to the commander of the garrison at Berwick.

This was undoubtedly the high tide of the Jacobite campaign. Apart from the castles of Edinburgh and Stirling and the Highland forts, Scotland was virtually theirs. It is understandable if Charles thought everything was going his way. Yet recruits were surprisingly slow to come in and the Campbells in the west and the Sutherlands, Mackays, and Munros in the north remained loyal to Hanover. Even the Mackintoshes, Mackenzies, Gordons, and Grants were divided, some for and some against the Prince, while Macleod and Macdonald of Skye came out in open opposition to him. Even so, within six weeks, the Prince had raised 5,000 men and 500 cavalry with the promise of French support. On the other hand the Government had large numbers of troops returning from Holland and considerable support in the English countryside.

On 3 November Charles started southwards, convinced that he would gather more supporters as he marched south. On 15 November, amid heavy snow, Carlisle, undergarrisoned and no longer fortified, surrendered without a shot fired, but this was the sole success of the march. By 3 December they had reached Derby with none of the hoped-for support forthcoming, and with only 5,000 men Charles was faced with three armies with about 30,000 men in

Representatives of the Macpherson (*top left*), Grant (*top right*), and Mar (*bottom left*) clans prior to the '45. Rob Roy Macgregor (*bottom right*) appears to be wearing the Campbell tartan as the Macgregor was proscribed

William Augustus, Duke of Cumberland (1721–65), whose memory is besmirched by his excesses after Culloden

all, two of which were approaching him from different directions. Despite his protests his advisers confirmed that there was no choice but retreat and on 6 December they started to retrace their footsteps northwards.

On Christmas day the Jacobite army entered Glasgow, the 'Whig' capital of the north, which had raised a regiment of Hanoverian militia, where they retaliated by requisitioning clothing for their forces. Meanwhile a further 4,000 Jacobite supporters had rallied at Perth. United with them the Jacobite forces were approximately equal to the Hanoverian army in the south of Scotland. The Hanoverian commander at this stage was General Henry Hawley, a blustering Englishman who had fought at Sheriffmuir and had a poor opinion of the Highlanders.

On 16 January Hawley, with a force of 8,500 men, including cavalry and artillery, arrived at Falkirk. The Jacobites with a force of some 8,000 advanced against him there on the morning of the 18th. Hawley, who had dined well the previous night, refused to believe that they would dare to attack him and took no notice of the first warning of their approach. When he finally accepted that the Jacobites were attacking it was nearly too late. With rain driving into their faces and wetting their ardour and their powder, the Hanoverian regiments broke when the Highlanders charged. Only their rearguard remained steady and provided covering fire as the remainder beat a disorderly retreat to Linlithgow in pouring rain.

Even the Jacobites were surprised by their victory and on 1 February their retreat to the Highlands began. It was the beginning of the preordained end. Like a Greek tragedy the entire episode had unfolded remorselessly from the moment of Prince Charles Edward's landing at Eriskay. After his initial victories the tide now turned in full flood against him.

By this time the young and energetic Duke of Cumberland, an experienced field commander, if somewhat limited tactician, was in command of the Hanoverian forces. Based at first in Aberdeenshire, he began his advance in April. By the 14th he was camped at Nairn and the speed of his advance had taken the disunited Jacobite commanders by surprise. Without pay, arms, and ammunition, with their leaders divided and distrustful of each other, the Jacobite army was steadily disintegrating, even if the Highlanders' morale remained as yet unimpaired.

The Battle of Culloden

Since the retreat from Derby the Prince had shown increasingly less interest in matters, but with that fatal Stuart ability to listen to the wrong man at the wrong moment, he agreed with O'Sullivan, his Irish evil influence, contrary to Lord George Murray's advice, that they should make a surprise attack on Cumberland's camp at dawn. Previous to this the utterly indefensible battlefield at Drummossie Moor near Culloden had been chosen by O'Sullivan, although Lord George Murray had advised a good defensive position near Dalcross Castle. Through sheer inefficiency at this stage the Jacobite army was without provisions and after a long, badly organised, and ill-guided night march which took them within three kilometres of the Hanoverian camp they were forced to withdraw once more to Drummossie Moor, tired out, dispirited, and still unfed.

16 April brought a freezing cold north-easterly gale with accompanying rain and sleet, blowing straight into the faces of the waiting Jacobite army. They were only 5,000 strong as opposed to Cumberland's 9,000 well-trained troops equipped with cannon. With the two armies drawn up some five hundred metres apart, from one in the afternoon the Jacobites were subjected to a long and sustained bombardment.

It was a heroic waste of lives and men. The Jacobites stood little or no chance. The wind was so strong that their own gunsmoke blinded them. Even so they charged and drove home their attack against odds of double their number, piercing Cumberland's left wing. Despite such gallantry inevitably the end had to come. Cannon and sheer weight of numbers decided the day. By 2 pm it was all over. An estimated 1,200 Highlanders were killed on the Jacobite side and some 364 Hanoverian soldiers of Cumberland's forces. The death knell of the Highland clan system had sounded.

Cumberland might have been remembered for his victory at this last battle on British soil had he behaved with anything like normal honour after the battle. As it was he refused quarter to prisoners or wounded and encouraged the senseless cruelty which blackened the day and earned him the title of 'Butcher' and the notoriety which still clings to his name. Yet this was merely a precursor of his merciless persecution of the Highlands which followed.

The Prince, urged to fly from the field and save himself, thereafter spent five months in the heather protected by the loyalty of the Highlanders, who despised the £30,000 put on his head. One example of the loyalty of his followers was that of Roderick Morrison, who bore a considerable resemblance to the Prince. Chased by Hanoverian soldiers, shot, and mortally wounded, he cried out in his last moments: 'You have slain your Prince.'

Eager to claim the reward, the soldiers cut off his head and took it triumphantly to Fort William. From there it was taken to London for definite identification and in the meantime the hunt for the Prince slackened at a time when he was hotly pursued.

Improbably disguised for a few days as 'Betty Burke', Flora Macdonald's serving wench, in a lilac-sprigged gown, he had a hazardous time in the islands before returning to the mainland. He had learned to smoke tobacco and had become accustomed to drinking whisky. Wearing the kilt, both belted-plaid and *philabeg,* and other disguises he had also suffered from lice and frequent wettings as he slept rough in the heather or some half-ruined bothy, to escape the attentions of patrolling soldiers. Yet he bore it all with remarkable aplomb and resilience.

Amongst the best-known incidents in the Prince's wanderings was the occasion when, against the advice of his companions, he entered a bothy in Glenmoriston. Inside were seven ragged and desperate men, outlaws like themselves, who today would merely have been considered partisans in occupied territory. The 'Seven Men of Glenmoriston' (eight in number in all) swore an oath not to betray him and despite the vast reward offered stood by their word. At this time the Prince was described by the Revd John Cameron as 'barefooted, had an old black kilt coat on, philabeg and waistcoat, a dirty shirt and a long red beard, a gun in his hand, a pistol and dirk by his side. He was very cheerful and in good health and in my opinion fatter than when he was in Inverness.'

The months he spent wandering in the Highlands, when he owed his life to countless known and unknown Highlanders of either sex, were the period when the legend and romance which surround his name were born. On 19 September he embarked from Loch-nan-Uamh, from the identical spot at which he had landed fourteen months earlier. With the departure of Prince Charles Edward Stuart the twilight descended on the heroic age of the Highlands.

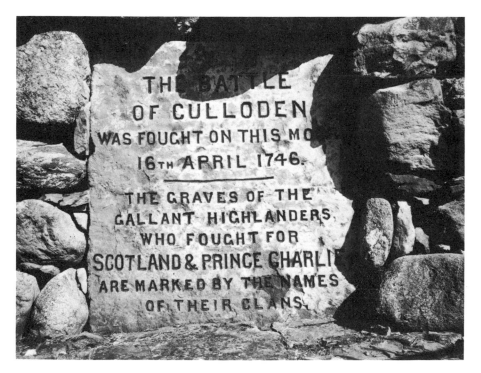

The memorial at Culloden marking the site of the battle. Near by are the individual clan graves marked by boulders

Chapter 5

The Emigrations Begin

By 1745 the last wolf in Scotland had been killed, but who exactly had killed it and when is a matter of some doubt. One claimant was Cameron of Lochiel in 1680, but the likelihood is that this was merely the last wolf in Lochaber. Another wolf is said to have been killed in Loth in Sutherland by a hunter named Polson in 1700. Yet another claim is that a wolf was killed in Morayshire as late as 1743 by a famous hunter named MacQueen.

The story goes that the chief of the clan Mackintosh had arranged a *Tainchel* to kill a large 'black beast', supposed to be a wolf, which had killed two children. MacQueen had some fine hunting dogs and was acknowledged by all to be such a fine hunter that the *Tainchel* waited for him to arrive even though it was soon long after the time when they would normally have started the hunt. When he finally arrived he was met with irritation at his lateness. 'What is the hurry?' he demanded. Then lifting the corner of his plaid he threw down the bloody head of the wolf in front of them.

In 1746 the effect of the battle of Culloden on the Highlands was to release a horde of ravening wolves in human form on the countryside, for, encouraged by the Duke of Cumberland's example, the Hanoverian soldiers did not hesitate to plunder and rape when the opportunity arose and the innocent suffered along with the guilty. For months after the battle fugitives were scattered throughout the Highlands and Islands, concealed in the open, or in the houses of friends, while the search for them and for the Prince continued relentlessly.

The Hanoverian soldiers were by no means all Lowlanders, however, for there were many Highlanders amongst them. Loudon's Highlanders, raised to fight on the Continent, had fought at Culloden on the Government side before being embarked for Flanders, fighting at Bergen-op-Zoom and being disbanded in 1748. Between 1745 and 1747 there were also two companies of Campbell, or Argyll Highlanders, raised in Argyllshire and the west, amounting to some 1,200 men. There were twenty companies of 100 men

Highland soldiers wearing the belted plaid and armed with smooth bore muskets, bayonets, broad swords, and dags each raised in Inverness and Ross serving with the Government forces. In addition MacLeod of MacLeod raised 200 men and Grant of Grant 98 for the Hanoverians. When houses were burned and many rendered homeless throughout the Highlands it was not always necessarily the red-coated soldiery who were responsible, but a case of old debts being paid off on erstwhile enemies by fellow Highlanders.

Worse still was the behaviour of many of the Lowland Scots such as the notorious Captain Ferguson of the Royal Navy and his Lieutenant Dalrymple. A month after Culloden by their orders their men burned the laird's house on Raasay and 300 cottages on the island, as well as slaughtering the stock and raping women. At Gairloch on the west coast Hector Mackenzie, the laird, had taken no part in the rising. His house, Tigh Dige, newly built in 1738 and with a slated roof, then an innovation, was bombarded by a naval vessel for no other reason than sheer wantonness. One of the balls stuck in the thick walls close to a hiding place beneath the rafters where a fugitive friend, Fraser of Foyers, was concealed for many months.

The rule of fire and sword with accompanying acts of aggression on guilty and innocent alike was deliberately allowed to continue for some time with little check. Under the guise of military occupation, the enforcement of the Disarming Acts and the Proscription of Highland Dress, the process of terrorising the Highlands into submission continued much longer, although probably only the first decade saw real victimisation and hardship. The acts themselves were not repealed for nearly forty years and garrisons were maintained for much of that time, long after there was any need for them. By then the acts were being ignored with impunity.

The Act for the 'Abolition and Proscription of the Highland Dress' was aimed at the core of the Gaelic being. It read:

That from and after the first day of August . . . one thousand seven hundred and forty seven, no man or boy within that part of Great Britain called Scotland, other than such as shall be employed as Officers or Soldiers in His Majesty's Forces, shall on any pretext whatsoever wear or put on the clothes commonly called Highland clothes (that is to say) the Plaid, Philabeg, or little Kilt, Trowse, Shoulder belts or any part whatsoever of what peculiarly belongs to the Highland Garb; and that no tartan or Part-coloured plaid or stuff shall be used for Great Coats, or upper Coats . . . every person so offending . . . shall suffer imprisonment . . . of six months . . . and being convicted of a second offence . . . be transported . . .

The act was not applied against those chiefs and clans who had supported the Government, but was enforced with brutal severity against the Jacobite clans. In the first days of enforcement orders were given to patrolling troops to 'kill upon the spot any person whom they met dressed in the Highland garb'.

Those suspected of evasion of the acts were forced to take an oath of abjuration as follows:

I swear as I shall answer to God at the great day of judgement, I have not and shall not have in my possession any gun, sword, or arms whatsoever, and never use tartan, plaid or any part of the Highland garb, and if I do so may I be accursed in my undertakings, family and property, may I never see my wife, nor children, nor father, mother, or relations, may I be killed in battle as a fugitive coward, and lie without christian burial in a foreign land far from the graves of my forefathers and kindred; may all this come upon me if I break this oath.

Even that ardent Hanoverian supporter, Forbes of Culloden, Lord President of the Council, whose family had gained the immensely profitable right to distil whisky on his estate at Ferintosh free of duty after its destruction by Graham of Claverhouse in 1689, protested against the act. He wrote to a Member of Parliament:

The garb certainly fits men inured to it, to go through great fatigues, to make very quick marches, to bear out against the inclemency of the weather, to wade through rivers and shelter in huts, woods and rocks, upon occasions which men dressed in the low country garb could not possibly endure . . . it seems to me an utter impossibility without the advantage of this dress for the inhabitants to tend their cattle and to go through the other parts of their business without which they could not subsist, not to speak of paying rents to their landlords . . .

There can be little question that the Government in Westminster over reacted after their fright at the near success of the Prince supported only by the Highlanders. In their determination to subdue the Highlanders they determined to mould them in their own image. They completely failed to appreciate that they were a different race with entirely different values. They would no doubt have banned the use of the Gaelic language except for the utter impossibility of enforcing such an act.

The subjugation of the Highlands was a lengthy process and much depended on the local military commanders. Some were undoubtedly more severe than others. This may be seen by the extremely dubious advice of Lieutenant-Colonel Watson, clearly a Lowlander, the commander at Fort Augustus in 1747, who wrote to his subordinates:

How soon the posts are fixed the commanding officer at each station is to endeavour to ingratiate himself in the favour of some person in his neighbourhood by giving him a reward, or filling him drunk with whisky as often as he may judge proper, which I'm confident is the only way to penetrate the secrets of these people.

In certain respects the aftermath of the Rebellion may have set back Highland developments. In 1726 Burt had surveyed the route for the Caledonian Canal, but work on it did not start until after the turn of the century. In 1735 it was proposed that a road should be built between the Spey valley at Kingussie and Braemar on Deeside, but this has still not been started. In 1737 the Duke of Atholl introduced larch into his estates at Blair, but it was not until 1764 that they were being planted systematically. On the other hand many important developments would have taken far longer to evolve.

Perhaps one of the most important and far-reaching of the acts passed after the 1745 Rebellion was that removing the chieftains' powers over their clansmen. The immediate effect of this was that the chieftains, with their feudal powers circumscribed, became purely and simply landlords, dependent on their cattle and their rents rather than on the number of men they had as followers. The Tacksmen, or chief tenants, found themselves with their rent being raised and there was a natural slow groundswell of discontent, which in due course was to lead to considerable emigration.

The Commissioners appointed to manage the forfeited estates after the 1745 Rebellion were also a potent force in introducing new ideas. By granting longer leases of twenty-one years, by enforcing the enclosing of land, by stipulating that tenants should introduce new methods of crop rotation and compelling the herding of sheep and cattle in winter to prevent them straying, they enforced the adoption of their methods. Inevitably their ideas were copied elsewhere in the Highlands. It was largely due to them that the potato was introduced to the Highlands, where it quickly became a staple crop.

Although it had been reduced to peace-time proportions, service in the Black Watch, as an opportunity to wear the kilt and bear arms, remained popular. There was no difficulty in obtaining recruits. In 1755, when war with France appeared increasingly likely they were promptly put back on a war-time footing and General Stewart of Garth recorded:

The Laird of Mackintosh, then a Captain in the Regiment, had charge of all the recruiting parties . . . to the Highlands and quickly collected 500 men, the number he was desired to recruit. Of these he collected 87 men in one forenoon.

One morning as he was sitting at breakfast in Inverness, 38 men of the name Macpherson from Badenoch, appeared in front of the window with an offer of their services to Mackintosh; their own immediate chief, the Laird of Cluny, being then in exile, in consequence of his attainder after the Rising. The late General Skinner of the engineers was at Breakfast with Mackintosh that morning; and being newly arrived in that part of the country, the whole scene, with all the circumstances, made an impression on his mind, which he never forgot.

In 1757, when the Seven Years War with France finally broke out, numerous other Highland regiments were raised. The Black Watch, or 42nd Regiment, soon to be awarded the distinction of becoming the Royal Black Watch, Montgomerie's Highlanders, or 77th, and Fraser's Highlanders, or the 71st and 78th, all fought with honour and renown in America against the French. Fraser's Highlanders fought under General James Wolfe at Louisburg and Quebec; the same James Wolfe, who while only a lieutenant after Culloden had offered his commission to Cumberland rather than despatch a wounded Highlander when ordered by him to do so.

Other Highland regiments raised during the war were Keith's and

Campbell's Highlanders, the 87th and 88th who fought in Germany with great distinction. The 101st, or Johnstone's Highlanders, were also raised to reinforce them, and the 89th or Gordon Highlanders were raised to fight the French in India, serving throughout the war with outstandingly good discipline. In addition independent companies were again enrolled in the Highlands during the war and recruits obtained for new regiments in the south, including the 100th and 105th Regiments of the Line and two other regiments of Highland Volunteers. Two fencible regiments were also raised in 1759, the Argyll Regiment and the Sutherland Regiment, each numbering around 1,000 men.

On the conclusion of the war in 1763 all these regiments returned home and were reduced, but those who had served in America were offered the alternative of being given a grant of land and settling in America. Many of them chose to do so and their letters to their friends and relations at home were a potent stimulus to emigration.

It had not taken the Government long to realise that this was the way to channel the warlike instincts of the Highlanders in their own interests. As Robert Burns put it pithily:

> But bring a Scotsman frae his hill,
> Clap in his cheek a Highland gill,
> Say such is Royal George's will,
> An' there's the foe;
> He has nae thought but how to kill
> Twa at a blow.

The behaviour of the Highland regiments in action, both their discipline and their valour, had made a great impression on all who saw them and Pitt, as Prime Minister, was greatly in favour of them. This probably had a considerable influence on the relaxation of the restrictions on the Highlanders from the late 1750's onwards. While they were not repealed for over two decades from this date it is clear that they were scarcely enforced at all in the later stages. Doubtless so many Highlanders by this time had served in various regiments that the wearing of the kilt and even carrying of arms was fairly general.

Meanwhile, about 1740, sheep began to spread into the Highlands in considerable numbers. Hitherto they had been regarded as unable to withstand the rigours of the Highland winters and incapable of standing up to droving. Beef was more popular than mutton and only enough sheep were kept for wool. The introduction of new breeds from the south, especially the black-faced Linton sheep, with coarser wool, and the use of turnips for winter fodder changed the situation.

Cattle drovers in the early eighteenth century taking Highland cattle round the edge of the Ochils (Highland Boundary Fault) to the Falkirk tryst

By 1740 considerable numbers of sheep had been introduced into Argyll, and Cowall in particular had been turned over mainly to sheep by the 1760s. The first introduction of sheep north of Inverness was made in 1762 by Admiral Sir John Lockhart Ross of Balnagown. The younger son of Lockhart of Lee, he was a Lowlander, who took the surname Ross as a condition of inheriting the estate. He immediately retired from the navy and set about improving the estate, as a first step introducing the black-faced sheep from further south. Contrary to general expectation they prospered and his example was soon followed by others.

The Exodus Begins

Unfortunately, to make way for the sheep, tenants already on the land had to be dispossessed. Furthermore, since the Highlanders were inexperienced with sheep, the flocks were generally put in the charge of Lowland shepherds. Already the Highlanders had found themselves taking second place to cattle and now they found themselves being dispossessed to make way for sheep. Furthermore it was their landlords, their erstwhile chieftains, to whom they had looked for succour and support, who were responsible for their eviction.

This was the start of the infamous Clearances which were to continue for another hundred years.

Yet, although the Clearances have been blamed for the numbers of Highlanders who emigrated, the facts do not altogether support this supposition, or the argument that many Highlanders were transported after the 1715 and 1745 Rebellions. In practice only about 800 Highlanders seem to have been condemned to transportation as bond servants after the 1715 Rebellion and of those many do not seem to have served their full term and others may not even have gone. Curiously enough roughly similar numbers seem to have been involved after the 1745 Rebellion.

In 1732 three Highland Scots, James Innes from Caithness, Hugh Campbell, and William Forbes, all took grants of land in the Cape Fear district of North Carolina, where the climate was warmer than in Scotland with longer summers and shorter winters. The soil was easily worked and reasonably fertile. In 1734 James Innes became a Justice of the Peace and another Scot, Gabriel Johnston, became Governor of North Carolina. Working together they were to encourage many Scots, particularly Highlanders, to emigrate to North Carolina.

In 1739 350 Highlanders from Argyll, consisting of eighty-five families under some five leaders, or Tacksmen, emigrated to the Cape Fear region. The following year the Tacksmen took out grants of land and following the familiar pattern they had left behind them these were sub-let to the families who had come out with them. The same pattern followed the emigrations which took place after the 1745 Rebellion with the Tacksmen taking out entire parties under their leadership.

Owing largely to their common language the Highlanders appear to have preferred to settle in groups together and the Cape Fear region of North Carolina was one of their favourite areas. It was there that members of the various Highland regiments, who were offered grants of land after their service in North America in the Seven Years War, mainly settled. Here they might be found in their national dress of kilt and plaid, although with varied clan tartans, in a closely-knit ethnic group, speaking Gaelic and bearing arms, as if still in the Highlands of Scotland.

Between 1768 and 1772 somewhere around 3,000 Highlanders were estimated to have emigrated to the Cape Fear district alone. Ironically many seem to have settled in Cumberland County, named after the Duke whose name was anathema in the Highlands following Culloden. By 1775 it was estimated that some 12,000 Highlanders had settled in this area of North Carolina, quite apart from the numerous others who had settled elsewhere in North America in similar groups.

In 1771 the hard winter, followed by cattle blight and steadily increasing rents, resulted in 700 Macdonalds emigrating from Skye and in 1773 yet more. Letters from settlers already doing well in America were all that was needed to

The emigrant Highlanders were a favourite subject for nineteenth-century artists

encourage those who had suffered similar miseries at home but had not yet made up their minds to leave. The effect was like a snowball growing in size as it gathered momentum.

Taking into account the fact that of a total population of some 3,000,000 only about 300,000 lived in the Highlands, it would have seemed that the loss of such numbers would have been important. With the introduction of the potato and vaccination against smallpox at about the same period, however, with the result that there were fewer deaths in infancy, it is probable that the population remained the same, or even increased. Nevertheless emigration from the Highlands and Islands continued apace in the 1770s.

The reasons principally given for wishing to emigrate were the uncertainty of tenure, rising rents, and the desire to join relations already abroad. It is noteworthy that evictions were hardly ever given as the reason for wishing to leave. Increasingly, however, the landlords were attempting to prevent emigration, arguing that the country needed the people. It was unfortunately all too often the skilled craftsmen and men of ability, whose loss was sorely felt, who were choosing to emigrate.

It is significant that most of these Highlanders were reported as arriving in America in full Highland dress, wearing kilt and plaid, and armed with swords and pistols. The various Disarming Acts and the Proscription of Highland Dress do not seem to have had much significance or force by this time. Tartan cloth was certainly being produced by the weavers in Stirling throughout the eighteenth century. In the same way it would seem that the Disarming Acts did not apply to sword and pistol makers, but only to the carrying of arms. Thus anyone leaving the country was able to buy arms quite openly, aware that they would not be contravening the law by carrying them in the Highlands. This was indeed yet another factor favouring emigration.

Certainly the famous dag makers of Doune, the master craftsmen who made the famous long-barrelled pistols with butts terminating in a character-istic double scroll, or ramshorn, effect, with a perfect balance, were not affected by the acts. They continued to make their pistols from around 1700 to as late as 1790, throughout the whole of the period covered by the various Disarming Acts. Apart from their superb balance these pistols were works of art in the best sense. The delicate tracery and scroll work on some of the finest examples resembles silver lacework. The merging of the barrel and butt is an example of perfection of line and craftsmanship. Such names as the four generations of Caddells, Campbell and Christie, all of whom hailed from the small village of Doune, were rightly famed throughout Scotland.

Even by 1770, however, there was still surprisingly little known about the Highlands in the south. In 1769 Thomas Pennant, the Welsh naturalist and antiquary, first visited Scotland and in 1771 published a book on his journey. Encouraged by the popular reception it received he made a further visit, resulting in a two-volume *Tour of Scotland,* published in 1774. An observant and indefatigable traveller, he noted amongst other points the wearing of the kilt and tartan as apparently everyday occurrences in the Highlands. Of the Highlanders and their relations with their chieftains he wrote:

The manners of the native Highlanders may justly be expressed in these words; indolent to a degree, unless roused to war or any animating amusement; or, I may say, from experience, to lend any disinterested assistance to the distressed traveller, either in directing him on his way, or affording their aid in passing the dangerous torrents of the Highlands; hospitable to the highest degree, and full of generosity; are much affected with the civility of strangers, and have in themselves a natural politeness and address which often flows from the meanest when least expected . . . Have much pride and consequently are impatient of affronts, and revengeful of injuries. Are decent in their general behaviour, inclined to superstition, yet attentive to the duties of religion .

. . But in many parts of the Highlands their character begins to be more faintly marked; they mix more with the world and become daily less attached to their chiefs; the clans begin to disperse themselves through different parts of the country, finding that their industry and good conduct afford them better protection . . . than any their chieftain can afford; and the chieftain taking the sweets of advanced rents and the benefits of industry, dismisses from the table the crowds of retainers, the former instruments of his oppression and freakish tyranny.

Despite Pennant's book, when Dr Samuel Johnson was persuaded by his friend and biographer Boswell to make a tour of the Highlands with him in 1773, it was with difficulty that he was convinced that he would not require a pair of pistols. In practice Dr Johnson, although notably biased against the Scots, was deeply impressed by the hospitality and courtesy with which he was received throughout the Highlands. He wrote of the Highlanders with perception:

Their pride has been crushed by the heavy hand of a vindictive conqueror, whose severities have been followed by laws, which, though they cannot be called cruel, have produced much discontent, because they operate on the surface of life, and make every eye bear witness to subjection. To be compelled to a new dress has always been found painful. Their chiefs being now deprived of their jurisdiction, have already lost much of their influence and as they gradually deteriorate from partriarchal rulers to rapacious landlords, they will divest themselves of the little that remains.

It was Boswell, however, in the company of Dr Johnson, who noted the effects of emigration in Skye. He recorded:

We had again a good dinner and in the evening a great dance . . . And then . . . a dance which I suppose the emigration from Skye has occasioned. They call it 'America' . . . It goes on till all are set a-going, setting and wheeling round each other . . . It shows how emigration catches till all are set afloat. Mrs Mackinnon told me that last year when the ship sailed from Portree for America, the people on the shore were almost distracted when they saw their relatives go off; they lay down on the ground and tumbled and tore the grass with their teeth. This year there was not a tear shed. The people on the shore seemed to think that they would soon follow.

The outbreak of the American War of Independence in 1775 brought emigration to a halt for the moment. Yet again, however, there was an immediate response when the call went out for more Highland regiments. Prominent amongst these was the Royal Highland Emigrant Regiment formed on the outbreak of war from Highland emigrants in North America discharged from the 42nd Black Watch, or Fraser's and Montgomerie's Highlanders who had settled there after the Peace of Paris had ended the Seven Years War in 1763. Sir John Johnson also recruited another emigrant

Dr Samuel Johnson (1709–84)

regiment, mostly Catholic Highlanders, particularly MacDonells, who had emigrated from Glengarry, Glen Urquhart, and Glenmoriston to his lands in the Mohawk Valley.

In Scotland the 71st, or Fraser's Highlanders, were raised in 1775. They served at Brooklyn, Savannah, and York River. In 1777 the Argyll Highlanders, or 'old 74th', were raised and were stationed in Halifax, Nova Scotia, throughout the war. They saw action at Penobscot. In the same year, 1777, Lord Macdonald raised the Macdonald's Highlanders, or the 'old 76th', who fought in Virginia and were made prisoners when Cornwallis surrendered. None of them deserted despite inducements being offered to them to do so. The other regiments were reduced in 1783, but they were only reduced in 1784 on their return home.

In addition to these, a number of fencible regiments were raised during the war. These included the Argyll, or Western Regiment, embodied at Glasgow in 1778, the Gordon Regiment, raised by the Duke of Gordon in Aberdeen in 1778, and the Sutherland Regiment raised in 1779 in Sutherland and Caithness, which was mainly stationed near Edinburgh. All these were also disbanded in 1783, but many of the latter subsequently joined the 93rd Sutherland Highlanders.

While the war was in progress, William Gilpin, the Prebendary of Salisbury, also made a visit to the far north. In his *Observations on the Highlands of Scotland during the Year 1776* he wrote:

Nor are the cattle of this wild country more picturesque than the human inhabitants. The Highland dress (which notwithstanding an Act of Parliament is still in general use) is greatly more ornamental than the English. I speak of its form not its colour, which is checked of different hues and has a disagreeable appearance. The plaid consists of a simple piece of cloth three yards in length and half that measure in breadth. A common one sells for about ten shillings. The Highlander wears it in two forms. In fine weather he throws it loosely round him and the greater part of it hangs over his shoulder. In rain he wraps the whole close to his body. In both forms it makes elegant drapery and when he is armed with his pistols and Ferrara (Andreas Ferrara, a Spaniard, was invited to Scotland by James III to teach his countrymen the art of tempering steel; from him the best broadswords take their name) has a good effect . . .

By this time many of the Highland chiefs and gentlemen of influence were in the habit of sending their sons to be educated in Scottish universities, or even further south. Later they might be sent to London with a view to obtaining appointments through the influence of friends or relatives. One result of this was a considerable Highland population in London which resulted in 1778 in the formation of the Highland Society of London.

In 1782 this Society formed a committee with a view to obtaining the repeal of the Act against Highland Dress, which had clearly outlived its time. It was put to the house of Commons by the Marquis of Graham, subsequently Duke of Montrose, and seconded by Fraser of Lovat, who stressed the point that it would help to 'keep a useful body of subjects on this side of the Atlantic . . . and keep them happy at home'. This was indicative of the fact that the chiefs, who had in many cases previously been encouraging emigration were now becoming alarmed at the loss of so many of their best mechanics and craftsmen.

The act was repealed in 1782 without any dissent and the following proclamation written in Gaelic was posted throughout the Highlands:

> Listen, Men!
> This is bringing before all the sons of Gael that the King and Parliament of Britain have for ever abolished the Act against the Highland Dress that came down to the Clans from the beginning of the world to the year 1746. This must bring great joy to every Highland heart. You are no longer bound down to the unmanly dress of the Lowlanders. This is declaring to every man, young and old, simple and gentle, that they may after this put on and wear the trews, the little kilt, the doublet and hose, along with the tartan kilt, without fear of the laws of the land, or the spite of enemies.

A little of what the kilt and tartans meant to the Highlander may be gauged from this proclamation, although it is clear that they had been worn for some time with total disregard for the law throughout much of the Highlands. It was really an indication that the Highlander, chiefly owing to his outstanding services in wartime, had been fully restored to favour. The old fear of the Highlander had by this time been wholly dissipated, even if they were still by no means fully understood.

Following the end of the war in 1783 and a severe winter with famine conditions in much of the Highlands many seized the opportunity to emigrate. In 1784 that eccentric Yorkshire squire and sportsman, Colonel Thomas Thornton, who had been educated at Glasgow University, kept a sporting diary of a visit to the Highlands which with additions was finally published in 1804 as *A Sporting Tour through the Northern Parts of England and Great Part of the Highlands of Scotland, including Remarks on English and Scottish Landscapes and General Observations on the State of Society and Manners*. On visiting a church on Speyside he noted:

> I found a much thinner audience than I ever remembered, and, conversing upon this subject with the . . . gentlemen of the neighbourhood, they informed me that the spirit of emigration had seized the people of these parts and that many handicraftsmen and others, whose services I much wanted, had actually left the country . . .

His was the first book to concentrate on the sporting facilities available in the Highlands. He mentioned—among other feats— fishing the Leven above Dumbarton and catching five salmon, including one of over 18 kilograms, inside two and a half hours. He shot grouse, ptarmigan, and blackgame on Speyside. He caught a record pike below the Cairngorms. He also noted much of interest by the way, even if he had no compunction in plagiarising paragraphs at a time from Pennant.

Blair Castle, north of Pitlochry in Perthshire, the last castle in Britain to withstand a siege

He recorded the trial in Inverness of a sheep stealer named Kennedy, who lived in the wilds of Glengarry with a dozen followers. They were said to have stolen over 600 sheep from the forfeited lands of Cameron of Lochiel, which were being run by a government-appointed factor. Kennedy's men had threatened the witnesses so that they failed to appear and he had to be acquitted.

Amongst the great houses he visited, Thornton mentioned Blair Castle, which had been besieged unsuccessfully by Lord George Murray before Culloden, the last castle in Britain to withstand a siege. It had since had its battlements removed and, 'much reduced in height', had been converted into a Georgian house, only to be subsequently rebattlemented in the nineteenth century. Of Inveraray he noted that the castle was nearly finished. Planned in 1744 along with an ambitious plan for rebuilding the town, the castle was eventually completed in the 1790s. Thornton noted that the town 'consists of about two hundred houses, many of which though small, are neatly built'. Then somewhat irrationally he added Pennant's description of some fifteen years earlier to the effect that it was 'composed of the most wretched hovels'.

In the same year, 1784, Pitt the Younger's Government was induced by complaints from the English distillers about unfair competition to attempt to tax the Scottish distillers at the same rate. For the purposes of this act a distinction was drawn for the first time between the Highland and Lowland distillers, the latter being taxed more heavily. The boundary or so-called 'Highland Line' then drawn by Parliament between Highlands and Lowlands was defined thus:

A certain line or boundary beginning at the east point of Loch Crinan, and proceeding thence to Loch Gilpin; from thence . . . along the west side of Loch Fyne to Inveraray and to the head of Loch Fyne; from thence . . . to Arrochar . . . to Tarbet; from Tarbet in a supposed line eastward on the north side of Ben Lomond, to . . . Callander . . . from thence north eastward to Crieff . . . to Ambleree (Amulree) and Inver to Dunkeld; from thence along the foot and side of the Grampian Hills to Fettercairn . . . and from thence northward . . . to . . . Kincardine O'Neil, Clatt, Huntly and Keith to Fochabers; and from thence westward by Elgin and Forres, to the boat on the river Findhorn, and from thence down the said river to the sea at Findhorn, and any place in or part of the county of Elgin which lies southward of the said line from Fochabers to the sea at Findhorn.

Between 1750 and the 1790s there were several instances of the building of model 'planned' villages in various parts of the Highlands, generally by landowners with a view to the improvement of their estates. Such a one was the building of Kenmore at the foot of Loch Tay by the Earl of Breadalbane in the 1750s. Another was Grantown-on-Spey planned in 1765 by Sir Ludovic Grant and intended as a centre for wool and linen manufacture, also for timber and carpentry workers. In the 1792 Statistical Account the Revd Mr Lewis Grant wrote:

Grantown is a village erected under the influence of the Grant family, it being little more than twenty years since the place where it stands was a poor rugged piece of heath. It now contains from 300 to 400 inhabitants, some of whom are as good tradesmen as any in the kingdom.

In 1786 Pultneytown was built on lines laid out by Thomas Telford as the twin burgh alongside Wick, under the aegis of the British Fishery Society. The two towns developed side by side until finally merged in 1902. In 1788 the British Fishery Society also founded a village and fishing port at Ullapool on the shores of Loch Broom. This sea loch provided good shelter from gales and was favourably placed for the west-coast herring fishing. It is still obvious at first sight that Ullapool was a planned village and seen from the sea front it has a distinctly pleasing appearance. It is reminiscent in many ways of Inveraray, which, of course, was built at much the same time and was also intended as a base for herring fishing on Loch Fyne.

Less successful was Tomintoul, the highest village in the Highlands, of which the Revd Mr John Grant wrote in 1790:

Tammtoul . . . is inhabited by 37 families, without a single manufacture . . . All of them sell whisky and all of them drink it. When disengaged from this business the women spin yarn, kiss their inamoratos, or dance to the discordant sounds of an old fiddle . . . Here the Roman Catholic priest has an elegant meeting-house and the Protestant clergyman the reverse . . . A school is stationed at this village attended by 40 or 50 little recreants all promising to be very like their parents.

Clearly the Revd Mr John Grant had a good sense of humour as well as the ability to pen a telling phrase. He neatly underlined the characteristic Highland ability to throw a party, or ceilidh, with little or no excuse. The Highlanders always seem to have been able to hold a ceilidh at a moment's notice, when there would be dancing to the pipes or fiddle, singing, poetry recitations, and story-telling, with each person present taking their turn to entertain the company. Aided by the ever-present whisky barrel, a good time would be enjoyed by all, despite the poverty in which they lived and the comparative misery of their lives during the grim winter months.

In 1791 Sir John Sinclair of Ulbster introduced the first sheep in the far north on an estate named Langwell in Caithness. A progressive landlord and prolific letter writer he also introduced the *First Statistical Account of Scotland* in the 1790s with a survey of each parish written by the minister in answer to a questionnaire he sent to each one. On the subject of sheep he wrote at first with enthusiasm:

The Highlands of Scotland may sell at present, perhaps from £200,000 to £300,000 worth of lean cattle per annum. The same ground will produce twice as much mutton and there is wool into the bargain. If covered with the coarse woolled breed of sheep, the wool might be worth about £300,000 . . . whereas the same ground under the Cheviot, or True Mountain breed, will produce at least £900,000 of fine wool.

As late as 1792 the men of Ross and Sutherland banded together to try to check the steady invasion of sheep over what they regarded as their lands. Starting from Lairg some 400 strong the Highlanders marched south driving the Lowland shepherds who had come north with their flocks and their sheep in front of them. They had nearly reached Alness with some 6,000 sheep when word arrived that the military had been turned out against them. Like so many Highland armies before them they vanished away in the night and when the soldiers arrived there was no sign of them. Eventually five men, allegedly the ringleaders, were tried and received varying sentences up to seven years' transportation to Botany Bay, the newly-founded penal settlement in Australia.

Meanwhile the Clearances began to take effect throughout the far north and Sir John Sinclair was appalled at the results of his plan. He wrote in disgust:

The first thing that is done is to drive away all the present inhabitants. The next is to introduce a shepherd and a few dogs; and then to cover the mountain with flocks of wild coarse woolled and savage animals, which seldom see their shepherd or are benefited by his care.

Although there were attempts to reverse the process started by the introduction of sheep by the Campbells in the west and by Admiral Sir John Lockhart Ross of Balnagown in the north, none of them were immediately successful. In 1784 Mr David Dale, a Glaswegian businessman, founded the new town and mills at New Lanark. In the *First Statistical Account* of 1793 it was noted:

With a view to prevent their further emigration to America he notified the people of Argyllshire and the Isles, of the encouragement given to families at the cotton-mills; and undertook to provide houses for 200 families in the course of 1793 . . . and a considerable number of Highlanders have of late come to reside at New Lanark . . .

Mr George Dempster, a friend of David Dale's idealistic son-in-law Robert Owen, started a similar mill at Spinningdale on the shores of the Dornoch Firth on his estates at Skibo and Pulrossie. His idea was that women and children could be employed there while their husbands and brothers worked on the farms. In the *First Statistical Account* of 1793 Mr Dempster outlined his plans:

These estates contain about 1,800 acres of land . . . from about 500 to 700 feet above the level of the (Dornoch) Firth. There may be about 300 families living on these estates with the exception of the mains, or house farm, on each place. The farms are of small extent in regard to arable ground. They produce some corn and potatoes, hardly sufficient to maintain the families of the tenants. The tenants pay their rents by the sale of cattle, which are fed in their houses on straw throughout the winter and pick up a miserable subsistence on the waste and common ground of the estates during the summer . . . The estates furnish some wood, with which and the swarded surface of the ground cut into the form of large bricks they make houses . . . for themselves, covering them with some swarded turfs cut thinner and resembling slates in their form. Once in three years all the earthy part of these houses is thrown on the dunghill and new houses built again of the same materials. The cattle commonly occupy one end of the house during the winter season. Some holes in the walls and roofs serve for windows and chimneys. An iron pot for boiling their food constitutes their principal furniture . . .

As to the occupations of these people, the women begin to earn a little money by spinning. The young men go early in the spring to the south country and hire themselves for all kinds of country labour; towards harvest time many of the women go also in the same way to assist in cutting down and getting in the crop. They all return before winter and are said to pass the time round good fires of peat . . . and do very little work. In the south country however . . . they are remarked for their assiduity and are said to be indefatigable . . . It need hardly be mentioned that the inhabitants are in general poor . . .

It is not therefore the intention of the proprietors to exact for some time any increase in rents . . . but on the contrary to encourage them by every means possible to improve their little spots of land, to erect for themselves more comfortable houses and to build them of more durable materials . . . to establish the weaving of linen and to encourage the extension of the spinning of yarn . . . apprentices will be instructed in the art of weaving . . . by these means employment will be found for people of all ages and sexes . . .

Some have thought it would be a fitter use for the Highlands to convert them into sheep walks. That it might be better for the people to cultivate sheep instead of black cattle is probably true. That the sheep is a hardier and more useful animal than the ox may be true also. That the increase of rents by converting cattle breeding farms into sheep walks would be more sudden than the system here suggested is not to be disputed. But that the estates would ultimately become more valuable is by no means so clear a proposition . . .

As early as the 1750s one or two wealthier landlords, notably the Earl of Breadalbane, who had built miles of roads and numerous bridges round Loch Tay, had introduced spinning amongst his tenants as a cottage industry, distributing spinning wheels amongst them. Like Dempster's attempt, however, these attempts would unfortunately have been doomed to failure with the ultimate collapse of the weaving industry in the 1830s, owing to the introduction of the steam loom. As it was, the heirs of these well-meaning landlords failed to continue their efforts and accepted instead the economic advantages of turning the land over to sheep.

War with France

In 1793 France in the throes of the Revolution declared war against Britain and the war was to continue until 1815, draining the Highlands of men for the Highland regiments. The 74th Highland Regiment of Foot and the 75th Regiment, or 1st Battalion Gordon Highlanders, had been raised as early as 1787 for service in India. The 74th served at the battle of Assaye and of a total of 495 officers and men 164 were killed and 295 wounded, yet only two months later they were in battle again. Small wonder that with such fighting spirit the Highland regiments were called on in time of danger.

When the call came the Highlanders were not found wanting and it was soon proved that their chieftains' names could still attract men to battle. In 1793 Kenneth Mackenzie, grandson of the Earl of Seaforth attainted after the 1745 Rebellion, who had bought back the family estates and had his title restored by George III, raised the 78th Highlanders, or Ross-shire Buffs, later known as the 2nd Battalion, Seaforth Highlanders. The 79th Queen's Own Cameron Highlanders were raised in the same year by Alan Cameron of Erracht. In 1794 the 98th or Argyllshire Highlanders were raised by the Duke of Argyll, although in 1798 their number was altered to the 91st. Also in 1794 the Marquis of Huntly raised the 92nd or Gordon Highlanders. In 1800 Major-General Wemyss of Wemyss raised the 93rd or Sutherland Highlanders. All the Highland regiments had records of distinguished service and required a constant flow of fresh recruits to make good the losses they sustained in action.

There were also numerous fencible regiments raised. In 1793 these included the Argyll Regiment, raised by the Marquis of Lorne; the Breadalbane Regiment by the Marquis of Breadalbane; the Gordon Regiment embodied at Aberdeen, which served in Kent and was reviewed by George III; the Grant or Strathspey Regiment raised by Sir James Grant of Grant; and the Sutherland Regiment by General Wemyss of Wemyss. In 1794 the Caithness Regiment was raised by Sir John Sinclair of Ulbster; the Dumbarton Regiment by Colonel Campbell of Stonefield; the Reay Regiment by George Mackay of Bighouse; the Fraser Regiment by James Fraser of Belladrum; and the Glengarry Regiment by Alexander MacDonell of Glengarry (most of whom emigrated to Canada when reduced in 1802). In 1795 the Inverness-shire Regiment was raised by Major Baillie of Duncan. In 1796 the Ross-shire Regiment was raised by Major Colin Mackenzie of Mountgerald. In 1799 the Clan Alpine Regiment was raised by Colonel Alexander Macgregor Murray; the Lochaber Regiment by Cameron of Lochiel; the Regiment of the Isles by Lord Macdonald; the Ross and Cromarty Rangers by Colonel Lewis Mackenzie; and the Macleod or Princess Charlotte of Wales' Regiment by John Macleod of Colbecks. All these were reduced in 1802 at the Peace of Amiens.

It is clear from this formidable list that the Highlands had been constantly called on throughout the last decade of the century to produce its fighting men. Only the old men, the women, and children remained behind and they were fast being replaced by sheep, as Sir John Sinclair remarked. Once again with the declaration of war emigration had come to a halt.

One result of this was the inevitable tendency for the Highlanders remaining to attempt to pay their rents by illicit distillation of whisky. Throughout the latter part of the eighteenth century whisky distilling had increased. From 1725 when the Government under Sir Robert Walpole instituted the first tax on malt the effects had been far-reaching. Ale, which had been the most popular drink in Scotland, grew steadily less popular as the quality suffered or the price increased to absorb the new tax. Illicit distillation of whisky from malt which had not paid the tax increased as steadily and the popularity of whisky as the drink of the people grew apace. In the Highlands particularly the illicit distilling of whisky became a local craft.

Writing in 1796 for the *Statistical Account* the Revd Mr David Dunoon at Killearnan in Ross-shire noted:

Distilling is almost the only method of converting our victual into cash for the payment of rent and servants; and whisky may, in fact, be called our staple commodity. The distillers do not lay the proper value on their time and trouble, and of course look on all, but the price of barley and the fire added to the tax, as clear profit, add to these the luxury of tasting the quality of manufacture during the process.

In 1798, giving evidence before a Committee on Distilleries set up by the

DISTILLATION.

The double Apparatus for Distillation

Government to find out the reason for the decrease in tax returns, despite a steady increase in taxation which was merely forcing yet more small distillers to turn to illegal distilling, the Lowland distiller John Stein gave evidence on illegal distilling as follows:

It is not confined to great towns or regular manufacturers, but spreads itself over the whole face of the country, and in every island from the Orkneys to Jura. There are many who practise this art who are ignorant of every other, and there are distillers who boast that they make the best possible whiskey, who cannot read or write, and who carry on this manufacture in parts of the country where the use of the plough is unknown and where the face of the Exciseman is never seen. Under such circumstances, it is impossible to take account of its operation, it is literally to search for revenue in the woods or on the mountains.

Dr John Leyden in his *Journal of a Tour of the Highlands in 1800* noted with disapproval:

The distillation of whiskey presents an irresistible temptation to the poorer classes, as a boll of barley, which costs thirty shillings, produces by this process, between five and six guineas. This distillation had a most ruinous effect in increasing the scarcity of grain last year . . .

The Government could think of only one solution and in 1800 doubled the already penal tax of £54 to £108 on each licensed still. The effect, naturally enough, was to produce such an intolerable burden on the small distillers that they either went bankrupt or took to illegal distilling. By such unimaginative action the Government was in effect forcing the Highlanders to disobey the law.

In the first years of the nineteenth century this method of continuous distillation using two pot stills was devised, but it proved unsuccessful

A fine example of Landseer's remarkably accurate view of the Highlands

Chapter 6

The Royal Tourists

During the final years of the eighteenth century emigration had been continuing despite the war with France, once it had become apparent that Britain had command of the sea. It was by this time no longer a case of the Tacksmen emigrating with a group of followers and their families. In some cases priests went at the head of their flocks, but increasingly it was a case of contractors persuading people to take passage. It seems to have become an unsavoury racket.

In 1800 it was recorded that a certain Major Simon Fraser at Fort William had 'made a trade out of the business since 1799'. Sheriff-Substitute Brown of Inverness wrote about another contractor, George Dunoon, on whose ships fifty people died of cholera: 'I saw the ships when at Fort William. They were much crowded. When the passengers landed in America they were shut up in a point of land . . . to prevent the contagion of the disease.'

At that time the laws which controlled the number of slaves to be carried in a slave ship did not apply to emigrant ships and on occasions 700 emigrants would be carried in holds where only 500 slaves would have been allowed. Thomas Telford, who had been called on to establish the reasons for the high level of Highland emigration at this period, noted eleven ships sailing from Fort William in 1801, with as many as 3,300 emigrants. Another port from which they sailed at this time was Ullapool. The exact number of emigrants carried by each ship was hard to substantiate since they might easily stop at more than one port on their way before finally sailing across the Atlantic.

With the peace of Amiens in 1802 it seemed as if the war in Europe might have ended at last. The fencible regiments were all reduced and men began to return to their homes in the Highlands. For some it was to find that in the meantime their homes had been demolished, their families evicted, and that sheep now grazed where they had once lived.

As early as 1782 the first evictions of 500 tenants had been made in Glengarry by the mother of the Chieftain, Alistair Ranaldson MacDonell, during his minority. In 1802 he was himself responsible for another massive wave of evictions and the majority of the Glengarry men took ship for Pictou in Nova Scotia while Dunoon fattened on the profits. In the same year 800

The Crinan Canal as it is to-day. It was first opened in 1801 and completed in 1812

Roman Catholics from Barra in the Outer Isles sailed for Antigonish with their priests Alexander and Augustin Macdonald. In 1803 Thomas Douglas, eighth Earl of Selkirk and a firm believer in emigration as the answer for the Highlands, led 800 emigrants from Skye, Ross, Inverness, and Argyll to Prince Edward Island, where they settled successfully under his leadership.

This was the period for canal building in the Highlands. Even so it comes as something of a surprise to learn what one writer was proposing for Lairg in the Statistical Account of 1798:

The greatest improvement of which this part of the kingdom is capable (and indeed it is a national concern) is that of making an inland navigation through this parish from the E. to the W. sea. It is but 5 computed miles (or about $7\frac{1}{2}$ English) from the end of Loch Shin to a navigable arm of the Western Ocean . . . It would soon be the means of establishing fisheries, manufactures, commerce and industry, over all the neighbourhood. Perhaps it might also prevent the dangerous and circuitous navigation through the Pentland Firth.

James Watt (1736–1819)

The Crinan Canal was first proposed by the Glasgow magistrates who approached the Commissioners of the Forfeited Estates with the suggestion that a canal be built either at Crinan or Tarbert to save the long journey round the Mull of Kintyre to and from the Clyde. James Watt surveyed both routes and in 1793 an act was passed authorising the building of a canal at Crinan. The company promoting it ran into financial difficulties and the canal was only finally opened in an incomplete state in 1801. Still unfinished in 1804 the Government was approached for aid. In 1812 Thomas Telford, who was then working on the Caledonian Canal, was called on to give his views and estimates on costs. On his recommendation the canal was finally completed.

In the meantime the Caledonian Canal had also begun. In 1773 it too had been surveyed by James Watt, but at that time no further action had been taken. In his report on the reasons for emigration Thomas Telford had emphasised the fact that providing some form of public work, such as the building of the canal, would offer employment to those who might otherwise be forced to leave the country. Finally, in 1803, an act was passed setting up a commission to undertake the work and Telford was put in charge as chief engineer.

From the start, work on the Caledonian Canal was bedevilled by labour difficulties. Local labour from Inverness-shire frequently took time off for their own occupations, such as helping with the harvest, or herring fishing. An exception was those evicted by Cameron of Lochiel from their land around Loch Arkaig. It was in the end found necessary to employ men from as far afield as Skye, Morar, and the Moray Firth. It was also found necessary to build a brewery at Corpach at the southern end of the canal 'to induce the workmen to relinquish the pernicious habit of drinking whisky'. In addition, when war broke out again in 1803, it was unavoidable that costs rose steadily. It was to be ten years before the canal was even half-finished.

With the outbreak of war inevitably the Highland regiments were soon brought up to full strength again. By this time, however, the authorities in Whitehall were intent on bringing them into line with the others. The question was mooted in a letter to Colonel Cameron of the 79th Highlanders. A Mr Henry Thorpe writing on notepaper headed 'Horse Guards, 13th October 1804' asked him to state his 'private opinion as to the expediency of abolishing the kilt in Highland regiments and substituting in lieu thereof the tartan trews'. Colonel Cameron's fiery reply in four remarkably involved and lengthy sentences left no doubt as to his views on this suggestion:

Glasgow, 27th October, 1804.
Sir—On . . . the propriety of an alteration in the mode of clothing Highland regiments . . . I beg to state, freely and fully, my sentiments upon *that* subject, without a particle of prejudice . . . merely founded upon *facts* as applicable to these corps . . . as far as I am *capable,* from thirty years experience, twenty years of which I have been upon *actual* service in all *climates,* with the description of men in question . . . independent of myself being a Highlander and well knowing all the conveniences and inconveniences of our native garb in the field and otherwise, and perhaps, also, aware of the probable source and clashing motives from which the suggestion . . . originally *arose* . . . In the course of the late war several gentlemen proposed to raise Highland regiments . . . adulterated with every description of men . . . anything but real Highlanders, or even Scotchmen (which is not synonymous) and the colonels themselves being . . . accustomed to wear breeches, consequently *averse* to that free congenial circulation of pure wholesome air (as an exhilerating native bracer) which has hitherto so peculiarly befitted the Highlander for *activity,* and all the other necessary qualities of a soldier, whether for hardship upon scanty fare, *readiness in accoutring,* or making *forced marches* &c, beside the exclusive advantage, when halted, of drenching his kilt, &c, in the *next brook,* as well as washing his limbs, and drying *both,* as it were, by constant *fanning,* without injury to either, but, on the contrary, feeling clean and comfortable, while the buffoon tartan pantaloon &c, . . . sticking wet and dirty to the skin, is not very easily pulled off, and *less so* to get on again in case of alarm . . . absorbing both wet and dirt, followed up by rheumatism and fevers . . . in hot and cold climates; while it consists with knowledge that the Highlander in his

native garb always appeared more cleanly and maintained better health in both climates than those who wore even the thick cloth pantaloons . . . if anything was wanted to aid the rack-renting Highland landlords in destroying that source which has hitherto proved so fruitful for keeping up the Highland corps, it will be abolishing their native garb, which His Royal Highness the Commander-in-Chief and the Adjutant General may rest assured will prove a complete death warrant to the recruiting service . . . I sincerely hope His Royal Highness will never acquiesce in so painful and degrading an idea (come from whatever quarter it may) as to strip us of our native garb . . . and *stuff* us into the harlequin pantaloon, which take away completely the appearance and conceit of a Highland soldier . . . I would rather see him *stuffed* in breeches and abolish the distinction at once—

I have the honour to be &c (Signed) Alan Cameron.

Colonel 79th or Cameron Highlanders. To Henry Thorpe Esq.

While Colonel Cameron's fierce defence of the kilt saved the Cameron Highlanders and other regiments for the moment, Whitehall did not give up easily. In 1808 the Adjutant-General issued a memorandum which read:

As it would be an inducement to the men of the English Militia to extend their services in greater numbers to these regiments, it is in consequence most humbly submitted for the approbation of His Majesty, that His Majesty's 72nd, 73rd, 74th, 75th, 91st, and 94th Regiments should discontinue to wear in future the dress by which His Majesty's Regiments of Highlanders are distinguished and that the above corps should no longer be considered on that establishment.

Between 1730 and 1815 no fewer than 86 Highland regiments were raised and at long last the well to which the Government had been turning so often for fresh cannon fodder was beginning to run dry. Progressive disillusionment throughout the Highlands caused by the frequently broken promises of those in authority, by their own economic plight as the pace and extent of the evictions increased and sheep filled the land, as much as the prospect of being killed or maimed in action, were all points actively weighing against fresh recruitment at this stage in the war. An example of a recruiting poster of the period around 1811 indicates that even the more famous Highland regiments were having difficulty finding men of the right calibre:

The Gallant

Ninety Second

or Gordon Highlanders

who have so often distinguished themselves at Copenhagen, Spain, on the plains of Holland and the sands of Egypt, and who are now with Lord Wellington in Portugal, want to get a few spirited young men, lads and boys, to whom the greatest encouragement and

Highest Bounty will be given

From the character of the officers of the regiment who are from this part of the Highlands, they can depend that the interest and advantage of high spirited and well conducted soldiers from this part of the country will be particularly considered.

Printed at the Journal Office Inverness

Although costs were spiralling owing to the war the one thing the Highlanders were never without was whisky. In her *Memoirs of a Highland Lady* Elizabeth Grant recalled that in 1813, when she was only sixteen, she used to visit the timber workers on the Spey:

When the men met in the morning they were supposed to have breakfasted at home and had perhaps had their private dram, it being cold work in a dark wintry dawn, to start over the moor for a walk of some miles to end standing up to their knees in water; yet on collecting whisky was always handed round; a lad with a small cask—a quarter anker—on his back, and a horn cup in his hand that held a gill, appeared three times a day among them. They all took their 'morning' raw, undiluted and without accompaniment, so they did the gill at parting when the work was done; but the noontide dram was part of a meal. There was a twenty minutes' rest from labour, and a bannock and a bit of cheese taken out of every pocket to be eaten leisurely with the whisky. When we were there the horn cup was offered first to us, and each of us took a cup to the health of our friends around us, who all stood up. Sometimes a floater's wife or bairn would come with a message; such messenger was always offered whisky. Aunt Mary had a story that one day a woman with a child in her arms, and another bit thing at her knee, came up among them; the horn cup was duly handed to her, she took a 'gey guid drap' herself and then gave a little to each of the babies. 'My goodness, child,' said my mother to the wee thing that was trotting by the mother's side, 'doesn't it *bite* you?' 'Ay, but I like the bite,' replied the creature.

The timber-felling operations on Speyside and the floating of timber down to the river mouth were still continuing quite successfully in 1813, but that same year saw the last iron foundry in the Highlands closed down. This was the large ironworks on Loch Fyne at the village named Furnace, which had grown up around the operation. Founded as late as 1754, when most of the others had already closed, the Argyll Furnace Company was formed by a Lancashire concern. Local haematite was used and the abundance of local wood for charcoal. With ready access by way of Loch Fyne, the company continued until the use of coal and steam instead of water power and charcoal rendered it uneconomic and in 1813 it was dismantled.

The year 1814 saw the Government make yet one more effort to control the widespread illicit distillation of whisky taking place throughout the Highlands. In 1803 they had already doubled the tax on stills yet again to a ridiculous £168, which had merely made the problem worse. They now introduced a flat rate of £10 for a licence to distil, but prohibited all stills under 2,270 litres capacity; furthermore the Highland distillers were forbidden to sell whisky south of the Highland Line. General Stewart of Garth summed it up thus:

It is evident that the law was a complete interdict, as a still of this magnitude would consume more than the disposable grain in the most extensive county within this newly drawn boundary; nor could fuel be obtained for such an establishment without an expense which the community could not possibly bear. The sale, too, of the spirits produced was circumscribed within the same line, and thus the market which alone could have supported the manufacture was entirely cut off. Although the quantity of grain raised within many districts, in consequence of the recent agricultural improvements, greatly exceeds the consumption, the inferior quality of this grain, and the great expense of carrying it to the Lowland distillers, who, by a ready market, and the command of fuel, can more easily accommodate themselves to this law, renders it impracticable for the farmers to dispose of their grain in any manner adequate to pay rents equal to the real value of their farms, subject as they are to the many drawbacks of uncertain climate, uneven surface, distance from market, and scarcity of fuel. Thus hardly any alternative remained but that of having recourse to illicit distillation, or resignation of their farms and breach of their engagements with their landlords . . . Hence they resort to smuggling (i.e. illicit distillation) as their only resource. If it indeed be true that this illegal traffic has made such deplorable breaches in the honesty and morals of the people, the revenue drawn from the large distilleries, to which the Highlanders have been made the sacrifice, has been procured at too high a price for the country.

In 1815 came Waterloo and the final end of Napoleon's threat to the peace of Europe. The Highland regiments' heroic actions in the battle caught the imagination of the country and on their return, as they marched back to Scotland to be disbanded, or reduced to peace-time requirements, they received tumultuous receptions at every halt. A writer in the south, who had seen them marching past, using the pseudonym 'Near Observer', wrote enthusiastically, 'On many a Highland hill and Lowland valley long will the deeds of these men be remembered.' General Stewart of Garth felt compelled to comment acidly:

This 'Near Observer' perhaps did not know that, on many a Highland hill, and in many a Highland glen, few are left to mourn the death, or rejoice over the deeds of the departed brave. New views of Highland statistic have changed the birth-place of many a brave soldier and defender of the honour, prosperity and independence of this country, to a desolate waste, where no maimed soldier can now find a home, or shelter, and where the sounds of the pipes and the voice of innocent gaiety and happiness are no longer heard.

The year 1816 saw a significant trial take place in Inverness. Mr Patrick Sellar, factor of the Sutherland estates under the Commissioner, Mr William Young, was arraigned at the Circuit Court on charges of murder and arson resulting from the evictions he had supervised in the parishes of Kildonan and Farr in the year 1814. The evictions in Sutherland had begun reasonably mildly in 1807, under the aegis of Mr Young, with the ejection of ninety families from Farr and Lairg. In 1809 several hundred had been evicted in Dornoch, Loth,

Overleaf: Highlanders holding off heavy French cavalry at Waterloo, 1812

Golspie, and Rogart. With Mr Sellar's arrival the process continued annually until 1811, the land being turned over to sheep.

In 1813 Mr Sellar had made the only successful bid for the tenancy of the whole of the Kildonan and Farr lands. He was thus acting in three capacities, as factor for the estates and as legal agent for the proprietors, as well as in his own interest as incoming tenant when in 1814, amid scenes of considerable distress, he had personally supervised the eviction of some 2,000 people, burning their houses and supplies of corn. The death of a 100-year-old bed-ridden woman was directly attributed to this treatment. The Sheriff-Substitute of Sutherland, Mr Robert McKid, very courageously in the circumstances, indicted Mr Sellar on charges of murder and arson for trial at Inverness.

The trial itself was something of a farce. As it was held in English the witnesses who could only speak Gaelic were at a considerable disadvantage, but it scarcely mattered, since the facts were barely contested. The trial itself only lasted a day and a half, with a lengthy summing up in the defendant's favour on the morning of the second day. It only took the jury, composed mostly of local landowners, a quarter of an hour to find him not guilty. To the native Highlander the verdict was plainly that sheep were more important than human beings.

Following the trial Mr William Young ceased to be Commissioner for the Sutherland estate, but his successor, Mr James Loch, was also a Lowlander much in the same mould. His opinion of the Highlander was low:

Contented with the poorest and most simple of fare and, like all mountaineers, accustomed to a roaming unfettered life, which attached them in the strongest manner to the habits and homes of their fathers, they deemed no new comfort worth the possessing which was to be acquired at the price of industry; no improvement worthy of adoption if it was to be obtained at the expense of sacrificing the customs or leaving the home of their ancestors.

Unfortunately as Commissioner of the Sutherland estates Mr Loch was in a position of considerable power, as Mr Young had been before him, and he continued his predecessor's policies with unabated zeal. His portraits show him as a man with a mouth like a slit in a collecting box and the weak, but self-indulgent, jaw of an extremely obstinate, self-opinionated man. His utterances bear this out and in the matter of the Clearances in the far north he was certainly the evil genius in the background.

The Strathnaver Clearances

In 1819 he authorised the notorious Strathnaver Clearances when a further 2,000 Highlanders were evicted and once again Mr Sellar was present acting in his threefold capacity. The minister of Strathnaver, Mr Donald Sage, kept a diary of events and wrote:

To my poor and defenceless flock the dark hour of trial came at last in right earnest. It was the month of April, and about the middle of it, that they were all, man, woman and child, from the heights of Farr to the mouth of the Naver, on one day, to quit their tenements and go—many of them knew not whither. For a few some miserable patches of ground along the shores were doled out in lots without aught in the shape of the poorest hut to shelter them. Upon these lots it was intended that they should build houses at their own expense and cultivate the ground at the same time as occupying themselves as fishermen, although the great majority had never set foot in a boat in their lives . . .

The middle of the week brought on the day of the Strathnaver Clearance (1819). It was a Tuesday. At an early hour of that day Mr. Sellar, accompanied by the Fiscal, and escorted by a strong body of constables, sheriff officers and others, commenced work at Grummore, the first inhabited township to the west of the Achness district. Their plan of operations was to clear the cottages of their inmates, giving them about half an hour to pack up and carry off their furniture and then set the cottages on fire. To this plan they ruthlessly adhered, without the slightest regard to any obstacle that might arise while carrying out its execution.

At Grumbeg lived a soldier's widow, Henny Munro . . . She was a joyous, cheery old creature; so inoffensive, moreover and so contented and brimful of goodwill that all who got acquainted with old Henny Munro could only desire to do her a good turn, were it merely for the warm and hearty expressions of gratitude with which it was received . . . After the cottages at Grummore were emptied of their inmates and roofs and rafters had been lighted into one red blaze, Mr. Sellar and his iron-hearted attendants approached the residence of the soldier's widow. Henny stood up to plead for her furniture—the coarsest and most valueless that well could be, but still her earthly all . . . she was told with an oath that if she did not take her trumpery off within half an hour it would be burned. The poor widow had only to task the remains of her bodily strength and address herself to the work of dragging her chests, beds, presses and stools out at the door and placing them at the gable of her cottage. No sooner was her task accomplished than the torch was applied, the widow's hut, built of very combustible material, speedily ignited . . . the wind unfortunately blew in the direction of the furniture and the flame, lighting upon it speedily reduced it to ashes...

I had occasion in the week immediately ensuing to visit the Manse at Tongue. On my way thither I pass through the scene of the campaign of burning . . . The banks of the lake and the river, formerly studded with cottages, now met the eye as a scene of desolation. Of all the cottages the thatched roofs were gone; but the walls built of alternate layers of turf and stone remained. The flames of the preceding week still slumbered in their ruins and sent up into the air spiral columns of smoke; whilst here a gable end, there a long side wall, undermined by the fire burning within them, might be seen tumbling to the ground, from which a cloud of smoke and then a dusky flame slowly sprang up . . . nothing could more vividly represent the horrors of grinding oppression.

From this description and others of a similar, or earlier, date it is possible to obtain a vivid picture of the interior of these Highland houses built of 'alternate layers of turf and stone' with sod roofs and earth floors. As there was seldom, if ever, a proper chimney, but only a hole in the roof, the interior was generally half obscured by a blue haze from the permanently burning peat fire over which an iron tripod and chains supported a cauldron of the same metal containing water simmering for a thin broth or potatoes, or porridge. At least

Examples of chairs from Highland households dating from the early eighteenth century

the smoke kept away the midges, that scourge of the summer month's in so many parts of the Highlands, and then the broth might be enriched with fish, or even on occasions venison.

A simple table and chairs comprised the bulk of the furniture, with possibly a chest containing a spare plaid, or other garments. Towards the end of the eighteenth century there would also often be a spinning wheel beside the fire, but prior to that the same work was accomplished painfully slowly by hand. Against the wall would be box beds, with sliding wooden doors to allow the occupants some privacy, although in the poorer households a plaid hung from a rope would suffice for the same purpose. In these box beds many of the occupants of these houses coughed themselves to death with tuberculosis caused by infected milk, or else with pneumonia caused by the permanently damp conditions. Those who survived more often than not ended their lives prematurely crippled with rheumatism or arthritis.

This was not the sort of picture of the Highlands portrayed by Sir Walter Scott in such works as *Rob Roy,* or any other of the Waverley novels. Yet it was largely due to his novels that the mists of legend and romance began to be woven round the Highlands. The first historical novelist to become a best seller, the 'Wizard of the North', was responsible more than almost any other man for publicising the Highlands in the south of Scotland and in England.

A Royal Visit

Although thought of principally as a novelist and poet and possibly secondly as a lawyer, Scott was in fact an expert showman. He, more than anyone, in conjunction with General Stewart of Garth, was responsible for much of the background organisation of George IV's famous visit to Scotland in 1822, when he became the first reigning monarch to visit the country since the reign

Sir Walter Scott (1771–1832)

Above left: George IV and, *above right:* wearing the kilt on his visit to Scotland

of Charles II exactly 172 years previously. Brief as it was, his visit was a significant occasion.

Scott's son-in-law, J. G. Lockhart, described the arrival of the royal yacht at Leith in pouring rain on 14 August 1822:

... Sir Walter rowed off to the Royal George, and, says the newspaper of the day, 'To this record let me add, that, on receiving the Poet on the quarter deck, his Majesty called for a bottle of Highland whisky, and having drunk his health in this national liquor desired a glass to be filled for him ...'

By this time any Highland whisky had to be illicitly distilled since there simply were no Highland stills of 2,270 litres capacity as required within the terms of the Act of Parliament of 1814. Yet everyone in the Highlands drank whisky freely, from Members of Parliament like Sir Peter Grant, Miss Elizabeth Grant's father, and wealthy landowners like Sir Francis Mackenzie of Gairloch, down to the very poorest families. The law was completely ignored.

In the area around Glenlivet alone there were said to be over 200 illicit distillers, perhaps the greatest concentration in the Highlands, for the district was isolated and hard of access for excisemen, and the whisky distilled there was regarded as by far the best. Miss Elizabeth Grant recorded:

One incident at this time made me very cross. Lord Conynghame, the Chamberlain, was looking everywhere for the pure Glenlivet whisky; the King drank nothing else. It was not to be had out of the Highlands. My father sent word to me—I was the cellarer—to empty my pet bin, where was whisky long in the wood, long in uncorked bottles, mild as milk, and the true contraband gout to it . . . The whisky and fifty brace of ptarmigan all shot by one man went up to Holyrood House and were graciously received and made much of . . .

Thus George IV started off his visit to Scotland by consuming illicitly distilled whisky.

Corpulent and corseted as he may have been, George IV also had a fine sense of theatre. His visit created immense excitement throughout Scotland and people from all over the country came to Edinburgh to witness the event. By this time the secret of weaving many of the old tartans had been forgotten for during the repression after the 1745 Rebellion many of the old tally sticks, used by the weavers to record the setts of the tartans they wove, had been destroyed. Several Highland chieftains ordered tartan by the hundreds of metres for their followers from the well-known tartan weavers in Stirling and there are at least two tartans which are now claimed by several clans on the grounds that they were ordered for George IV's visit, but they are generally credited to the chieftain who paid for them. Even Lowland lairds such as the Duke of Hamilton appeared in the kilt, although in many instances, such as his, they were box pleated rather than the modern single pleats.

George IV, himself, superintended by Sir Walter Scott and General Stewart of Garth, was garbed as a Highland chieftain in the Royal Stewart tartan, with, it is said, pink silk tights beneath the kilt to preserve the decencies. The occasion is well described by Miss Elizabeth Grant:

The whole country went mad. Everybody stormed every point to get to Edinburgh to receive him. Sir Walter Scott and the Town Council were overwhelming themselves with preparations . . . The King wore at the Levee the Highland dress . . . Someone objecting to this dress, particularly on so large a man, 'Nay' said she (Lady Saltoun, noted for her wit) 'we should take it very kind of him, since his stay will be so short, the more we see of him the better.' Sir William Curtis (the Lord Mayor of London) was kilted too, and standing near the King, many persons mistook them, amongst others John Hamilton Dundas, who kneeled to kiss the fat Alderman's hand, when, finding out his mistake, he called out 'Wrong, by Jove!' and rising, moved on undaunted to the larger presence . . .

In October, to commemorate the King's visit to Scotland and also with a view to quietening the critics of the vastly increased costs of the venture, the Caledonian Canal was finally opened. Apart from labour difficulties and spiralling costs due to inflation, Telford had also run into strong opposition from MacDonell of Glengarry, who seized every opportunity of interfering with the work, despite the fact that he was awarded £10,000 compensation because the canal passed through 16 kilometres of his land. A tiresome poseur, appearing always in full Highland dress with a 'tail' of followers, he was ironically enough the great-nephew of the thirteenth chief 'Young Glengarry' of the '45, who acted as a Hanoverian spy on the Jacobites in France under the codename 'Pickles'. None of this prevented him taking a prominent part in the opening ceremonies.

In late 1822 the Duke of Gordon spoke out in the House of Lords on the measures to check illicit distilling in the Highlands. At this time he was one of the largest landowners in Scotland, particularly in the great whisky distilling areas of Banffshire and Inverness-shire. He pointed out that the Highlanders could not be prevented from distilling whisky and that it was natural they should do so. He went on to state that if realistic measures were passed to allow any distiller the chance of legally distilling whisky of as good a standard as was illicitly distilled, he and other large landed proprietors in the Highlands would do their best to encourage their tenants to take out licences and also to suppress illicit distilling.

In 1823 an act was passed setting a flat licence rate of £10 for stills of 182 litres capacity and over, with a duty of 2s. 3d. on each 4.5 litres distilled. The result was a gradual return to legal distilling, although it was to be many years before illicit distilling was finally suppressed. Before the act the total tax-paid whisky consumed annually was a mere 9,100,000 litres. Two years after the Act it had risen to 27,300,000 litres. In 1823 there were 1,400 seizures of illicit stills, but within a decade this figure had fallen to 692. Whisky distilling in Scotland had finally progressed from being a cottage craft to a burgeoning industry.

Meanwhile emigration continued for numerous reasons apart from the encouragement provided by letters from those who had already settled successfully. The kelp industry, which had provided alkali, in short supply during the war, collapsed soon after 1815 when it became available from Europe once more. This caused great hardship in the west coast and on the Islands where the seaweed kelp had mainly been harvested, providing one of the few sources of income. Clearances also continued either for reasons of

Opposite: MacDonell of Glengarry

Overleaf: The wild countryside of Sutherland, part of which was purchased from Lord Reay by the Duke of Sutherland

'improvement' as in Sutherland, or else due to the sheer extravagant living of the chieftain as in Glengarry. Then in 1824 came the 'Year of the Short Corn', when a disastrous harvest brought near famine to the Highlands relieved only by supplies of grain sent in via the military roads and the Caledonian Canal.

In 1828, as the final irony of a misspent life, Alistair MacDonell of Glengarry died as the result of misjudging a leap on to the rocks near Corran from a steamer which had gone aground there in the Caledonian Canal. He left £80,000 worth of debts and his son, Aeneas, was forced to sell all the Glengarry land which remained except for Knoydart in the west. Glengarry itself was bought by William Ward, the eleventh Baron of that name, who despite being English enthusiastically wore the kilt and plaid and held Highland Gatherings. He also introduced such English innovations as ploughing matches for those of his tenants not dispossessed to make way for sheep. In similar ways many parts of the Highlands were becoming available to speculators from the south.

Osgood Mackenzie, son of Sir Francis Mackenzie of Gairloch, in his book *A Hundred Years in the Highlands* about his family's life on the west coast, mentioned an extremely wealthy Englishman, who about 1830 bought a neighbouring estate of 28,000 hectares. 16–20,000 hectares were famed deer forest yet he never stalked it and let it to Osgood Mackenzie for £5 a year. At the first Inverness Gathering he attended, soon after his arrival from England, he wore a kilt which reached nearly to his ankles. When it was pointed out that it might be more becoming to his figure to wear one a little shorter he then had another made which was so short that he scandalised everyone at the Stornoway Ball.

At least he appears to have lived on his estate, which is more than many of the later southern landowners were prepared to do. Of course the Sutherland estates were an early example of land owned by largely absentee English landlords. The Countess of Sutherland had been orphaned at thirteen months, when her father, the last earl, and her mother, both died prematurely, probably from typhoid. After some lengthy litigation she finally inherited as a minor the title of Countess of Sutherland and some 2,200 square kilometres of land in the county. She was, however, brought up chiefly in the south by well-meaning guardians and when of age married the second Marquis of Stafford, George Granville Leveson Gower, the product of a mating three generations previously between wealthy Yorkshire wool merchants and coal owners.

In addition to his wife's immense estates in the north, the second Marquis inherited his father's large estates in Stafford and Shropshire and the wealth of his uncle the Duke of Bridgewater. He was, in effect, an absentee landlord, English to the marrow, and with absolutely no understanding of, or real interest in, the Highlanders who were his tenants in the north. In 1830 he added by purchase from Lord Reay, chief of the Mackays, the 960 square kilometres of Sutherland that he had owned in the north-west, thus obtaining ownership of virtually all of Sutherland and becoming the largest landowner in Britain. In 1833 he was made Duke of Sutherland, possibly his only ambition, and died within six months of achieving it, but the policies he had initiated through his Commissioners William Young and James Loch and his factor Patrick Sellars were continued by his Duchess-Countess after his death.

One of her first actions was to propose the renovation of Dornoch Cathedral, founded in the thirteenth century, but by this time much decayed and reduced to the status of the parish church, with a view to erecting a memorial to her husband. In her plans for the renovation she put forward these points:

1st. I will, at my own expense, restore in the manner I shall be advised, the nave, or west end of the Cathedral now in ruins . . .

2nd. I will repair, restore and reseat the north and south aisles in the manner shewn in a sketch . . . on the conditions herein expressed.

3rd. That the other Heritors will consent to the choir or east aisle being also repaired by me and to its remaining in all time hereafter my sole property and that of my successors . . .

In 1835 it was ruthlessly renovated by a Mr Burns, who had already dealt in a similar fashion with St Giles in Edinburgh. The ruined nave, with its pillars, aisles, and detached chapel, together with the gravestones with which it was filled, as well as tons of soil and human remains, were carted away with complete insensitivity for the feelings of the relatives of the dead. Referring to this, the Revd Donald Sage quoted the remark of an old parishioner who had suffered in the Sutherland Clearances as he buried his wife:

. . . As he took his last look at the rapidly disappearing coffin: 'Well Janet,' said he. 'The Countess of Sutherland can never flit you any more.'

Had he lived to hear of the dreadful doings at the reconstruction of Dornoch Cathedral by the orders of this heartless woman, he might not have been so sure that even in her narrow house, his Janet was altogether beyond another summons of removal from the same ruthless hand.

Meanwhile the year 1831 had seen the invention of the patent continuous still by Aeneas Coffey, ex-Inspector General of Excise in Ireland. Although not introduced into the Highlands for many years it was to have a very considerable effect on whisky distilling throughout Scotland. The new still, which was known as the patent-still, or Coffey-still, produced spirit in one continuous stream from any form of grain with only the addition of small amounts of malt in the fermenting process being required. There was no need for the time-consuming methods of double distillation using pure malted barley and two pot-stills in two separate processes, as was required to produce malt whisky in the time-honoured Highland fashion.

The advantages of the new patent-still were soon perceived by the large Lowland distillers who were already producing great quantities of much inferior whisky at lower prices than their Highland competitors. Already the market in the north was being affected by the sale of this inferior whisky, as a letter from a Major Cumming Bruce in the *Inverness Courier* of 1831 clearly indicated:

It is asserted that the rage for the use of whisky is still increasing, while to our sad experience we know that its quality is deteriorating among us. It is no longer the pure dew of the mountain which issued from the bothies of our free traders of the hills, healthful and as exhilerating as the drops which the sun's first rays drink up from the heathbell of the Cairngorms, but a vile, rascally, mixed compotation which fires the blood and maddens the veins without warming the heart, or, like the old, elevating the understanding.

The next twenty years were to see the Highland distillers struggling for their existence against strong competition from the large and powerful firms in the south of Scotland. Yet the same years also saw the development of many firms in the north which are today household names. In the south it is noticeable that the names belonged to individuals, often primarily merchants rather than distillers, who none the less became powerful figures, such as Haig, Dewar, Justerini and Brooks, Hill Thomson, Sandeman, Teacher, John Walker. In the north the names were those of distilleries, such as The Glenlivet, Talisker, Linkwood, Glenfarclas, Glenmorangie, Glen Grant and many others. There were still remarkably few outlets for industry in the Highlands and distilling remained the most conveniently suited to the Highland scene.

One industrial development which took place in 1841 was the formation of the Loch Fyne Powder Mills to produce gunpowder at Furnace in Argyll, close to the site of the old Argyll Furnace Company's erstwhile ironworks. This involved the erection of a whole series of new buildings, a mixing house, a mill house, a press house, a corning house, and a glazing house as well as a boiler house and a dusting house and finally two magazines. At the entrance to this complex of buildings there was a watch house where the workmen changed and were searched for combustible materials before starting work. With the advent of the young Queen Victoria to the throne in 1837 it seemed as if industrialisation might be reaching the Highlands at last.

Queen Victoria's First Visit

In fact Queen Victoria was to have a very different effect on the Highlands. Married in February 1840 to her cousin Prince Albert of Saxe-Coburg, she found the first few years of her marriage a period of considerable adjustment, even though she and her husband were undoubtedly very much in love with

Queen Victoria's first visit to Scotland. The royal couple are shown embarking for the north

each other. By late 1842, however, their eldest daughter, Victoria, was already eighteen months old and their initial household troubles were settled. During that time they had never really escaped from the atmosphere of the court. On their first visit to Scotland in September 1842 she and Albert were in effect experiencing the pleasure of a delayed honeymoon.

The highlight of their visit was their reception at Taymouth Castle by the Earl and Countess of Breadalbane, where they were greeted by a kilted guard of honour of the 92nd Highlanders and Lord Breadalbane's Highlanders also in full regalia. The Prince Consort found that the scenery reminded him of Germany and Switzerland and thoroughly enjoyed the shooting and deer stalking, killing amongst other game one of the capercailzies which had only been re-established in Scotland five years earlier by the combined efforts of the Earl and the English naturalist Fowell Buxton. The young Queen fell in love with the tartans and the kilts of the Highlanders as well as the scenery and ever afterwards regarded the Highlands as a place of enchantment. She read extracts from Scott's *Lay of the Last Minstrel* to Albert and the entries in her diary verged on the ecstatic at times. At the end of their first visit she wrote: 'We shall never forget it.'

It is interesting to note that during the period from 1820 to 1840 there had been a gradually increasing antipathy in some Highland regiments to the kilt. This was, of course, still the period when commissions were acquired by purchase and this discontent stemmed entirely from certain senior officers, not of Highland origins, who took every opportunity to avoid wearing it. Hearing their comments and having been issued by Whitehall with unsuitable hard tartan which chafed their legs, the men took up the complaints and a clamour arose in the press. This was promptly stilled by the provision of more suitable tartan material and an order that all officers and men should wear the correct dress on duty and on parade.

In the same year came the 'Disruption' of the Church of Scotland, which was to cause much heartsearching throughout the Highlands. This was a rebellion against the principle, which had been established by the Court of Session and passed by the House of Lords, that the patron of a living had the right to choose the minister. It was increasingly felt throughout the Church that the congregation should have the right to choose their own minister. The first rebellion was at Marnoch in Banffshire in 1841 when the entire congregation of 2,000 left the church rather than see a new minister inducted who was not of their choice. In 1843 at the General Assembly of the Church of Scotland 451 ministers out of 1,203 left to form the Free Church of Scotland.

Queen Victoria and the royal family on a typical Highland outing near Balmoral, painted by Landseer

The majority of ministers leaving the established Church to join the Free Church were in the Highlands. Very typical was the Revd Mr Donald Sage, who had earlier been at Strathnaver and by this time was minister of Ressolis on the Black Isle. He wrote subsequently: 'After . . . joining the Free Church I may truly say that I exchanged debt and poverty for peace of mind and a competency enabling me to supply my everyday wants and to pay all my debts.'

Although many of the ministers and congregations in the Highlands seceded from the established Church, a preponderance of the landlords remained in the Church of Scotland. The result was initially that the Free Church often found it difficult to obtain ground on which to build a church for their congregation, or a house for their minister. Thus in the early days of the Free Church the services were frequently held in the open air. On occasions this led to large gatherings of several thousand attending these services, some of whom had travelled as much as a hundred miles on foot.

At Strontian in Morvern almost the entire congregation seceded from the Church. On being refused permission by the landowner, an Episcopalian, to build a new church on his land, they first held their services in the open air, then ordered a floating church, appropriately ark-shaped, to be built in a shipyard at Port Glasgow. This was then moored in Loch Sunart and the congregation approached by boat. The floating church sank an inch for every hundred people on board and one minister noted:

Here I preached thrice on the Sabbath, twice in Gaelic, once in English. I was thanked by the office-bearers and told that their church had never been so deep down in the water before (six inches).

In 1844 Victoria and Albert again visited Scotland in September, this time visiting Blair Atholl where they were entertained by Lord and Lady Glenlyon. Here, in the hills around Glen Tilt, Victoria accompanied Albert stalking and they both found they enjoyed it even more than their previous visit. On their return Victoria noted 'The English coast appeared terribly flat' after 'the dear, dear *Highlands*'. She wrote:

There is a great peculiarity about the *Highlands* and the Highlanders; and they are such chivalrous, fine, active people. Our stay among them was so delightful. Independent of the beautiful scenery, there is a quiet, a retirement, a wildness, a liberty, and a solitude that had such charm for us . . .

During this period two early books of importance were written on sport in the Highlands. In 1838, in a racy, easy style, William Scrope, a wealthy dilettante and friend of Landseer, wrote *The Art of Deer Stalking*, filled with anecdotes of poachers, freebooters, and Highland superstitions. In 1845 Charles St John's *Wild Sports and Natural History of the Highlands* was published, which ran into nine editions before the end of the century. A

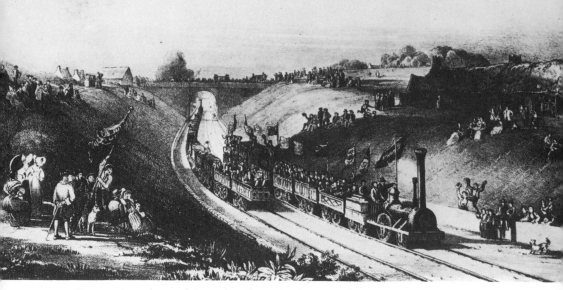

The opening of one of the early railways in the west of Scotland

naturalist-collector of the new school he wrote of stalking deer, shooting, and fishing as well as of the wild life he saw all round him. Full of delightful anecdotes it also contained original sketches by the author. Like the royal visits, these encouraged tourists from the south to go to the Highlands to admire the scenery and to enjoy the sport available.

This was also the period of railway mania throughout the country and in 1845 a scheme was passed by Parliament for a line from Aberdeen to Inverness, although it was not completed. In the same year two lines were proposed to link Inverness with Aberdeen and Perth. It was, however, a decade or more before these were completed, for the rugged terrain of the Highlands called for high standards of engineering and considerable investment.

From 1846 to 1848 the failure of the potato crop caused great hardship in the Highlands and Islands, which like Ireland had come to rely on this as their staple diet. There were riots on the east coast and many faced starvation. In the Gairloch area Osgood Mackenzie's mother, Lady Mackenzie, working in conjunction with his uncle Dr John Mackenzie, organised relief works. With some Government assistance, by fund raising and by using their own money, they raised £10,000 to pay for the building of a road from Gairloch and Poolewe to Loch Maree, thus providing wages for this public work so that no one would starve. The neighbouring proprietors followed their example so that a road was built from Loch Maree and Gairloch along the coastline from Poolewe through Aultbea, Gruinard, and Dundonnel to join the Garve to Ullapool road at Braemore.

Undoubtedly Lady Mackenzie was a woman of character for she taught herself Gaelic and insisted on her sons learning the language from a Gaelic-speaking nursemaid. Her sons were also all educated at home with tutors, rather than being sent south to a public school and university. They were thus able to understand their people and manage their estates successfully in a way that non-Gaelic speakers would have found almost impossible.

At this time, barely a hundred years after Culloden, the 'Erse language' had already been nearly 'rooted out' of the Highland regiments. Certainly the number of Gaelic speakers had declined radically. On joining the 92nd Gordon Highlanders in 1848 Lieutenant-General Sir John Ewart, then a Captain, wrote, as a matter of pride, that they were 'about the most exclusively national of any in the Highland Corps, about half the men at the time I joined speaking Gaelic'.

In 1848 Victoria and Albert first stayed at Balmoral and found it so much to their taste that they returned each year thereafter, and by 1850 they had bought it. By this time Victoria regularly wore a tartan plaid, or sash, and Albert wore the kilt, as did the royal children. They all learned Highland dancing, including Victoria. The castle itself was decorated with tartan throughout. The curtains, the carpets, the chair covers, everything was tartan. There were also thistles everywhere, in carvings, needlework, and paintings. Enough, as the Earl of Clarendon commented, to feed many donkeys, if any of them had borne any resemblance to nature. Although Balmoral was at first too small, by 1853 it had been remodelled on a larger scale and Victoria always regarded it as her favourite home.

Before the royal family had made it their permanent home, with considerable foresight, as well as foreboding, the Revd Thomas Maclauchlan, Gaelic scholar and Presbyterian minister, wrote in 1849:

Much as we rejoice in our beloved Sovereign's visits to our country, we fear that they may hasten the consummation of making our Highlands a great deer forest by inducing a large number of our English aristocracy to flock to them for the purpose of sport.

Like many other converts to the Highlands the royal couple became more Highland than the Highlanders. From their first arrival they regularly attended the Braemar Gathering and Highland Games. They approved of the bagpipes and by their example encouraged the wearing of the kilt and started the enthusiasm for tartan which has grown steadily ever since. English newcomers to the Highlands, following the royal example, were to embrace not only the kilt but the pipes and the Highland games, as well as the field sports available. They also embraced what they imagined to be the romantic Scottish architecture. Gothic monstrosities with pepperpot towers, crow-stepped gables and battlements proliferated. The Balmoralisation of the Highlands had begun.

It is an intriguing point that it was not until George IV's visit to Scotland in 1822 that interest in the tartans revived. The first book on the tartans was

Above: Balmoral, the royal home established by Victoria and Albert in the mid-nineteenth century

Right: Wilkie's romantic portrayal of the corpulent, corseted Prinnie without his 'pink silk tights'

published in 1823 written by J. Smith. By 1850 there had been six more written, including *Vestiarium Scoticum* by the Sobieski brothers, which even more than the others, although an enormous tome, was an obvious fake. Undoubtedly many of the tartans produced in it had simply been invented. This did not stop people wearing them enthusiastically and the tartan mania is not a disease which has grown less virulent over the years.

In 1854 the Crimean War broke out and the second Duke of Sutherland

called a meeting in Golspie. Some four hundred or so men attended and cheered the Duke politely. He then addressed them on the necessity of defeating Russia and the Czar. On a table beside him there was a pile of gleaming sovereigns for recruits, but when he called for volunteers no one came forward. When he realised none were forthcoming he indignantly stood up and demanded to know the reason. According to Donald MacLeod's *Gloomy Memories in the Highlands of Scotland* eventually one old man stepped forward and leaning on his staff addressed the Duke thus:

I am sorry for the response your Grace's proposals are meeting here today, so near to the spot where your maternal grandmother by giving some forty eight hours notice marshalled 1,500 men to pick out the 800 she required, but there is a cause for it and a genuine cause and, as your Grace demands to know it, I must tell you as I see none else is inclined in the assembly to do so. These lands are now devoted to rear dumb animals which your parents considered of far more value than men. I do assure your Grace that it is the prevailing opinion of this county that, should the Czar of Russia take possession of Dunrobin Castle and Stafford House next term that we could not expect worse treatment at his hands than we have experienced at the hands of your family for the past fifty years. Your parents, yourself and your Commissioners have desolated the glens and the straths of Sutherland where you should find hundreds, yea thousands of men to meet and respond to your call cheerfully had your parents kept faith with them. How could your Grace expect to find men where they are not and the few of them that are to be found have more sense than to be decoyed off by chaff to the field of slaughter. But one comfort you have; though you cannot find men to fight, you can supply those who will fight with plenty of mutton, beef and venison.

*Opposite:*In fact the Highland regiments fought gallantly in the Crimea and yet again did themselves great credit

Chapter 7

The English 'Invasion'

It is revealing to learn from Osgood Mackenzie's recollections how self-sufficient the life was on the west coast of the Highlands as late as the 1850s. The houses were, of course, all lit by candles which were manufactured in considerable quantities from tallow obtained from sheep's fat, or else by boiling down the livers of fish, and were naturally somewhat evil smelling. Knives, forks, and spoons were extremely uncommon and in the poorer parts only hands were used for eating since not even plates were available. Spoons were mostly of horn, made by travelling tinkers who melted down cow and sheep horns for the purpose. Flax was carded and spun to provide linen. Hemp was grown and spun to provide herring nets and rope, although rope was also made from heather, or pounded bog-fir roots. Since few roads existed sledges were built from birch trees and proved capable of crossing heather and boggy ground, being used to move peats, crops, fish, lime, manure, or hay where no cart could have gone. Food, such as deer and mutton tongues, was preserved by smoking, or by salting, and fruits were dried and candied.

As there were virtually no sacks to be had, everything was carried in bags made of sheepskin. Sheepskin drawn tight over a frame, with holes burned through it with red-hot needles, was also used to make sieves to riddle corn or meal. Although the Highlanders merely had their hand-held ploughs to break up the soil and had to carry most of their seed, crops, or manure in wickerwork creels, they were according to him, anything but lazy as has often been suggested. Despite the handicaps of the run-rig system they made the most of their ground, using seaweed as mulch and penning cattle on the ground they intended to sow to provide manure. They also took care to cultivate every available piece of ground, however rocky, using the old *cashcrom*, or foot plough.

The Mackenzies were, of course, more closely integrated with the countryside than many non-Gaelic-speaking landlords. Commenting on the Disruption, for instance, Osgood Mackenzie wrote:

A crofter family near Ullapool, West Ross *c.* 1880

No wonder the people rebelled when worthless men were appointed to big parishes by lay patrons, quite regardless of their being suitable, or unsuitable. This was the case at Gairloch, when an old tutor who had hardly a word of Gaelic tried to make up for his want of the language by the roaring and bawling he kept up in the pulpit while attempting to read a Gaelic sermon translated from the English by some schoolmaster . . .

Holding such views it is not perhaps surprising that the Mackenzies joined the Free Church. This in itself was unusual since the Disruption led to a split between many tenants and their landlords, who mainly remained Episcopalians. The Disruption also led to a narrowness of outlook and a rigid observance of the Sabbath which resulted in occasional absurdities. Osgood Mackenzie noted some of these with humour.

For instance the Free Church minister at Aultbea preached on alternate Sundays at Gairloch. Due to his exertions in the pulpit he sweated profusely and always required a change of underclothes, but these had to be sent ahead during the week for 'nothing would induce him to carry the smallest parcel in his trap on the Sunday'. Another Free Church minister forbade anyone to attend communion who was 'a frequenter of concerts or dances'. Such narrowness of outlook and rigidity of mind led to a good deal of hypocrisy, thus water had to be drawn from the well on Saturday and by Sunday might be flat, therefore it became advisable to take plenty of whisky with it to counteract the flatness.

In 1852 a lasting economic venture was started at Crarae on Loch Fyne, where a quarry was opened to produce improved paving stones for the streets of Glasgow and other cities. Although termed granite, the stone was in fact porphyrite, extremely durable and hard to extract from the ground without considerable blasting. Very large amounts of gunpowder were required to blast the required amounts of stone, producing immense explosions, which in course of time became a tourist attraction.

In the same year the death of the chieftain Aeneas MacDonell, son of the ill-fated Alistair MacDonell of Glengarry, after he had returned disillusioned from an attempt to settle in New South Wales, led to further evictions. His widow decided to raise sheep in Knoydart, the last remaining MacDonell lands. Over 400 families were forcibly evicted from Airor, Doune, Inverie, and Sandaig. As had been the case in Sutherland, their homes were destroyed and the people dispersed.

In 1853 Mr R. Alister, author of *Barriers to the National Prosperity of Scotland*, entered into public controversy with the Marquis of Breadalbane, on the subject of the eviction of his tenants. In July Mr Alister wrote:

Your lordship states that in reality there has been no depopulation . . . In Glenquoich, near Amulree, some sixty families lived where there are now only four of five . . . On the braes of Taymouth at the back of Drummon Hill . . . some forty or fifty families resided, where there is not one now! Glenorchy by the returns of 1831 showed a population of 1,806; in 1842, 831;—is there no depopulation there? Is it true that in Glenetive there were sixteen tenants a year or two ago, where there is not a single one now? Is it true, my lord, that you purchased an island on the west coast called *Luing*, where some twenty five families lived at the beginning *of this year*, but who are now cleared out to make room for one tenant . . . ? . . . from everything I have heard your lordship has done more to exterminate the Scottish peasantry than any man now living; and perhaps you ought to be ranked next to the Marquis of Stafford in the unenviable clearing celebrities. If I have overestimated the clearance of five hundred families please correct me.

Perhaps wisely, the Marquis of Breadalbane did not reply, although another writer, Mr Duncan Campbell, in his *Reminiscences and Reflections of an Octogenarian Gael* explains why the Marquis was not publicly pilloried for his evictions as the Marquis of Stafford had been. He recorded:

When such a loud and continued outcry took place about the Sutherland clearances, it seems at first sight strange that such small notice was taken by the Press, authors and contemporary politicians, of the Breadalbane evictions . . . One reason—perchance the chief one—for the Marquis's immunity was the prominent manner in which he associated himself with the Nonintrusionists and his subsequently becoming an elder and liberal benefactor of the Free Church . . . His Free Church zeal . . . may . . . have been . . . genuine . . . but . . . it covered as with a saintly cloak his eviction proceedings in the eyes of those who would have been his loud denouncers and scourging critics had he been an Episcopalian or remained in the Church of Scotland . . .

In 1851 the Sheriff-Substitute of Skye, Mr Thomas Fraser, formed the Highlands and Islands Emigration Society. The idea was promptly taken up and in 1852 it had been transformed into the Society for Assisting Emigration from the Highlands and Islands of Scotland with a London headquarters under the chairmanship of the Assistant-Secretary to the Treasury, Sir Charles Trevelyan, and Prince Albert as patron. When it was wound up in 1859 it had already assisted over 5,000 from the Highlands and Islands to emigrate. By this time the increasing depopulation of the Highlands and Islands was again causing alarm.

During the Crimean War from 1854 to 1856, despite the continuing evictions and the ever-increasing depopulation of the Highlands, the Highland Brigade, consisting of the 42nd, or Royal Black Watch; the 79th, or Queen's Own Cameron Highlanders; and the 93rd, or Sutherland Highlanders, 'the thin red streak, tipped with a line of steel', distinguished themselves with honour under General Sir Colin Campbell. They went on to cover themselves with even greater glory in the Indian Mutiny in 1857 under the same commander. At the Relief of Lucknow alone, the 42nd won eight VCs and the 93rd seven VCs, all well earned.

Overleaf: Ben More and Glen Dochart in the 1870s

Hunting, Shooting, and Fishing

By this time the regular tourist trade was becoming established during the summer months in the Highlands. Such Spas as Ballater, originally started at the Wells of Pannanich in 1790, and Strathpeffer, which had opened in 1820, had regular visitors from Aberdeen, Edinburgh, and Glasgow, as well as further south, once their fame had spread. It was, however, increasingly to view the scenery, or to sample the sport available, on moor, river, and loch, or deer forest, that the visitors were coming from the south.

Noblemen such as the Dukes of Gordon and Atholl, or the Marquis of Breadalbane would invite housefuls of guests to enjoy the sport. Others might lease from them or similar large landlords, outlying houses, or lodges, on their estates for the same purpose. Already the Revd Thomas MacLaughlan's prognostications were being fulfilled as the idea of buying an estate in the Highlands for the summer months was beginning to take a hold on society where the Royal example was often slavishly followed.

In the main the modern methods of stalking deer were employed, although in some places deer were still occasionally driven past the waiting guns in the manner of the old *Tainchel*. During the autumn of 1858 an even older method of hunting deer was demonstrated at least on one occasion. Samuel White Baker, author of *The Rifle and Hound in Ceylon*, was staying with the Duke of Atholl at Blair Castle amongst a large house party. He was urged to give a demonstration of hunting deer with hounds, armed only with a knife, as he had portrayed the sport in Ceylon. It was argued that hounds trained as Scottish deer hounds were, merely to bay the wounded deer, could not be urged on to hold him while the knife was used. Baker wrote subsequently:

The arguments had interested the ladies of the party, and it was arranged that I might select any two of the deer hounds and hunt down a fresh stag, run it to bay, and kill it with a knife. To myself the affair appeared exceedingly simple . . . but others disbelieved that the two hounds would bring a fresh deer to bay, as they had always been accustomed to follow animals that were wounded . . .

By the advice of the head forester, Sandy Macarra, I chose my old friend Oscar and another hound . . .

We were a large party . . . The afternoon was perfect . . . the presence of many ladies brought us luck . . . we were suddenly delighted by the almost magical appearance of a stag . . . about 1,000 yards distant.

This was in Glen Tilt, notable for its length and straightness, and Baker, accompanied by two keepers with the hounds, climbed the hill until they were above the stag and spectators on the road below. Within a hundred metres of the stag they released the hounds:

This must have been a lovely sight from the carriages . . . For a few seconds the stag took up the hill, but the hounds ran cunning and cut him off; he now took a straight course along the face towards the direction where the carriages were waiting below. The hounds were going madly and gaining on him . . . and away we went as hard as we could go . . . The deer . . . turned down the hill towards the river with the two dogs within yards of his heels . . . after running about a quarter of a mile down the road we heard the bay and shortly arrived at the spot where the stag was standing in the middle of a rapid and the hounds were baying from the bank . . . Patting both the excited hounds upon the back, and giving them a loud halloo, I jumped into the water, which was hardly more than hip deep, but the stream was very rapid . . . The two keepers had followed me and Oscar and his companion no longer thought of baying from the bank, but carried onward by the torrent, together with ourselves were met by the stag with lowered antlers. I never saw dogs behave better, although for a moment one was beneath the water. Oscar was hanging to the ear, I caught hold of the horn to assist the dog and at the same moment the other dog was holding by the throat. The knife had made its thrust and the two gillies were holding fast by the horns to prevent the torrent carrying away the dying animal. This had been a pretty course, which did not last long, but it was properly managed and in my opinion ten times better sport than shooting a deer at bay.

The year 1860 saw the introduction of the breech-loading shotgun, which was to facilitate shooting enormously. With the ability to reload speedily and fire both barrels without fear of misfires the sport of shooting was re-volutionised. Instead of only shooting over dogs on the moors, the principle of driving the birds over butts was soon developed and between the 1860s and 70s this became increasingly practised. The 'Glorious Twelfth' was on its way.

In the whisky industry meanwhile, the practice of blending malt whiskies with each other to achieve a smoother taste had been introduced. When the Spirits Act of 1860 permitted the blending of spirits in bond the merchants in the south soon took the opportunity of mixing grain, or patent still, whisky with malt whisky and this blended whisky very quickly became popular. The power of the merchants to order what they wished gave them a measure of control over the distillers, particularly in the north, where the malt distillers were struggling to survive against the competition of the larger Lowland distillers with their patent stills.

By 1860 for the first time more patent still whisky was produced than malt whisky, for the pot-still malt distillers in the north, individualists to a man, had not yet learned the importance of combining, while the Lowland distillers had already entered into trade agreements. In addition the tax on whisky, which had been raised to 6s. od. per gallon in 1855 and 8s. od. in 1856 was raised in 1860 to 10s. od. Already the Government in the south had discovered that it formed a useful milch cow for taxation purposes.

With the ready availability of cheap labour in the Highlands this was a period of considerable building. Working as a stonemason was one of the commonest occupations in the Highlands, either building walls dividing the new estates which were being formed, or building new houses of stone to replace the old turf houses from which so many were evicted. Slates too were in great demand and the quarries at Ballachulish, formed originally at Easdaile

Bas relief in marble over the ballroom at Balmoral showing the royal family at the Highland games

in 1697, employed somewhere in the region of 400 men and boys producing over 15 million slates a year by mid-century.

Stones, of course, had always played an important role in the Highlands. From the earliest days the lifting or throwing of stones had been regarded as a test of manhood. The Manhood Stone, or *Clach Cuid Fir*, was generally a large stone weighing anything from 51 kilograms upwards which had to be raised from the ground and lifted waist high, then placed on a wall. A stone of this kind was often to be found close by a chieftain's house or castle, where it could be used as a test of the strength of visitors, or young men claiming manhood.

There are still numbers of these *Clach Cuid Fir* to be found in the Highlands. One well-known example, called the Putbrach, is outside the churchyard at Balquhidder. There is one weighing 129 kilograms at Inver near Braemar, but the two most notable are the Stones of Dee at the Bridge of Potarch, where they were used for tethering horses. These two together weigh more than 356 kilograms and were once lifted and carried five metres by the famous athlete and stonemason Donald Dinnie when he was repairing the bridge in the 1870s.

Another type of stone was the *Clach Neart*, or Stone of Strength, which generally weighed about 14 kilograms and was thrown, or putted, competitively. In the same competitive spirit races would be run to the summit of a nearby hill and back. Tossing the caber is thought to have originated with the 'floaters', or early lumberjacks, engaged in floating logs down the Spey. The concept of competitive piping had by this time been established for many years and skill in Highland dancing was also hotly contested. From such simple sports the early Highland Games developed, one of the earliest being the Braemar Gathering, first held in 1817 due to the promptings of officers and men returned from the army after Waterloo.

From her first visit to Balmoral in 1848 Queen Victoria and her family had made an annual visit to the Braemar Gathering and with such an example it cannot have been long before numerous other Games were being formed in a spirit of emulation. In 1861 the Royal family visited Balmoral as usual and appear to have had a particularly pleasant visit, making various expeditions. To begin with they visited Fettercairn and Invermark travelling to the best of their ability incognito. In her diary Victoria wrote:

Friday September 20th . . . At a quarter past seven o'clock we reached the small quiet town, or rather village, of *Fettercairn*, for it was very small—not a creature stirring and we got out at the quiet little inn, 'Ramsay Arms' quite unobserved and went at once upstairs. There was a very nice drawing room, and next to it, a dining-room, both very clean and tidy—then to the left our bed-room which was excessively small, but also very clean and neat . . . We dined at eight, a very nice, clean, good dinner. Grant and Brown waited. They were rather nervous, but . . . they had only to change the plates, which Brown soon got in the way of doing . . . The landlord and landlady knew who we were, but *no one else* . . . and they kept the secret admirably . . .

Saturday September 21 . . . We passed . . . *Fasque*, belonging to Sir T. Gladstone, who has evidently done a great deal for the country, having built many good cottages . . . The harvest and everything seemed prosperous and the country was very pretty . . . We got back to *Balmoral* much pleased with our expedition at seven o'clock. We had gone 42 miles today and 40 yesterday, in all 82.

In October they made another similar expedition to Dalwhinnie and Blair Atholl. Queen Victoria noted:

Tuesday, October 8, 1861 . . . At *Kingussie* there was a small, curious, chattering crowd of people—who, however, did not really make us out, but evidently suspected who we were. Grant and Brown kept them off the carriages, and gave them evasive answers, directing them to the wrong carriage which was most amusing . . .

At Dalwhinnie they did not fare as well as at Fettercairn and the next day they started off again for Blair Atholl:

. . . We passed many drovers, without their herds and flocks, returning, Grant told us, from *Falkirk* . . . A few miles from *Dalnacardoch* the Duke of Athole (in his kilt and shooting jacket as usual) met us . . . We passed by the *Bruar*, and the road to the *Falls of Bruar* . . . near which I cannot help regretting the railroad will come . . . The Duke offered to lead the pony on one side and talked of Sandy for the other side, but I asked for Brown (whom I have far the most confidence in) . . . Sandy McAra the guide and the two pipers went first, playing all the time . . . We emerged from the pass upon an open valley . . . with the hills of *Braemar* before us . . . We got home safely at a quarter past eight . . . We had travelled 69 miles today and 60 yesterday. This was the pleasantest and most enjoyable expedition I *ever* made . . . Did not feel tired . . .

In December 1861 Albert died and the grief-stricken Victoria retired to the seclusion of Windsor and Balmoral for more than a decade. John Brown, in whom she had so much 'confidence' was to become much more friend and adviser than servant, to the annoyance of her family and the courtiers who attended her. The relationship was to become such that she was lampooned in the press as 'Mrs Brown', but anyone who imagined that the relationship went further than that of trusted and loyal, if typically outspoken, Highland servant could not have understood the Highlanders, or, for that matter, Queen Victoria.

As she noted in her diary the railway was approaching Blair Atholl and by 1863 the line from Perth to Inverness was at last completed. The result was an increase, both in tourist traffic throughout the north and also in a certain amount of goods traffic, particularly the regular fish trains, carrying consignments of herring from the north. These were the boom years in Wick where as many as 1,100 boats were to be seen engaged in the herring fishing.

In 1868, surprisingly, there was the discovery of gold in Kildonan, on the property of the Duke of Sutherland. The area in south-east Sutherland is mainly moorland with streams running into the Helmsdale river from boggy ground. For the next two years there were some 400 miners panning for gold in the area and something like £12,000 worth of gold is supposed to have been extracted during this period. Permission for further gold mining was then withdrawn.

Some idea of the scale of many of the Victorian Highland sporting parties of this period may be gained from a letter written by Lady Baker, second wife of Sir Samuel White Baker, to her step-daughter Edith, while a guest of the Duke of Atholl at Blair. Since last visiting Blair Atholl a decade previously Samuel White Baker had been knighted for discovering the sources of the Nile, where at one point he had electrified the natives by appearing in full Highland dress, wearing the Atholl kilt and plaid with sporran and bonnet to match. Lady Baker wrote:

My dearest Edith . . . It is very annoying that we cannot manage to be together, but it can't be helped. Papa returned yesterday; he had been away deer stalking since

Victoria and John Brown. He became more a friend and adviser than a servant to the dismay of her friends and the court

Above: The Pultneytown Harbour, Wick *c.* 1880. In the herring boom years over 1,000 boats would fish from here

Right: A rare early photograph of crofters on the Isle of Skye grinding corn with a hand quern

Monday. Altogether he shot six stags. We shall be at a very gay party the week after next, as there will be two balls given for the Prince of Wales. It is so very kind of the Duchess to insist upon our staying so long. We shall have been here for nearly a whole month by the time we leave . . .

Throughout the Highlands there were new landlords, from England or even further afield, who were adapting the Highland ways, adopting the kilt, and building new houses, sometimes evicting the tenants, but more often than not finding that this had already been accomplished. Such names as Sir Thomas Gladstone at Fasque, or Sir Dudley Couttes Marjoribanks, to take only two examples amongst many, were scarcely Highland in origin. The latter's memorial on a fountain outside his gothic baronial mansion at Tomich explains all that needs to be said. It read:

To the Memory of Sir Dudley Couttes Marjoribanks Bart
1st Lord Tweedmouth
Born Dec 19th 1820
Died Mar 4th 1894
Whose home was at Guisachan 1854–1894
Who built the village of Tomich and whose chief delight was to work
for the improvement and development of this district
And also to the memory of Isobel Lady Tweedmouth who was a mother
to the People of the Guisachan property from 1854 to 1904
This fountain is erected by their children
Edward 2nd Lord Tweedmouth and Ishbel Countess of Aberdeen.

Such small model estate villages as that at Tomich, sufficient to house the requisite number of employees required on the estate during the summer and autumn period, when the absentee landlord came up for the enjoyment of his sport, were being built throughout the Highlands. This purely seasonal employment was, of course, extremely bad for the economy. If there had been any other than employees left on the property it is more than probable that the monument would have been erected by 'grateful tenants', with the alternative of eviction had they not contributed their allotted share. Where the English had not taken over completely, they were diluting the blood of the original Highland landowners and chieftains by inter-marriage.

The old crofting tenants had almost entirely been evicted and such farming as was done was restricted to the Mains, or home farm of the estate. The old crofter tenant had more often than not degenerated into a paid employee. On the other hand sheep were already giving way to grouse and deer to provide sufficient sport for the annual visits of the absentee southern landlords and their friends. The farming slump of the 1860s and 70s merely accentuated this trend. While lip service might be paid to 'improvements' these were generally simply a matter of running the estate on the southern model, not of producing a way of life for the Highlanders which would provide them with the type of life they had been accustomed to of old.

In 1870 the West Highland railway reached Strome opposite Skye and a large pierhead was constructed for steamers operating to the Hebrides. For a time this hitherto tiny village became one of the more important ports on the west coast, regularly sending train-loads of sheep, cattle, and fish from the Islands to the south. This was sufficient, however, to bring about the first of not infrequent similar scenes when in 1873 the so-called 'Sabbatarian Riots' occurred.

Two cargoes of fish had arrived in the early hours of Sunday morning and

Opposite top: The royal family ascending Loch-na-Gar

Opposite bottom: The little house at Glassalt Shiel, from a watercolour by W. Simpson, 1882

when they were being off-loaded fifty or so local men appeared and forcibly stopped all work on the dock. An attempt to enlist the aid of the local policeman found him 'not available'. The following day the Chief Constable and six policemen arrived from Dingwall, but were unable to move the Free Church protesters, who were determined that no work should take place on the Sabbath.

In the end police reinforcements were obtained from as far south as Perth and Lanark and as far north as Elgin and Inverness, providing a show of force of 160 men, but too late to be of use. Had it not been for the intervention of the local Free Church ministers, however, there would certainly have been a serious confrontation the following weekend when 2,000 Free Church followers had been summoned to a mass rally of protest. Fortunately in this instance commonsense triumphed and the fish went to market fresh, instead of rotting over the week-end. Such instances of narrow Sabbatarian observance throughout the Highlands, however, continued to be a source of wonderment to visitors from the south who found themselves unable even to obtain a sandwich on the Sabbath unless it had been made the previous day.

In 1875 the introduction of the hammerless shotgun, much as it is to be found today, resulted in even more intensive shooting. The moors were strenuously keepered. Eagles, hawks, wild cats, martens, polecats, and foxes were shot, trapped, and poisoned mercilessly until few were to be seen except in the wilder regions of the north-west. On the other hand rabbits, which had been introduced by Osgood Mackenzie's father as early as the 1850s in the west and by other landlords elsewhere, flourished without hindrance. Butts for shooting grouse criss-crossed the moors and the shooting holiday in Scotland became a subject for satire in *Punch*. Leech's drawings give a good impression of the sporting scene in the Highlands at this period. The changeover from sheep to sport was more or less complete.

One writer of this period had already sounded the warning over undue sheep grazing in 1877:

We could point to one or two hirsels which carried stocks of 1,000 to 1,100 over winters some twenty years ago which will now scarcely winter 800. The cause of this we believe, is the covering of the land for so long a period exclusively by sheep, without any cattle being allowed on it . . .

Queen Victoria, by this time recovered from the death of her beloved Albert and roused from her seclusion, in the same year, 1877, built herself a little house at Glassalt Shiel by the end of Loch Muich, 3 kilometres from Balmoral,

Opposite: The Torridon Mountains from Flowerdale, Gairloch

Overleaf: A beautiful period photograph of deer stalking in the 1880s

A photograph of Queen Victoria's Glassalt Shiel *c.* 1895

to which she could retire with a lady-in-waiting. John Brown still occupied a favoured place as her chief factotum, but the period of her unpopularity during her prolonged seclusion had ended with the attempt on her life in 1872 and the national alarm when her heir Prince Edward's life had seemed in danger from typhoid in the same year. The Victorian hold on the country was once again complete.

It would be wrong to think of this as an age of stagnation, for there were many developments in industry and other spheres in the south, but in the Highlands there was little except tourism to enliven the scene. With the development of the Highland season came the growth of the Highland inn. Those who had no friends in the Highlands to visit and who did not wish to go to the expense of leasing a shooting or fishing lodge for the season found the Highland inn providing precisely what they required.

Catering primarily for sportsmen rather than travellers, these inns were generally sited near good stalking, fishing, or shooting. Inside they were varnished a dark brown, which grew darker with each passing year and were furnished with comfortable leather armchairs for the tweed-clad, often kilted, sportsmen who visited them. On the walls were hung glass cases with record trout and salmon and heads of exceptional deer shot in the vicinity. Glass cases containing stuffed wildcats, martens, capercailzie, and ptarmigan, or other fauna of the Highlands were another favourite decoration. Along the walls the bound volumes of *Punch* steadily accumulated year by year to provide reading material for the sportsmen on the Sabbath when all other forms of occupation were strictly forbidden.

Changes in the Whisky Trade

An important event occurred in the whisky industry during the same year, 1877, when the Distillers Company Limited was formed from a merger of six large Lowland whisky companies, John Reid, John Haig, Macfarlane, MacNab, Robert Mowbray, and Stewart and Co. Latterly known simply as the DCL, this was to become the most powerful force in the whisky industry. Meanwhile in 1874 the North of Scotland Malt Distillers Association had been formed and a number of individual firms were flourishing, even if the weaker had already gone to the wall. Among those which were to survive as household names were George Smith's Glenlivet, Talisker on Skye, Robert Hay's Glenfarclas, William Mathieson's Glenmorangie, and John Macdonald's Ben Nevis.

John MacDonald, founder of the Ben Nevis distillery in 1825, was known throughout Scotland as 'Long John'. By this time the distillery had its own pier on the shores of Loch Linnhe and was producing something approaching 13,638 litres a week. In 1878 they expanded and built another distillery, employing altogether over 200 in their labour force. Within six years their production had soared to somewhere in the region of 1,181,960 litres a year.

The 1870s were the years when the insect *Phylloxera Vastatrix* devastated the vineyards in France with the result that by the end of the decade brandy was virtually unobtainable. The opportunity to sell their product was seized by the leading merchants of Scotch, such as the Dewar brothers and James Buchanan, with his noted 'Black and White' whisky. By the end of the decade the upper classes in England had changed over to drinking whisky. The boom years of the 1880s and 90s for the Scotch whisky industry followed.

It should not be imagined because the worst of the Clearances and evictions had taken place between the years 1780 and 1850 that they were by this time finished. Throughout the Highlands and the Islands they continued, if generally on a lesser and more subdued scale. Fairly typical was the eviction of twenty-three families in the Lochbroom area from a property named Leckmelm by a paper manufacturer from Aberdeen named Pirie, who bought the estate in 1879. Using the letter of the law, Mr Pirie was careful only to take all the land, which was his by right of purchase. The crofters, thus rendered homeless, were allowed to retain their cottages, but once they had lost their means of livelihood were, of course, unable to survive except as his employees. They were not allowed to keep any livestock and thus were entirely dependent on Mr Pirie's wishes for survival. The leader of those who opposed him was unceremoniously evicted in 1880 and several others immediately followed, but all within the strict limits of the law, despite a storm of protest in the northern newspapers.

In the same year, 1880, the Malt Tax, which had been such a source of bitterness after its introduction in 1725 following the Union, was repealed. Although the repeal was welcomed by the whisky industry it resulted in an increase in illicit distilling. Since making malt was no longer illegal it meant that the excise officers had to catch the illicit distiller in the act of brewing or distilling, which was a period of only some four to six days, as opposed to three weeks. The high standard of legal distilling by this time, however, ensured that the cruder products of the illicit stills did not find a ready market and the brief upsurge was soon quelled.

The reforms of the British Army introduced by Mr Edward Cardwell, later Viscount Cardwell, Secretary of State for War, received the Royal Warrant in 1881. These included the abolition of the system of purchasing commissions and other sweeping changes in the British Army. Amongst these were the dropping of the old system of numbering regiments and the merging of many regiments into two battalions so that theoretically one might serve abroad while the other remained at home. At the same time recruiting areas were strictly defined to prevent wasteful overlapping in recruiting campaigns.

By amalgamation the Highland regiments were reduced to six. Thus the remains of the eighty-six Highland regiments recruited between 1730 and 1815 became the Royal Highland Regiment, or Black Watch; the Gordon Highlanders; the Seaforth Highlanders; the Highland Light Infantry; the Argyll and Sutherland Highlanders; and, the only one to remain a single battalion, the Queen's Own Cameron Highlanders. The percentage of Gaelic speakers amongst all ranks in these six remaining Highland regiments was predictably by this time extremely small, being in many cases less than a platoon. Significantly too the old nicknames of the Highland regiments, which were 'Donald', 'Rory', or 'Her Nainsel', had already given way to 'Jock', essentially a Lowland nickname, unknown in the Gaelic, which had hitherto been reserved for the Lowland regiments.

To Queen Victoria's distress, but that of few others in the court circles, her faithful attendant John Brown died in 1883. If this event caused a singular outburst of relief amongst her family and retainers, it was nothing compared with another explosion that year. As already noted, the large blasts required to remove porphyrite from the quarry at Crarae on Loch Fyneside had become something of a tourist attraction. In June of that year a 'Monster Blast' with some 4 tonnes of gunpowder was advertised to coincide with the arrival of the tourist paddle steamer *Lord of the Isles*.

The 2nd Battalion Royal Highlanders (The Black Watch)

Three months later there was an explosion of a different nature in the vicinity. Despite the 1875 Explosives Act regulating the control and production of explosives, by which the Loch Fyne powder mills at Furnace should have been condemned, they had been allowed to continue operating, on the grounds that they had already operated for thirty years. Unfortunately the buildings were much too close to each other and on 29 September due to a chimney having caught fire and setting the boiler house alight there was a violent explosion. By a minor miracle the only person killed was the manager. Two shinty teams and a crowd of spectators had just left the playing field nearby to go to the assistance of a horse and cart which had overturned on the road nearby. Six cartloads of boulders were subsequently removed from the deserted pitch. Thereafter the powder mills were closed.

In 1885 there were welcome signs that at last the Government was becoming aware of the effects of the Clearances, rather more than a shade too late. In a speech at Inverness Mr Joseph Chamberlain indicated his willingness to lock the byre door after the cow had been stolen, stating:

The history of the Highland Clearances is a black page in the account with private ownership in land, and if it were to form a precedent, if there could be any precedent for wrong-doing, if the sins of the fathers ought to be visited upon the children, we would have an excuse for more drastic legislation than any which the wildest reformers have ever proposed. Thousands of hard-working, industrious, God-fearing people were driven from their lands which had belonged to their ancestors, and which for generations they had cultivated; their houses were unroofed and burnt down and they were turned out homeless and forlorn, exposed to the inclemency of the winter season, left to perish on the hillsides or to swell the full flood of misery and destitution in places overseas to which they were driven for refuge. They suffered unbearably; very many died. However, as time went on the descendants of those who did survive have contributed in no mean degree to the prosperity of the countries in which they finally settled. The Highland countryside was depopulated by those clearances. The general condition of the people left behind suffered and it has gone on deteriorating until it has become at last a matter of national concern. If I am correct in the statement in which I have endeavoured to summarise what I have read and learned upon this subject, I ask you whether it is not time that we should submit to careful examination and review a system which places such vast powers for evil in the hands of irresponsible individuals and which makes the possession of land not a trust but a means of extortion and exaction? . . .

In the following year, 1886, the Crofters Act offered the crofter security of tenure. On the other hand while providing the crofters with an assured foothold they were so circumscribed by officialdom that they had little or no scope for improving their position. Furthermore they were thereafter under the sway of bureaucracy, which was sited in Edinburgh at a considerable distance from their crofts and the crofters themselves. Moreover it was operated by officials who were neither natives of their region nor understood their language so that the act was thus one of somewhat doubtful worth.

Between Queen Victoria's Jubilee in 1887 and her Diamond Jubilee in 1897 there was considerable development in the Highlands. The West Highland railway, running across the wild Moor of Rannoch to Fort William and thence by a magnificent feat of Victorian engineering over a lengthy viaduct alongside Loch Shiel to Mallaig, was eventually completed between the years 1891 and 1894. With the addition of the railway Fort William became an even more important centre than previously. It was already the base for the Caledonian Canal and now it was the centre for much of the through traffic from Mallaig and the Isles.

In 1896 the first stage in an even more important step for Fort William's future was taken. A hydro-electric scheme was introduced to harness the Falls of Foyers to produce power to process bauxite into aluminium for the recently formed British Aluminium Company. This was the first attempt in Britain to use water power on such a scale. There was then no village at Foyers and supplies for the scheme had to be transported directly from the Caledonian Canal. By 1898 there was a village on the site and the company proudly produced a pamphlet stating:

At Foyers the Company has built a village which now counts a population of some 600 souls, all of whom are dependent on the new industry for their daily bread. The impoverished crofters and fisherfolk of the Western Highlands acclaim with gladness the advent of this industry into their midst, offering as it does a thrice-welcome

Three generations of a crofting family on the island of St Kilda

addition to their scanty opportunities of wage earning. It inspires them with a genuine hope that the devastating tide of emigration may be stayed, and that their beautiful but desolate glens may ere long witness a prosperity hitherto unknown.

With the extension of the West Highland railway to Kyle of Lochalsh in 1898 there was a considerable expansion of this tiny village. As had been the case with Strome nearly two decades earlier piers and railheads were built to form a reasonable port. The Kyle of Lochalsh which had previously merely served as a crossing to Skye suddenly became important to the fishing trade as a port where fish could be sent by rail to market and Strome faded into insignificance once more.

Towards the end of Queen Victoria's reign in 1899 came the outbreak of the Boer War. Amongst the troops in action were the famous Highland Brigade, consisting of the 2nd Battalion the Royal Highlanders, or Black Watch; the 1st Battalion the Highland Light Infantry, the 2nd Battalion the Seaforth Highlanders; and the 1st Battalion of the Argyll and Sutherland

The Caledonian Canal at Fort Augustus *c.* 1880

Highlanders, commanded by Major-General Wauchope. At Magersfontein, faced with Boer sharpshooters entrenched behind barbed-wire entanglements, then a novel form of warfare, the Highland Brigade attacked time and again with consummate bravery. They lost somewhere in the region of 750 officers and men, including General Wauchope—amongst the first to be killed. Although defeated with honour on this occasion, they went on to distinguish themselves in subsequent campaigns, adding lustre to the fighting record of the Highland regiments.

The End of an Era

In January of 1901 Queen Victoria died, bringing an era to an end. King Edward VII, who succeeded her at long last, was known for his womanising, his sporting proclivities—in particular shooting and racing—and for his dubious companions. In practice he turned out to be a great ambassador for

Britain, and the Edwardian era became one of prosperity and growth in many fields, even if it was to be the last peaceful era of the century, the final lull before the storm.

In 1902, after the coronation on 9 August, the King and Queen attended the Braemar Gathering. Accompanying the King, clad in the Royal Stewart tartan, were his sons, the Prince of Wales, Edward, and Albert. The royal carriages, it is reported, arrived shortly before four, driving through a double line of Farquharson, Duff, Dee, and Balmoral Highlanders, the latter headed by William Campbell, the King's piper. After half an hour or so the royal party departed, but not before Queen Alexandra, an enthusiastic photographer, had taken pictures of many of the participants in the Games.

An interesting sidelight on the life at Balmoral and Windsor is that when clearing out the debris left by his mother, including numerous busts of John

Queen Victoria at the Braemar Gathering shortly before her death

Brown, it appears that the King found a Highland dress outfit which had been worn by the late Emperor Frederick III of Germany. At Christmas he had it sent to his nephew, Kaiser Wilhelm, Frederick's son and heir, who sent him the following letter:

Dearest Uncle,
I hasten to offer you my sincere and warmest thanks for the . . . most touching and splendid gift of dear Papa's Highland dress. It was a most kind thought and gives me great pleasure. I will remember having often stood as a boy in Papa's dressing room and enviously admiring the precious and glittering contents. How well it suited him and what a fine figure he made in it! I always wondered where the things had gone to . . . The last time I wore Highland dress at Balmoral was in 1878 in September, when I visited dear Grandmamma and was able to go out deer stalking at Lochnagar . . . I am deeply sensitive to the kind thoughts that prompted you to send the things back to me . . .

During the Victorian era the 'Highland Dress' had undergone a deep-sea change which would have staggered some of the Highlanders of old. The sporran in particular had developed into an immense hairy object, often decending below the wearer's knees. The *Skein dhu*, or small knife, carried by the Highlander of old in his armpit, had now descended to the knee, tucked in the stocking. In itself there was no objection to this, except that the handle had also been developed into an ornate thistle with a large cairngorm, or similar stone embedded in the head.

Certain shibboleths had grown up regarding the way the kilt should be worn. The fact that most of the tartans bore anything but a close resemblance to those worn before 1745 appeared of little interest. The kilt jacket, however, had to have double cuffs, shoulder straps, and braided pockets in the style of the old uniform jacket worn by soldiers in the eighteenth century. The shoes had to be black, as worn in the army. Both these sacred cows, of course, were perpetuated by those who had served in the army and known nothing else.

All these details of dress were earnestly copied by the new Highland chieftains from England who had taken over the land. With this outfit, the crook, its ornate head carved, inevitably, in the shape of a thistle, was always carried, despite the fact that no Highlander of old would have been seen associating with sheep if he could possibly have avoided it. Furthermore it became a rule that no Highlander wore the kilt south of the Highland Line. That all Highlanders had once worn it south of the Highland Line, or wherever else they might go, largely because they had no other clothes; that they had worn shoes, if at all, of brown untreated skin, and had a purse attached to their belt as a sporran, were all facts that were unknown, or conveniently ignored. The Victorian era was one of rigid class distinctions and no one dared to question them. In the matter of Highland dress there were few original Highlanders left qualified to act as arbiters.

Highland evening dress in 1902 showing the new-look sporran

The year 1904 saw the closure of the lead mines at Strontian after a lengthy, if fitful, period of working. At the same time the development of the British Aluminium Company's ambitious plant at Kinlochleven was begun with the setting up of the Loch Leven Water and Electric Power Company. The Blackwater Dam was built; for many years the largest dam in Britain with a 6·4-kilometre-long reinforced concrete conduit and six lines of pipe 1·6 kilometres long leading to a power house for an aluminium works. A village was built to house the workers and for five years, from 1904 to 1909, a workforce of between three and four thousand men was employed. By 1907 the Kinlochleven works were in production. The hydro-electric scheme was by far the most ambitious yet developed and the works empoyed over 300 men, who were settled in the newly-built village of Kinlochleven. The British Aluminium Company had produced the most ambitious industrial plan for the Highlands yet conceived. Furthermore it worked.

Apart from the invention of aeroplanes, the introduction of the motor car was one of the most important changes in the Edwardian era. The 1906 edition of Black's *Shilling Guide to Scotland* included this warning on motoring in Scotland:

Owners of large cars fitted with costly pneumatic tyres would do well to aviod certain of the rougher roads, such as that between Tyndrum and Ballachulish, and still more the one leading from Tyndrum to Oban through Glencoe. Whatever the rugged grandeurs of the scenery, they can scarcely compensate for the ruining of tyres worth £20 apiece.

The years from 1905 to 1909 were of immense importance to the whisky industry and to the Highlands, due, surprisingly enough, to a judgement by the Islington magistrates in London in 1905. They had upheld the prosecution against a publican for selling grain whisky as Scotch whisky, maintaining that: 'Whisky should consist of spirit distilled in a pot still, derived from malted barley, mixed or not with unmalted barley, and wheat, or either of them.' The judgement continued: 'Patent still spirit made largely from maize, has been sold as whisky in a largely increasing manner for years . . . as . . . Scotch.'

This decision naturally came as a very nasty shock to the patent still distillers, particularly the Distillers Company Limited. The malt distillers in the north, on the other hand, were triumphant. It was, however, pointed out to them that if they insisted on a pure malt regulation becoming law it would end up against their own interests since more malt would be produced in the Lowlands and Highland malt would be displaced to keep the price right. In the end the entire whisky industry requested a Royal Commission to decide what was Scotch whisky. In 1908 the Commission began its task and in 1909 reached its conclusions after hearing 116 expert witnesses over seventeen months. It concluded:

. . . 'whiskey' [the spelling at the time] is a spirit obtained by distillations from a mash of cereal grains saccharified by the diastase of malt; that 'Scotch whiskey' is whiskey, as above defined, distilled in Scotland and that 'Irish whiskey' is whiskey, as above defined, distilled in Ireland.

This was eventually to prove of enormous importance to the Scotch whisky industry as a whole since the definition established by law has since ensured that no other country can attempt to produce 'Scotch' without infringing international law. The Highlands and the malt pot-still distillers were ultimately to gain considerably by this judgement. As a result it is only in the Highlands that a Highland malt whisky can be produced today.

The death of Edward VII in 1910 brought that lavish, short-lived era to an end. The reign of George V saw the outbreak of the First World War in 1914.

In August the regular battalions of the Highland regiments which had been in training camp at Blair Atholl were ordered to their war depots. The Cameron Highlanders were sent to Edinburgh Castle, the Argyll and Sutherland Highlanders to Fort George. The county of Moray provided a full territorial battalion of the Seaforth Highlanders. The 1st Battalion of the Black Watch were at Aldershot and the 2nd in India, nor was either soon to return to Scotland. All over Scotland, Highlands and Lowlands alike, men were marching to the colours. Unfortunately the Highlanders had few enough to send.

Once again, in the service of their country, thousands of Highlanders died in the Highland regiments. It was not only those from Scotland who died, but countless second, third, fourth, and fifth generations of men descended from Highland ancestors. From Canada, from Australia, from New Zealand, and from South Africa they came in kilted regiments. Here indeed was the ultimate proof of the Highlander's worth which had been so carelessly discarded.

Kilt-makers of the Gordon Highlanders in barracks prior to the 1914–18 war

Chapter 8

Past, Present, and Future

The First World War from 1914–18 had considerable economic effects on the Highlands. Like everywhere else in Britain, farming, which had slumped in the 1870s and 80s with the introduction of cheap imported grain and refrigerated meat, boomed when the U-Boat blockade brought a demand for home-grown food. The aluminium industry, based on Foyers and Kinlochleven, also boomed. During the six years from 1914 to 1919 the British Aluminium Company's production rose from 70,000 tonnes per annum to 130,000 tonnes.

On the other hand the Highland pot-still malt whisky distillers suffered considerably during the war years. In the initial stages of the war severe rationing of grain and their inability to produce industrial alcohol like the Lowland patent-still distillers, had resulted in many being shut down, or being taken over by more powerful concerns such as the Distillers Company Limited. Finally the U-Boat blockade reached such a pitch that pot-still malt distilling was temporarily halted altogether. An increase in taxation in 1918 from 14s. 9d. per proof gallon to 30s. also affected the industry very adversely. When distilling was allowed again in 1919 a further swingeing increase in taxation to 50s. per proof gallon resulted in more closures and take-overs throughout the industry.

The boom in farming did not last long after the war with the return of cheap imported grain and refrigerated meat from the Antipodes and the Argentine in the 1920s. The demand for aluminium, however, remained firm and the British Aluminium Company promoted a bill in 1918 to drive a tunnel through the hills from Loch Treig to enlarge the Kinlochleven project. This was objected to on the grounds that it would be 'taking water from Inverness-shire for the benefit of Argyllshire', and this resulted in re-planning and re-siting the proposed works outside Fort William, so that it was 1921 before the act received royal assent.

The whisky industry made a brief recovery from the effects of the war in 1919 and 1920, but this minor boom did not last long. The effects of yet

A typical scene from a Highland malt distillery with the gleaming copper pot stills

another fierce increase in taxation to 72s. 6d. per proof gallon combined with
the introduction of Prohibition in the United States of America were
disastrous. By 1921 the production of Scotch whisky had slumped from 31
million to 27 million litres and the product had virtually been priced out of the
home market. A side effect was that whisky, which had previously almost
always been sold by the gallon, now began to find ready sales in bottles and by
the end of the decade it was generally sold in·this form.

The early post-war years saw the intervention of the state in various forms
in the Highlands. The re-settlement of ex-servicemen on the land, which had
been promised, led to the state ownership of land for crofts administered by
the Crofters Commission. The year 1919 also saw the formation of the
Forestry Commission. Formed with a view to ensuring that in the event of
another war Britain would not have to rely on imports of timber, the new
Commission took over the Crown forests. The largest of these in the
Highlands was Inverliever Forest in Argyll on the western side of Loch Awe.
In the same year the Ministry of Transport took over responsibility for the
Caledonian and Crinan Canals. In both the latter cases this meant that effective
control moved to London.

The 1920s saw the nadir of the Highlands' economic recovery. Crofting
and fishing were unable to pay their way, the distilleries were in the doldrums
and even the large estates on which many Highlanders had relied during the

A scene on the Crinan Canal at the time of the First World War

Victorian and Edwardian eras were cutting back on staff in the face of penal taxation. Emigration, that old panacea, continued, resulting in even greater depopulation. The 'Highland Problem' was there for all to see, but as yet no one was prepared to look very hard. Successive governments faced with grave post-war problems preferred to turn a blind eye to an area where there was little political capital to be gained.

One of the side effects of the war and the recession which followed was that, especially in the western Highlands, foxes in particular, but other predators as well, were allowed to proliferate unchecked with few of the estates able to afford the luxury of gamekeepers to keep their numbers under control. As a result partridges, grouse, and blackgame, which had been plentiful on the west coast, were reduced to the stage of being almost unknown in many areas. Osgood Mackenzie noted the total absence of many other birds he had known in previous years. Only the rabbit was to be found in enormous quantities nearly everywhere.

The mid-1920s saw the start of the ambitious hydro-electric scheme promoted by the British Aluminium Company. In 1924 the Lochaber Power Company was formed, to be followed by the North British Aluminium Company, and with Government support a labour force of 2,000 men was soon at work. A tunnel with a 4·5 metre diameter was driven 24 kilometres through the Ben Nevis range from Loch Treig to Inverlochy near to Fort William and by 1929 it was complete; the longest of its kind in the world, using water from an overall catchment area of 488 square kilometres. The result was the production of 10,000 tonnes of aluminium a year, but this was only the first phase of the project and the 1930s saw further continuous development. During this period of general slump and stagnation it was the only large-scale industrial investment to be found in the Highlands. Fort William benefited from this scheme with the growth of the adjacent Inverlochy village containing 300 houses for the 600 workers in the new plant.

One of the first attempts at harnessing hydro-power to provide domestic electric light and power was made at Loch Luichart in Easter Ross. In 1926 a local limited company was formed with Government backing and was soon providing electricity for Dingwall, Strathpeffer and the surrounding area. The scheme soon proved profitable and the Government loan was quickly repaid. Within a decade, merged by then with the Scottish Power Company, it was providing electricity to an area stretching from Golspie in the north to Beauly in the south.

Despite the effects of the General Strike and the financial depression that followed at the start of the 1930s, these were years that saw a slow but steady improvement in the Highlands. The early attempts at introducing hydro-electric power, the gradual re-growth of the whisky industry, saved at the eleventh hour, and the steady growth of tourism were amongst the more

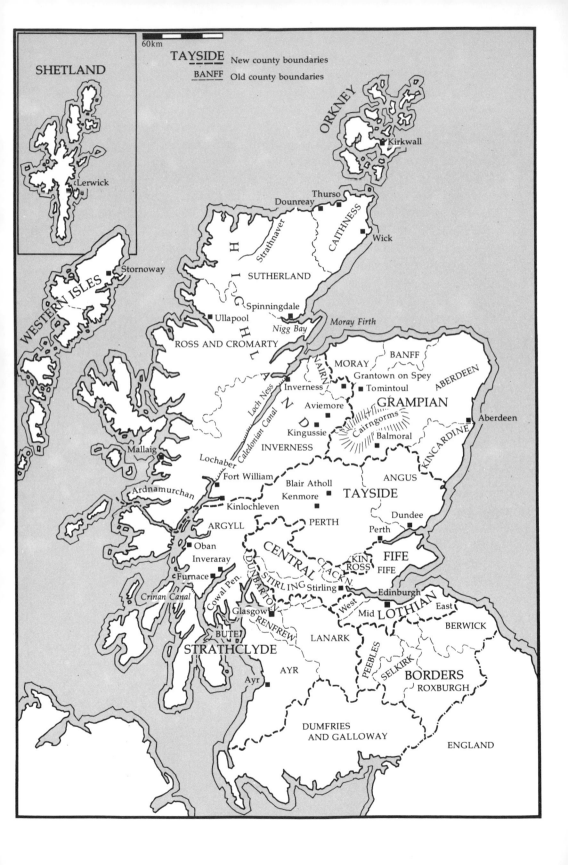

SHETLAND

Lerwick

60km

TAYSIDE New county boundaries
BANFF Old county boundaries

ORKNEY

Kirkwall

WESTERN ISLES

Stornoway

Thurso
Dounreay

CAITHNESS

Wick

Strathnaver

H
I
G
H
L
A
N
D

SUTHERLAND

Spinningdale

Ullapool

Nigg Bay

Moray Firth

ROSS AND CROMARTY

NAIRN

MORAY

BANFF

Grantown on Spey

ABERDEEN

Inverness

Tomintoul

Loch Ness

GRAMPIAN

Aviemore

Caledonian Canal

Cairngorms

Aberdeen

Kingussie

Balmoral

INVERNESS

KINCARDINE

Mallaig

Lochaber

ANGUS

Fort William

Blair Atholl

TAYSIDE

Ardnamurchan

Kenmore

Kinlochleven

Dundee

PERTH

Perth

ARGYLL

KIN
ROSS

FIFE

Oban

CENTRAL

CLACK'N.

FIFE

Inveraray

DUNBARTON

STIRLING

Furnace

Stirling

Edinburgh

Crinan Canal

Cowal Pen.

West

Mid

LOTHIAN

East

Glasgow

RENFREW

BERWICK

BUTE

LANARK

PEEBLES

STRATHCLYDE

AYR

SELKIRK

BORDERS

Ayr

ROXBURGH

DUMFRIES
AND GALLOWAY

ENGLAND

welcome factors. The development of the motor car during the 1930s in particular led to a big increase in tourism, despite the still generally execrable state of the Highland roads.

In 1930 the Grampian Electricity Company opened a hydro-electricity station at Rannoch, near Killichonan, using Loch Ericht as its principal reservoir. In 1933 this was joined to another station at Tummel Bridge at the eastern end of Loch Rannoch, using water from Loch Rannoch and Loch Laidon. This was the start of one of the more ambitious hydro-electric schemes, which in due course was to provide electricity over a large area.

The second phase of the North British Aluminium Company's hydro-electric development plans at Fort William was begun in 1931, involving the raising of the level of Loch Laggan. By the time this work had been completed after seven years the loch had been lengthened by 6 kilometres and had a storage capacity of 40 million tonnes of water. The water level of the river Spean was much reduced during these operations, but the main result was that the production of aluminium was doubled to 20,000 tonnes a year in 1938 at a critical period just prior to the outbreak of the Second World War.

One immediate effect of the ending of Prohibition in 1933 was a welcome increase in the export of Scotch whisky with a corresponding steady return to normal working conditions in the distilleries. By this time the industry had reached the sad state of affairs when only fifteen distilleries were working in the whole of Scotland and some of them only part-time, compared with 150 in 1900. Indeed in 1933 the Pot-Still Malt Distillers Association of Scotland, which included all the Highland distilleries, had recommended to its members that there should be no distilling that year. Not all of them heeded this advice, but it is an indication of how bad matters had become. Excessive taxation had brought the industry to a state of near collapse and only the providential re-opening of the American market prevented total disaster. By this time the Distillers Company Limited controlled thirty-three Highland distilleries, but even massive amalgamations of this kind did not help greatly, more especially since many were merely closed down to prevent over-production.

The Sighting of Nessie

The year 1933 saw the completion of a new road along the north side of Loch Ness, from Fort Augustus to Inverness, which had involved a considerable amount of blasting of rock out of the mountainside. Large areas of scrub and forest had also been cleared and the new road skirted Castle Urquhart on its promontory above Urquhart Bay, where a fortress had stood since the Iron Age. Built in the thirteenth century the castle had been blown up by English soldiers in the 1690s and remained a picturesque ruin ever since. About 5

The old and new county boundaries

Loch Ness where the 'monster' was sighted on 14 April 1933. Whether or not the Loch Ness Monster is really lurking below the calm waters is still open to debate

kilometres beyond the castle and the small village of Drumnadrochit lies Abriachan pier. It was here, while motoring to Inverness on the sunny afternoon of 14 April 1933, that the owners of the Drumnadrochit hotel were astonished to see 'an enormous animal rolling and plunging' in the waters of the loch.

On 2 May the *Inverness Courier,* a paper of considerable and well-earned repute, carried the story of this strange sighting in Loch Ness, using the word 'monster' for the first time. In fact this was by no means the first time mention of a strange object seen in the loch had been printed, for the *Northern Chronicle* in 1930 had recorded something unusual seen in the loch and on appealing for information a number of letters had been sent to the paper telling of strange sightings in the loch.

It has since been established that one of the earliest known sightings of a creature in the loch was in 1889, when two young boys named Craig, fishing off Urquhart Castle, saw a huge form rear out of the water. Rowing hurriedly to the shore they were told by their father never to repeat the story. As early as the First World War and the 1920s there were also sightings made, which were subsequently recalled, but at this time these had not been recorded.

It was not until October that *The Scotsman* took up the story and sent an experienced reporter to write a series of articles. After carefully interviewing the various witnesses he became convinced of their veracity and concluded that there must indeed be something strange in the loch. The London papers soon took up the story and the Caledonian Canal suddenly found its traffic considerably increased. Despite the lateness of the season, tourism also experienced a sharp boost and special express bus services were run between Glasgow and Inverness alongside the loch.

This did not, however, please everyone. The Revd Murdo Campbell of the Free Church in Fort Augustus predictably wrote:

One of the most pathetic sights which came under the observation of sane people in these parts within recent months was the presence of a number of people who arrived from the South last Lord's Day with a view to seeing a harmless animal which is supposed to reside in the depths of Loch Ness. It now appears that a wise Providence prevented the animal from gratifying the eyes of these breakers of the Lord's Day. This leads me to say that the word 'monster' is really not applicable to the Loch Ness animal, but it is truly applicable to those who deliberately sin against the light of law and revelation.

By November there had been numerous sightings and the general picture had emerged of an animal with a long neck and a small head, a large body and long tail, which generally showed two or three humps in the water and could swim at great speed leaving a considerable wake or commotion behind it. Bertram Mills offered a reward of £20,000 for the live capture of 'the Monster'. The excitement grew intense. Questions were asked in Parliament and the Secretary of State for Scotland was asked to guarantee the beast's safety from 'pot hunters'.

In late 1933 the first practical jokers cast doubts on the whole matter by faking tracks of the monster with a hippopotamus foot. The hoax was quickly uncovered, but the doubters seized on any explanation such as 'mass hallucination', 'a school of otters', 'floating vegetation', 'seals, or porpoises'. Despite many further sightings the aura of a hoax surrounded any mention of the beast in the papers.

In April 1934 a remarkable photograph was taken by a Harley Street surgeon while on holiday. One of the best photographs ever obtained of the beast, it effectively silenced many critics, although there were still sceptics in plenty. The mounting number of thoroughly reliable witnesses by this time should have convinced anyone with an open mind that there was indeed a strange animal in the loch. Unfortunately the press and many of the public were sceptical and many subscribed to an opinion voiced in *The Observer*: 'The whole business is a stunt foisted on a credulous public and only excused by a certain element of low comedy.'

Nevertheless the Loch Ness Monster, or 'Nessie' as it became affectionately named, remained a first-class tourist attraction, so much so indeed that the Austrian Government indignantly described it as a trick to keep tourists away from Austria and attract them to Scotland. A minor industry grew up around the beast, with Nessie toys, brooches, and post-cards. It became the subject of numerous music-hall jokes, but despite widespread and mainly good humoured scepticism it continued to attract hopeful watchers to the lochside and occasional sightings continued to be reported.

In 1935 the first national forest park was opened by the Forestry Commission in Argyll. The Argyll Forest Park lies in the Cowal peninsula between Loch Long and Loch Fyne. Extending to 24,000 hectares it includes the forests of Ardgartan, Glenbranter, Loch Eck, Glenfinart, and Benmore, as well as the Glasgow Corporation's estate at Ardgoil. From north to south it

Below: A group of tourists in the early 1930s at Braemar

Opposite above: Red deer at rest in the Highlands

Opposite below: A Scottish wild cat at bay

Overleaf: Loch Duich and the Kintail and Affric Mountains

measures 29 kilometres. As the forerunner of other similar national parks this was a new venture for the Forestry Commission.

From the start this proved to be a popular tourist attraction, although, of course, by no means the only one. Fishing and to a lesser degree shooting and deer stalking continued to bring their devotees to the Highlands. The more affluent leased shooting lodges, but an increasing number regularly visited the Highland sporting inns. The scenery continued to attract many from the south and from overseas, as did the annual Highland Games and the traditional royal visits to Balmoral and Deeside.

The outbreak of the Second World War in 1939 brought tourism to an abrupt halt as many parts of the Highlands, particularly the western Highlands, were declared restricted areas for one reason or another. The area around Spean Bridge was used as a training ground for Commando warfare and subsequently a monument overlooking the foot of the Great Glen was erected to the memory of those of the Commando forces who fell in action. In other areas experiments took place with new bombs, aircraft, guns, and similar secret war-time weapons. Overseas troops from Poland, Canada, Australia, and New Zealand, as well as latterly from the USA, were to be found billeted throughout many parts of the Highlands. Ironically, amongst these there must have been many descendants of Highlanders evicted during the Clearances.

Inevitably the 1940s, including six years of war and its aftermath, saw considerable changes in the Highlands. Amongst these were the opening up of the deposits of white cretaceous sandstone at Loch Aline in Morvern, which had been discovered by the 1925 Geological Survey. With the outbreak of war in Europe these became Britain's sole source of optical glass and, as such, of considerable importance to the war effort. Because of the importance of obtaining the sandstone no effort was made to control the effects of the mining operations, which remain a considerable eyesore.

Another grim reminder of the war is to be seen opposite Gruinard Island on the west coast, where signs still warn that the island is dangerous to visit and that landing is prohibited. The reason for this is that the island was sprayed during the war with anthrax germs as an experiment in chemical warfare and remains highly dangerous. Although visited annually by a team of scientists clad in protective clothing to check the degree of infection remaining, it is thought likely that it will be a full century before it can be declared safe.

A more constructive result of the war years was the completion of the third phase of the Lochaber scheme at Fort William, in 1943, when Canadian troops assisted with the damming of the headwaters of the river Spey. On the completion of this final phase in the North British Aluminium Company's

The ruined castle of Kilchurn, a Campbell stronghold built in 1440 on an island at the north end of Loch Awe

operation the output increased to 30,000 tonnes a year. Even during the war this industry proved itself capable of expanding.

The whisky industry was not so fortunate. Once again the pot-still malt distillers were seriously affected. In the initial year of the 'phoney war' distilling was merely restricted. Due to the lack of imported maize, patent-still distilling was prohibited, but limited pot-still malt distilling continued until 1941. Thereafter, until 1945, distilling was banned completely. During the entire six years of war the total distilling output of the industry amounted to less than a single year pre-war.

Finally in the year 1944–45, limited distilling by pot-still malt distillers was again permitted. It was not, however, until 1949 that full-scale distilling was again allowed and by then the tax had been raised to an unprecedented £10 10s. 10d. per proof gallon. It was not until as late as 1953 that the Government's method of rationing supplies of grain to distillers was finally ended and the Scotch whisky industry began to return to full operation. The overseas boom, which had been slowly developing, was by this time a reality, but the home market had almost ceased to exist due to the high rate of taxation and the lack of supplies.

The Development of Water-Resources

The year 1943 witnessed one of the most important and far-reaching developments for the Highlands when the Hydro-Electric Development (Scotland) Act was passed by Parliament, promoted principally by Tom Johnston, then Secretary of State for Scotland. By this act the North of Scotland Hydro-Electric Board was established with the task of developing the water-resources of the Highlands and Islands. It was given the task of supplying electricity to the consumer, to industry, and to the existing electricity suppliers. It was also given wide-ranging powers to collaborate in the social improvement and economic development of the north of Scotland. With the nationalisation of electricity in 1947 the north of Scotland was left out of the national scheme and all local authority or private company stations north of a line from the Clyde to the Tay were taken under the aegis of the Hydro-Electric Board.

The first turbine station built by the Board was opened in 1948 in Morar, but since then evidence of their work is to be seen throughout the Highlands. As well as providing electricity in the remotest areas of the Highlands, they have built in three decades some 644 kilometres of roads and some 400 houses for their workers. It is estimated that some 4,000 industrial consumers of electricity employ over 13,000 people in the area. Throughout the Highlands new dams, overhead cables and turbine stations, generally built to merge with their background in local stone, are evidence of their industry.

The 1950s saw the gradual resurgence of tourism as the rationing of petrol

A winter scene in the Cairngorms Nature Reserve

was eased. The decade also saw many developments under various public bodies in the Highlands, which encouraged this trend. The Nature Conservancy, founded in 1949 with a view to providing advice on the conservation and control of the natural flora and fauna of Great Britain, as well as to establish and manage nature reserves and develop research related to them, turned its attention first to the Highlands. The Beinn Eighe Nature Reserve near Kinlochewe in Ross-shire, consisting of 4,200 hectares, was the first to be formed in 1951. It was acquired primarily for the preservation and study of one of the largest remains of the old Caledonian Pinewoods. Amongst the animals preserved there are pine martens. This was only the first of nearly a dozen nature reserves of varying sizes to be formed in the Highlands covering by far the largest area of such reserves in Britain.

In 1954 the Nature Conservancy created the Cairngorms National Nature Reserve. Extending eventually to 26,000 hectares this is the largest reserve of its kind in Britain, including a large area over 1,220 metres high. It extends from Loch an Eilean about 260 metres above sea level to the top of Ben Macdhui 1,310 metres high. Such birds as ptarmigan, capercailzie, blackgame, peregrine falcons, and golden eagles and such mammals as red deer, roe deer, wild cats, foxes, badgers, and otters are to be found in the area as well as many rare species of flowers. The adjacent Craigellachie Nature Reserve of 256 hectares was established later in 1960.

Nearby, to the east, the Forestry Commission controls the Queen's Forest, the Glenmore Forest National Park and Rothicmurchos Forest, all of which had been acquired as early as 1923 from the Duke of Gordon. In 1955 the Forestry Commission also acquired the Crarae Forest Garden on Loch Fyneside, when it was gifted to the nation by Sir George Campbell, whose father, his namesake, had developed it since its purchase in 1920. Although small, this forest garden, or arboretum, contains many unusual conifers and other exotica, all encouraged to grow well by the softer climate of the west coast, affected by the nearness of the Gulf Stream.

The National Trust for Scotland, founded originally in 1931, also expanded into the Highlands during the 1950s when in 1952 they took over Osgood Mackenzie's gardens at Inverewe in Wester Ross. The gardens were first started by Osgood Mackenzie in 1862 when he had acquired the estate. He carefully nurtured them until his death in 1922, when they were taken over by his daughter until she decided to pass them on to the National Trust for Scotland in 1952. Here rare shrubs from all over the world can be seen flourishing under the benign influence of the Gulf Stream. In such a bleak landscape the gardens come as more than something of a surprise and attract many visitors throughout the year.

The hydro-electric stations built at Pitlochry and Clunie in 1950, with the later addition at Glen Errochty completed in 1957, provided another useful addition to the national grid. They also provided a tourist attraction at Pitlochry, where the salmon ladder draws many visitors to watch salmon making their ascent. In addition the new loch at Faskally provided further fishing opportunities for visitors. With the National Theatre established at Pitlochry since the 1950s and the attractions of a distillery open to visitors, as well as golf courses set in magnificent scenery, it is not surprising this has developed into a well-known tourist centre. Nevertheless Pitlochry owes much to the Hydro-Electric Board for its development over the past two decades.

During the 1950s there was also a resurgence of interest in the Loch Ness Monster. Numerous sightings were claimed and the papers continued to treat the story with humorous scepticism. Then, in 1957, Mrs Constance Whyte, a qualified doctor and wife of the manager of the Caledonian Canal, published her book *More Than A Legend*, which for the first time collated the various sightings and demonstrated to any unbiased reader that there must be some animal of unknown type in the loch. It also appeared that there was another similar animal, which had been sighted on several occasions, in Loch Morar, at over 1,000 feet the deepest loch in Scotland, above Arisaig on the west coast.

This book was undoubtedly the inspiration for numerous groups which set out to film the beast in Loch Ness during the 1960s. It also, of course, did no harm to the tourist trade, which was increasing yearly as more and more caravans headed north.

Another feature of the 1950s, particularly, was the increasing number of American firms entering the Scotch whisky industry. Taking full advantage of Government grants for overseas firms setting up industries in development areas, they built a number of new distilleries. In effect the Government were financing new industry which was setting up in competition with their own home-based firms. In 1950, for instance, Seagrams took over Strathisla distillery. In 1956 Schenley Industries of New York bought Seager Evans. In the Lowlands there were other examples.

Perhaps one of the most significant developments of the 1950s, however, was the building, by the Atomic Energy Research Authority in 1954, of the first Atomic Reactor at Dounreay, near Thurso in Caithness. From being merely the principal market town in the area, Thurso expanded quickly with the expenditure of around £40 million in that area. Since the Dounreay station eventually employed some 2,500 high-grade scientists and technicians as well as other staff, the United Kingdom Atomic Energy Authority became easily the largest employer in the district and in the ensuing two decades some 2,000 new houses were built, creating considerable prosperity. The building of a fast breeder reactor in the early 1970s ensured that this will remain an industrial development area as long as nuclear power is regarded as essential. The problems of storing strontium-90, which retains its dangerous radio-activity for several thousand years, remains, however, unsolved as yet and as such raises the question of safety inevitably in many people's minds, despite the assurances of scientists.

At Altnabreac, near Halkirk, in Caithness the Hydro-Electric Board, in conjunction with the Scottish Home Department developed a scheme for a peat-fired power station. First conceived in 1948, work was not begun on this project until 1954 and it was not until 1959 that the site was ready at a cost of £500,000. When it began operating that year, however, the turbines quickly became choked with peat ash. Further costly problems continued to arise, which it was claimed made the plant uneconomic. In 1962 it was finally wound up and the plant dismantled and sold. Whether in fact this was the right decision is still debatable, since so much public money has been spent on other ventures with less ultimate potential.

This was one of the Hydro-Electric Board's few failures and it has generally set high standards in the Highlands not always matched by other public bodies. The Forestry Commission, for instance, has on occasions acquired land by compulsory purchase orders and this has not always been appreciated by those whose land has thus been taken over and out of their own use. The crofters in the area of Roy Bridge near the famous Parallel Roads, the Ice Age formation, long a puzzle to the inhabitants and visitors, were among those thus affected. In 1959 the Forestry Commission acquired land in this area for the Inveroy and Glenspean Forests. This involved taking over land on which crofters grazed sheep. Rightly or wrongly, many felt that they were thus reduced to the stage where they could no longer earn their living on the land remaining to them and were forced to turn to the Forestry Commission for work. This in turn meant that the Forestry Commission bought their crofts and they remained as tenants, subject to accepting work where the Forestry Commission required them.

Although provided with work and a regular wage, as well as the offer of housing in the neat Forestry Commission villages to be found in many parts of the Highlands, this, understandably enough, did not always satisfy those who had been uprooted by these latterday Clearances. During the 1950s and early 1960s the Forestry Commission undoubtedly considered that public relations were not of great importance in their overall task of providing yet more timber to satisfy the needs of the future. That this attitude has undoubtedly changed and the monolithic juggernaut of the Commission has now appreciated that it has a duty to the public as well as to the nation is one of the developments of the 1960s and 70s to be applauded. It remains true, however, that any Clearances in the Highlands today are invariably due to statutory authority invoked by some public body rather than by private individuals. Today the State is by far the largest landowner in the Highlands and all too often decisions are still made from afar.

Throughout the 1950s and 60s onwards, tourism in the Highlands was steadily increasing. Various bodies were working together, or separately, to promote this end. The Scottish Tourist Board was, of course, primarily responsible, working in conjunction with the British Travel and Holidays Association. The Forestry Commission opened National Forest Parks and encouraged its workers to offer bed and breakfast facilities. The Nature Conservancy encouraged visitors to its Nature Reserves. The National Trust for Scotland also naturally encouraged visitors to its properties and also organised tours by bus and boat. The Scottish Council for Physical Recreation, the Scottish Youth Clubs Association and numerous other bodies were actively interested in encouraging tourism, quite apart from those individuals, or firms, financially involved in one way or another. During the 1960s the developments in this field were particularly spectacular.

Tourism was by no means the only aspect of the Highland economy booming during the 1960s. In 1960 an interesting venture started at Wick in Caithness, with the formation of Caithness Glass, a company producing high-quality blown-glass work. Instructors skilled in the art were brought in from Europe and a local labour force was trained in this work. Despite financial difficulties in the early years and various technical problems which arose, the firm built up a reputation for high-quality work and in 1967 began to show a profit. From then on it expanded and even opened a subsidiary firm in Oban, called Oban Glass. A decade later it was one of the principal sources of employment in Wick with a staff of over eighty.

Nor was the Hydro-Electric Board found lacking in promoting new ventures during the 1960s. In 1961 the Cruachan hydro-board scheme was started. This involved excavating a cavern inside Ben Cruachan in the Pass of Brander 91 metres long and 24 metres high, requiring the removal of over 200,000 tonnes of rock. Inside this vast artificial cavern are four reversible turbines and normal generating equipment. All this is hidden under the outwardly unchanged grass and scrub-covered slopes of the mountainside. A matter of 400 metres above the turbines is the white concrete of the dam for this £24 million project. Stretching away from the site the pylons and cables girdle the mountain.

The scheme involved three distinct sections. Two conventional plants are sited at Inverawe and Nant and this pump storage system at Cruachan. The system works by pumping water up to the reservoir, using electric power at off-peak periods to fill the dam. This is then used at times of high demand to generate electricity for the national grid. The turbines in the heart of the mountain thus work both ways, either pumping water from the loch to fill the reservoir, or as conventional producers of electricity. The cables also work both ways, passing electricity to work the turbines as pumps, or feeding electricity some 77 kilometres to the grid when the turbines are operating conventionally. This principle of pump-storage is unique in Britain and has produced an estimated saving of £1 million a year throughout the grid system. It has also been estimated that Cruachan could, if required, produce the equivalent of the entire output of the Hunterston Nuclear Power Station, the most modern in Scotland. It began operating in 1967 after having taken only six years to build. This is a major engineering feat and an installation of which both the Highlands and Scotland may well be proud.

In 1965 the Highlands and Islands Development Board was formed with very wide powers 'for the purpose of assisting the people of the Highlands and Islands to improve their economic and social conditions and of enabling the Highlands and Islands to play a more effective part in the economic and social development of the nation'. It has powers to prepare, concert, promote, assist and undertake measures for the economic and social development of the crofting counties. It can acquire land by compulsory purchase and may hold and manage or dispose of land, erect buildings, provide equipment and services, as well as establishing businesses or disposing of them. It can promote training schemes, produce publicity, give grants or loans which may promote the economic or social development of the area. It can also undertake research and borrow money.

Probably the principal weakness of the Board has been that it has been seen as a political stalking horse and this is highlighted by the fact that the members are appointed by the Secretary of State for Scotland and not elected. Even so, the Board has accomplished a great deal, particularly for the fishing industry. As well as the launching of over thirty trawlers, it has established twenty-four fish-processing plants and eleven boat-building yards, as well as vastly aiding the Highland fishing fleet. It has invested some £10 million in over 1,800 new projects and some £11 million in private enterprise. In promoting tourism and encouraging oil exploration the Board may well have involved itself somewhat beyond its depth in long-term developments which may not ultimately be in the best interests of the Highlands, but on the whole it has proved itself effective in terms of improving investment in the Highlands and attracting more people to the Highlands. It may equally be argued that it is merely one more bureaucratic element in the control of the Highlands, but that is another matter.

During the middle sixties there was a period of immense and excitingly diverse investment in the Highlands. Among these was the development of Aviemore as a holiday centre. The conception was originally that of Lord Fraser of Allander, who formed a £3 million consortium. In 1965 the Rank

Aviemore sports and holiday centre

Organisation opened a large hotel at Coylumbridge, close to Aviemore, and the Aviemore Centre, operated by the Highland Tourist (Cairngorm Development) Ltd., was also opened. This controls an entertainment and sports complex with a heated swimming-pool, a skating and curling rink of international standard with seven lanes, a plastic practice ski-slope, a nine-pin bowling alley, a cinema, theatre and conference hall, combined with a large hotel. Numerous other hotels, lodges and motels were built in the same area. With the ski-slopes and ski-lifts close at hand this became an integral part of a vast tourist project.

A small new township developed and something like 500 new jobs were available. At the same time the police force increased from one to eleven. The whole area from Grantown-on-Spey as far south as Dalwhinnie benefited from the scheme, but it is also argued that it has changed the characteristics of the community. While this is undoubtedly true it is also true that the Clearances a hundred years previously, or more, also altered the characteristics of the community. It is as true to say that the re-introduction of a herd of reindeer by Mikel Utsi in 1948 altered the characteristics of the Cairngorms. Another argument against these innovations is that the money earned does not go to benefit the community, but is syphoned off to the investors in the south. While this may be true there is no doubt that the community also benefits and this is better than merely stagnating.

By far the largest distillery investment of the decade in the Highlands began to take shape in 1965 with the formation of Invergordon Distillers Limited. Begun in 1961, the construction of a new distillery complex in this south-eastern corner of Ross and Cromarty, facing the Black Isle, was a landmark for the whisky industry. By the time it was in operation it was the largest single distillation unit in Europe, with an annual production in the region of 45 million litres of grain whisky. One of the first patent-stills to operate successfully in the Highlands it was also easily the largest.

Another new venture in 1965, in an entirely different part of the Highlands, was at Ardtoe at the tip of the Ardnamurchan peninsula, where the White Fish Authority established a pilot fish-farming scheme. As a result, the growth of plaice from around 2·5 centimetres long, reared in laboratories, to a marketable size is beginning to appear a profitable possibility. Such salt-water fish farming clearly has immense potential for the Highlands and this could prove to be one of the most important experiments yet started.

The following year, in 1966, at Kinlochailort, an experimental fish farm was started by Unilever to breed salmon and sea trout commercially. Starting in a similar way as a pilot scheme, this has since proved its worth and considerable benefits are likely to accrue from this method of rearing these fish. One result of the experiment is that it has provided employment in an area where it is badly needed.

The same year, 1966, saw the opening of the vast new Scottish Pulp and

Paper Mill at Annat near to Fort William. As well as building the plant, this also involved providing some 450 new houses for close on 1,000 workers and three new schools for their 640 children. It also required the building of a new quay at the foot of the Caledonian Canal to receive shiploads of timber from home and abroad. In addition the West Highland Railway, threatened with closure, remained open to provide essential supplies of logs from Crianlarich. Although of enormous size this plant was regarded as the smallest viable unit of its kind. Naturally this also had an immense effect on the prosperity of Fort William.

With the co-operation and advice of the Highlands and Islands Development Board, Invergordon was chosen as the site for a new smelter built by the British Aluminium Company at a cost of £37 million, employing 600 workers. Designed to produce 100,000 tonnes annually it was completed in 1971 at a time of reduced world demand for aluminium. By 1972 it was producing 72,000 tonnes and later began developing its full potential.

The 1970s saw a decade of expansion in the Highlands with some unfortunate retrograde steps. Much of the decade, naturally, was concerned with the development of off-shore oil and gas finds and with their shore-based effects. The vast and unsightly rigs and oil platforms developed at Nigg Bay and around Cromarty and further along the Moray Firth are examples on the debit side of the ledger. The improvement of communications throughout the Highlands are on the credit side. The dual carriageway from Perth to Inverness and the enormous bridge over the Moray Firth itself seems likely to be followed by the steady improvement of the roads all the way to Thurso and these are merely a foretaste of what the future must hold.

In 1972 the project of the Feshie road, that hardy decennial, first mooted by General Wade in 1726, was again raised and approval at first seemed almost universal. Then objections were raised on the grounds of the likely disturbance to the area and finally the project was shelved yet again. As an example of the opposing forces constantly at work against any progressive action in the Highlands this could hardly be bettered.

In the same year, with the aid of sonar equipment, echo sounders, and underwater cameras, an American team of scientists at last succeeded in photographing the Loch Ness Monster at close quarters. By this time it had been established to the satisfaction of almost everyone that several of these beasts, unknown to science, existed in Loch Ness and this appeared to be the ultimate proof, short of producing one of the creatures alive. Even so, it was not sufficient for the scientists of the British Museum, who still adhered stubbornly to the theory that it was merely a log of wood.

Although appealed to for assistance, the Highlands and Islands

The BP oil rig *Sea Quest* on the Forties oil-field

A photograph of the 'monster' taken in 1977

Development Board allowed the Brora coalfield, employing some thirty workers, to close down in 1973. Concentration on oil-field interests was blamed for what appears to have been something of an error. The coalfield, which had been operating since the sixteenth century, was latterly worked on a co-operative basis outside the National Coal Board and only required some £10,000 to open up a fresh seam of coal. Merely as a source of local employment likely to be still operating after the North Sea oil has been exhausted it seems to have been a mistake to allow it to close.

A Highland Wildlife Park, employing only eight full-time staff and additional seasonal workers, was opened at Kincraig, near Kingussie, in the same year with backing from the Highlands and Islands Development Board. Here in 80 hectares it is possible to see animals which live and which once lived in the Highlands, such as beavers, boars, wolves, bears, red deer, roe deer, wildcats, and martens, also birds from partridges and blackgame to capercailzie. Possibly more to the taste of many is the Highland Folk Museum nearby at Kingussie. Founded originally in 1935 it was enlarged in scope by the Pilgrim Trust in 1962 and given to the four principal Scottish Universities. It includes items of interest to the sportsman and naturalist as well as to the social historian, including examples of domestic articles used in the Highlands at varying periods with reconstructions of old Highland interiors as they might have been.

Into the Future

The way of life so convincingly re-constructed at Kingussie has, however, gone for ever. The Highlands must look to the future and expand wherever possible. One example of largely self-aided regeneration and expansion is to be seen in the fishing port of Mallaig on the west coast. In the 1960s it was merely one of several such small west-coast fishing ports with a total return of fish landed worth some £450,000. A £700,000 re-construction of the harbour completed in 1972 was followed by Associated Fisheries building a large cold store and by similar local investments. By such determined efforts on the part of its own local businessmen the landings increased in value in 1973 to somewhere in the region of £3 million. Not content with this, further improvements costing around £900,000 were begun, with a grant of 35 per cent from the Highlands and Islands Development Board. By 1973 it was regarded as the leading herring port in Europe and it had built up its shellfish facilities enormously. Thirty-two-ton refrigerated lorries regularly leave the port to take fish to market on the still largely inadequate roads. Here indeed is

A wolf in the Highland wildlife park at Kincraig near Kingussie

an example of development largely by the Highlanders themselves without outside aid.

During the 1970s it was clearly seen by many that the continued expansion of tourism in the Highlands was in danger of defeating its own ends. The hotels, motels, bed-and-breakfast units and even the caravan sites were on occasions filled to capacity during a season which began to extend over ever longer periods from the early spring right through the summer and winter months. Caravans, nose to tail on the narrow Highland roads, frequently blocked the way for commercial traffic and caused whole areas in the Highlands to grind almost to a standstill. The improvement in the roads, which is already slowly taking place, can only cope with a part of the problem. The fact is that no economy should become entirely dependent on

A wintry scene in the Spey Valley near Newtonmore

one industry, especially one such as tourism, which is essentially ephemeral. Already it is clear that the Highland economy is too dependent upon this as a means of existence.

Such events as the International Clan Gathering of 1977, when some 20,000 overseas Scots were scheduled to meet in Edinburgh in May and then disperse to their clan birthplaces in the Highlands, are only one aspect of a problem which is growing increasingly fast. The tartan image has to some extent been dispelled and such institutions as the Tartan Museum at Comrie will swiftly remove any misconceptions on the 'correct' tartans, or the 'correct' ways of wearing the kilt. Yet still the myths of the Highland way of life linger on, helped largely, it must be admitted, by the scenery and, occasionally, the climate. In the exceptional evening light of the west Highlands it is a dour and unimaginative clod who does not feel some sort of magic in the air; but it is impossible to live on that alone.

There is still a very considerable market for the sport to be had in the Highlands. Grouse-shooting commands very high returns and deer stalking, red and roe, is also a valuable asset. The concept of farming red deer as a means of utilising the land more economically has also proved reasonably viable in pilot schemes in certain suitable places. Ski-ing and mountaineering are also sports eminently suited to parts of the Highlands. Yet all this still leaves a great deal of land available, which could in many cases be put to a better use and with the pressure of population in these islands clearly this is a matter requiring urgent thought and action.

The late 1970s saw two contrary developments in the west coast. In 1976 the Ballachulish road bridge was opened, thus ending the perpetual bottle-neck which had been caused by cars queueing for the ferry. By facilitating traffic between Glasgow and Fort William this was undoubtedly a major improvement. Then in 1979 came the news that the Scottish Pulp and Paper Mill at Fort William would be forced to close because it was running at a loss. The effects of such a closure on Fort William are, of course, bound to be considerable and underline the importance of not relying too much on a single industry. It has indeed been suggested that for the £37 million spent by the British Aluminium Company on their smelter at Invergordon, employing 600 workers, a series of small industries might have been created employing somewhere in the region of 22,000 people. This, although essentially sound, rather begs the question of where these people might be housed.

It has been proposed that a new deep-water port should be established at Kinloch-Eriboll on the north-west coast. Loch Eriboll provides deep-water anchorages and has the largest undeveloped feldspar deposits in Europe. A new town developed here could well be a major base for small industries as well as creating an entirely new centre. With the pressure on these islands, it is important to look for any such opportunities and the Highlands certainly have the space available which is not to be found elsewhere.

Natural Scots pines flourishing under the aegis of the Nature Conservancy at Loch Maree

The difficulty with all such schemes is that the Highlands for the past fifty years, if not the past two hundred and fifty years, have been the patball of politicians. They are now also the cockpit of committees. Those authorities, or commissions, which have some interest in the Highlands include the Highlands and Islands Development Board, the North of Scotland Hydro-Electric Board, the Forestry Commission, the Nature Conservancy, the National Trust for Scotland, the Scottish Wildlife Trust, the Countryside Commission for Scotland, the Small Industries Council for Rural Areas of Scotland, the Scottish Council of Physical Recreation, the Scottish Tourist Board, and numerous others. The Forestry Commission is the largest landowner in the Highlands with something like one and a half million acres under its control. Naturally any major step taken in the Highlands is likely to affect several of these bodies and it becomes necessary to form a committee to decide, or debate, the issue, with sub-committees formed by each authority to present their view. Thus bureaucracy abounds and too often little is achieved.

For nearly a thousand years from the introduction of Christianity by St Columba the Highlands and the Highland way of life remained unchanged and virtually unchanging, unaffected by developments elsewhere. Cocooned by their separate language and their impenetrable mountains, without roads or communications, the Highlanders existed in their own separate world. That it may have been nearly pagan and almost wholly savage, governed by rules and customs which no longer applied in the developing world outside, is almost by the way.

With the Union of the Crowns in 1603 outside events began to impinge ever more strongly on the remoteness of the Highlands. For a hundred years the balance was held with difficulty. With the Union of the Parliaments in 1707 came the beginnings of real change. The 1715 Rebellion brought General Wade and military roads intersecting the Highlands. The 1745 Rebellion brought the Duke of Cumberland and Culloden. The old Highland way of life was finally at an end, even if it took a further hundred years to vanish completely.

The century from 1747 to 1847 saw cataclysmic changes for the Highlanders. The Highland regiments, the Clearances, and above all em-igration, emptied the glens and left only deer behind. The Balmoralisation of the Highlands from 1847 onwards brought in new English landowners to replace the old chieftains and introduced the gothic Highland architecture and tartan mania. Apart from these introductions the century from 1847 to 1947 saw mostly stagnation with frequent comments on the Highland problem, but little done to solve it.

Although there are many names associated with the Highlands from St Columba, MacAlpin, and Bruce to Montrose and Prince Charles Edward Stuart, none have been responsible for lasting change to the land itself. While there are few names relating to the past thirty years in the Highlands likely to be remembered a century from now there has never been a period of such constant innovation and development as the three decades since 1950. During that period there have been new roads and motorways driven through the mountains, thousands of hectares have been afforested, new national parks have been created, ambitious dams and hydro-electric schemes built, while new villages have been erected for workers and old ones revitalised. These changes have been accomplished by faceless men, by committees, and by public bodies faced with the challenge of North Sea oil, of nuclear power, and the sheer demand for land enforcing development. At present these changes may not be immediately apparent to the visitor, even if the pressures enforcing them are obvious enough.

More apparent today are the results of yesterday's errors. Today the Highlands are nearly emptied of Highlanders. The Gaelic language is almost

A ruined croft in the Highlands—a familiar symbol of past neglect

extinct. The Highland regiments that remain are proudly manned by Scots, whose origins may be well below the Highland Line, but who honour the traditions of their Highland predecessors. The kilt has been taken over by the Scottish nation as the national garb and the tartans have multiplied. Yet the Highlands themselves remain still strangely untouched, despite the dams, the oil rigs, the oil platforms, and all modern man's mechanical toys. With the development of the existing roads and the pressures of expanding population there will inevitably come new towns and new industries and perhaps the glens will be peopled once again. It is to be hoped that too many errors affecting the landscape will not be perpetrated and that something of the old magic will survive.

Acknowledgments

My thanks are due, as usual, to many librarians around the British Isles who have supplied me with material for this book, but particularly to the staff of the National Library of Scotland and the Central Library in Edinburgh, also Mr Brian M. Gall and the staff of the East Lothian County Library. For his help in the tiresome task of reading and commenting on the typescript I would particularly like to thank Kenneth H. Grose MA. As ever, I would also like to thank my wife, Evelyn, for her assistance, which extends far beyond the normal wifely spheres.

The publishers wish to thank the following for their kind permission to use their illustrations:

Aerofilms: p. 224. K.M. Andrew: pp. 17 (bottom), 24. Courtesy of Sir James Hunter Blair/National Galleries of Scotland: p. 93. Janet and Colin Bord: pp. 14, 234. Bodleian Library: p. 46. British Library: p. 36. British Tourist Authority: p. 41. J. Allan Cash: pp. 99, 117, 170, 230. Raymond E. Chaplin/Netherfield Visual Productions: pp. 213 (both), 229. City of Aberdeen Library: pp. 184, 198. Officer Commanding Coldstream Guards/Michael Holford: p. 170. Conservateur du Service de Sceaux, Paris: p. 38. Ernest J. Cooke: pp. 158–9, 188, 214–5, 216. Cooper Bridgeman Library: pp. 148–9. Corpus Christi College: p. 40. The Distillers Compay Ltd: p. 204. Edinburgh City Libraries: Endpapers, pp. 104, 112 (all), 172, 176–7, 190–1, 203. Mary Evans Picture Library: p. 201. Fortean Picture Library: p. 228. Highland Folk Museum: p. 152. Michael Holford: pp. 17 (top), 110–1. A.F. Kersting: Frontispiece. Mansell Collection: pp. 28, 71, 74, 114, 140, 154 (left). National Galleries of Scotland: pp. 54, 68, 80, 87, 153, 156. National Museum of Antiquities Scotland: pp. 15, 18 (both), 26, 51, 62 (both). National Portrait Gallery: p. 109. Nature Conservancy Council: pp. 219, 232. Courtesy of Sir David Ogilvy: p. 35. Planair: pp. 64–5. Popperfoto: p. 226. Reproduced by Gracious Permission of Her Majesty Queen Elizabeth II: pp. 84, 164, 169, 180, 183, 187 (both), 192, 195, 199. Radio Times Hulton Picture Library: pp. 43, 45, 48, 52, 95, 97, 107, 118, 124, 126, 128, 138, 143, 154 (right), 163, 166, 197, 206, 212. Scottish Record Office: p. 82. Kenneth Scowen: pp. 90–1. Edwin Smith: pp. 8, 19, 50, 56, 96, 210. John Topham Picture Library: pp. 132, 142, 185.

Picture Research: Faith Perkins
Maps: A.R. Garrett

Select Bibliography

Adam, Frank. *The Clans, Septs and Regiments of the Scottish Highlands* (Johnston & Bacon, 1908)

Adam, M. I. *The Causes of the Highland Emigrations of 1783–1803* (Scottish Hist. Review, 1920)

Barnard, A. *The Whiskey Distilleries of the United Kingdom* (Harper, 1887)

Boswell, James. *Journal of a Tour of the Hebrides* (London 1856)

Brander, Michael. *The Scottish Highlanders and Their Regiments* (Seeley, 1971); *The Original Scotch* (Hutchinson, 1974); *Scottish Crafts & Craftsmen* (Johnston & Bacon, 1974); *A Guide to Scotch Whiskey* (Johnston & Bacon, 1975); *Scottish and Border Battles and Ballads* (Seeley, 1975)

Buchan, John. *Montrose* (London, 1928)

Burns, Robert. *Complete Works* ed. William Scott Douglas (1890)

Burt, Captain. E. *Letters from a Gentleman in the North* (London, 1754)

Colier, A. *The Crofting Problem* (Cambridge University Press, 1953)

Darling, F. Fraser. *The West Highland Survey* (OUP, 1953); and Boyd, K. M. *Highlands and Islands* (Collins, 1969)

Dinsdale, T. *The Loch Ness Monster* (Routledge & Kegan Paul, 1961)

Graham, H. G. *The Social Life of Scotland in the 18th Century* (Black, 1950)

Grant, Elizabeth, of Rothiemurchos. *Memoirs* ed. John Mirray (1950)

Grant, I. F. *Highland Folk Ways* (Routledge & Kegan Paul, 1961)

Gray, M. *The Highland Economy* (Oliver & Boyd, 1957)

Haldane, A. R. B. *New Roads Through the Glens* (David & Charles, 1968); *The Drove Roads of Scotland* (1952)

Laing, Andrew. *A History of Scotland* (Edinburgh, 1900–6)

Leyden, Dr. *Journal of a Tour of the Highlands* (Edinburgh, 1805)

Lindsay, J. *The Canals of Scotland* (David & Charles, 1973)

Linklater, Eric. *The Prince in the Heather* (Hodder & Stoughton, 1965)

Loch, James. *An Account of the Improvements . . .* (1820)

Mackenzie, Alexander. *A History of the Highland Clearances* (Glasgow, 1883)

Mackenzie, Osgood. *A Hundred Years in the Highlands* (Bles, 1921)

MacKenzie, W. C. *The Highlands and Isles of Scotland* (Edinburgh, 1949)

MacLauchlan, Thomas. *The Depopulation System in the Highlands* (1849)

MacLeod, Donald. *Gloomy Memories of the Highlands* (Edinburgh, 1860)

McLintock, H. F. *Old Irish and Highland Dress* (Dundalk, 1950)

O'Dell, A. C. and Walton, K. *The Highlands and Islands of Scotland* (Nelson, 1962)

Pennant, Thomas. *Tour in Scotland* (1771)

Prebble, J. *The Highland Clearances* (Secker & Warburg, 1963)

Robertson, Alexander. *Where are the Highlanders?* (Edinburgh, 1856)

Sage, Donald. *Memorabilia Domestica* (Ed.1889)

Simpson, W. D. *Portrait of the Highlands* (Hale, 1969)

Sinclair, Sir John. *General View of the Agriculture . . .* (1795)

Stanford Reid, (ed.). *The Scottish Tradition in Canada* (McLelland, 1976)

Stewart, General Sir David, of Garth. *Sketches* (1822)

Thomson, D. and Grimble, I. *The Future of the Highlands* (Routledge, 1968)

Thomson, Francis. *The Highlands and Islands* (Hale, 1974)

Thornton, Thomas. *A Sporting Tour* (1804)

Whyte, Constance. *More Than a Legend* (Hamish Hamilton, 1957)

Wilson, John. *Scotland's Malt Whiskies* (Dumbarton, 1975)

Witchell, Nicholas. *The Loch Ness Story* (Dalton, 1974)

Index